TERRA

TALES OF THE EARTH

Also by Richard Hamblyn

The Invention of Clouds

TERRA

TALES OF THE EARTH

Four Events That Changed the World

RICHARD HAMBLYN

PICADOR

First published 2009 by Picador
an imprint of Pan Macmillan Ltd
Pan Macmillan, 20 New Wharf Road, London N1 9RR
Basingstoke and Oxford
Associated companies throughout the world
www.panmacmillan.com

ISBN 978-0-330-49073-3

1 3 5 7 9 8 6 4 2

A CIP catalogue record for this book is available from
the British Library.

Printed in the UK by CPI Mackays, Chatham ME5 8TD

For Ben and Jessica

It seemed to me that I could feel the indifferent
threat of the earth through the soles of my feet,
the volcanoes, earthquakes, tsunamis,
terrors of nature's fact.

WILLIAM GOLDING

CONTENTS

List of Illustrations xi

PREFACE *xv*

PART ONE

EARTH

The Lisbon Earthquake, 1755

1

PART TWO

AIR

European Weather Panic, 1783

63

Part Three

FIRE

The Eruption of Krakatau, 1883

123

Part Four

WATER

The Hilo Tsunami, 1946

181

Afterword *239*

Notes *247*

Acknowledgements *260*

Index *262*

List of Illustrations

PICTURE SECTIONS

1 Lisbon before the earthquake, c. 1750. Mary Evans Picture Library.

2 The monastery at Mafra, coloured engraving, c. 1850. Author's collection.

3 How subduction works. David A. Hardy/Science Photo Library.

4 *Auto da fé*, Terreiro do Paço, Lisbon, 1717. Mary Evans Picture Library.

5 An imaginary view of the Lisbon earthquake and tsunami, wood engraving, 1887. Science Photo Library.

6 Refugee camp on the outskirts of Lisbon, anon. German engraving, 1755. Courtesy of the National Information Service for Earthquake Engineering, EERC, University of California, Berkeley.

7 The ruins of the Royal Opera House, Lisbon, engraving by J.-P. Le Bas, 1757. Courtesy of the National Information Service for Earthquake Engineering, EERC, University of California, Berkeley.

8 A before and after view of Lisbon from a German atlas published in the 1770s. Courtesy of the National Information Service for Earthquake Engineering, EERC, University of California, Berkeley.

9 Benjamin Franklin in his backwoodsman's hat, engraved from the portrait by C. N. Cochin, 1777. Mary Evans Picture Library.

10 A page from Edward Pigott's notebooks. By kind permission of York City Archives.

11 The Meteor of 18 August 1783, as it appeared from the NE Corner of the Terrace at Windsor Castle', aquatint by Thomas Sandby after

a watercolour by Paul Sandby, published October 1783. Science Museum/SSPL.

12 The first public manned balloon ascent, 21 November 1783. Coloured etching, Germany. Science Museum/SSPL.

13 Map showing the extent of the Laki Fissures eruption, Iceland, 1783. From Saemund Magnussen Holm, *Om Jordbranden paa Island i Aaret 1783* (1784). By permission of the British Library: BL 233.d.8.(1.).

14 Photograph of Sidney Tucker Baker aged eleven. With kind permission of Dr Richard S. Fiske of the Smithsonian Institution's National Museum of Natural History.

15 View of Krakatau before the eruption, from the *Illustrated London News*, 8 September 1883. Corbis.

16 Krakatau in eruption, 27 May 1883, from the *Graphic*, 11 August 1883. Corbis.

17 The stranded paddleship *Berouw*, in an engraving from the *St. Nicholas Magazine*, March 1900. Mary Evans Picture Library.

18 Death Ship, from Camille Flammarion, *La Fin du Monde* (1893). Mary Evans Picture Library.

19 'Twilight and afterglow effects at Chelsea', pastel sketches by William Ascroft, dated 26 November 1883. Science Museum/SSPL.

20 Rogier Verbeek and his team on the remains of Krakatau, chromolithograph from Verbeek's *Krakatau* (1885). By permission of the British Library: BL x 439.

21 Anak Krakatau, satellite image (1998). Geoeye/Science Photo Library.

22 Laupahoehoe Point, Hawaii, *c.* 1930. Vintage postcard, author's collection.

23 Downtown Kamehameha Avenue, 1930s. Vintage postcard, author's collection.

24 Tsunami coming in, Hilo, 1 April 1946. Jeanne Johnston Collection, Pacific Tsunami Museum.

25 Running from the wave, Hilo, 1 April 1946. Cecilio Licos Collection, Pacific Tsunami Museum.

26 Café 100, Hilo, 1 April 1946. Pacific Tsunami Museum.

27 Railroad car, Hilo, April 1946. Lee Hatada Collection, Pacific Tsunami Museum.

28 The rebuilding begins, Hilo, April 1946. Eklund Collection, Pacific Tsunami Museum.

29 Tsunami memorial, Laupahoehoe Point, Hawaii. Mila Zinkova.

30 Tsunami warning siren, Laupahoehoe Point, Hawaii. Author's photo.

31 Sightseers waiting for the wave on the night of 22 May 1960. James Hamasaki, Pacific Tsunami Museum.

32 Parking meters bent by the force of the 1960 tsunami, Hilo. US Army Corps of Engineers, provided by the National Geophysical Data Center, Pacific Tsunami Museum.

33 The DART system. NOAA/National Weather Service.

34 Site of Shinmachi, Hilo Bay, Hawaii. Author's photo.

35 Waiakea Town clock, Hilo Bay, Hawaii. Author's photo.

FIGURES IN THE TEXT

i Earth's principal tectonic plates. *page 14*

ii The dynamics of P-waves and S-waves. Gary Hincks/Science Photo Library. *page 16*

iii Map of the Sunda Strait, with the placement of the various ships. Royal Society Report on *Krakatau* (1888). By permission of the British Library: BL 7105.g.10. *page 145*

iv Map of the Big Island of Hawaii, with inset showing Hilo Bay. *page 185*

v 'Seismic Wave Havoc', from the London *Times*, 3 April 1946. *The Times*/NI Syndication. *page 204*

vi Tsunami transit times across the Pacific Ocean. *page 228*

PREFACE

When I first set out to write this book I imagined finishing it in time for the two hundred and fiftieth anniversary of the Lisbon earthquake in November 2005, but by Christmas 2004 I had only just begun work on the fourth and final section, which describes the impact of the 1946 Fool's Day tsunami, the event that led to the establishment of the Pacific Tsunami Warning System – an impressive combination of technology and surveillance that has contributed to the safety of tsunami-prone communities for more than half a century. Sixty years on from the Fool's Day disaster, the success of the Pacific warning system seemed a suitably optimistic note on which to end this historical account of the social and scientific consequences of natural disasters.

But, as all the world recalls, that Boxing Day morning broke with the news that another massive tsunami had struck, this time in the Indian Ocean, and that tens of thousands of people were likely to have been killed. Hour by hour, as more detailed reports came through, the sheer scale of the devastation seemed hard to take in; by the end of the day some ten countries on two continents had declared a state of emergency, and by the end of the week the death-toll had risen to almost two hundred and fifty thousand people, with several millions more rendered homeless and dispossessed. It was the worst natural disaster of modern times. Suddenly, the historic success of the Pacific Tsunami Warning System seemed a hollow achievement, given the failure to alert any of the devastated coastal communities of the imminent arrival of the waves. The scientists on duty at the Pacific Tsunami Warning Center on Ewa Beach, Oahu, had received preliminary information on the tsunamigenic earthquake even as it was still in progress: the magnitude 9.15 submarine earthquake had lasted just over four minutes – an extraordinary length of time for a single seismic event – but the absence of tide gauges or sea-floor sensors in any of the affected areas meant that they had no way of knowing if a tsunami had been generated. Their advance-warning system had been equipped to monitor only the coastlines of the Pacific. So as the coastal towns and villages of north-west Sumatra were being destroyed by the first of the giant waves that had been initiated by the undersea rupture, all that could be done in faraway Hawaii was email a general information bulletin to the twenty-six Pacific nations on the warning centre's contact list, and wait for further details to emerge.

By the time the first wave had reached the west coast of Thailand, some fifty minutes later, staff at the centre had already emailed a second, upgraded warning bulletin to the contacts on their list, and were now beginning a hopeless search for the telephone numbers or email addresses of civil-defence coordinators across the entire Bay of Bengal and Indian Ocean regions, but, as Barry Hirshorn, one of the geophysicists on duty that day, explained in an interview with *Channel 4 News*, 'there were no contact points, no organizations, no warning systems that I knew of in the area' – and so, as the sun continued rising on that Boxing Day morning, the waves powered towards the waking towns and villages along the densely populated coastlines of India, Sri Lanka and the Maldive Islands, with no alarms or warnings given out by the only people on the planet who could have known, at that moment, just how powerfully the events of the following few hours would come to haunt and horrify the world.

The parallels with the book that I was writing were, of course, painfully apparent, and as the weeks went by, during which a vast and apparently uncoordinated relief effort swung into action all over the world, yet another chapter in the history of disaster had started to unfold. But in spite of the overwhelming scale of the event, and the numerous public policy failures that exacerbated its effects – including the deliberate destruction of coral reefs and mangrove forests: natural coastal barriers that do much to absorb the energy of incoming waves – I was determined that this book should retain at least some of its original optimism. Earlier disasters, after all, had yielded crucial insights and understanding that were rapidly deployed in mitigating the dangers of their inevitable recurrence. The Lisbon earthquake of 1755 had led to the development of antiseismic building designs which continue to save lives throughout the world, while the Pacific Tsunami Warning System had been implemented within eighteen months of the Hilo disaster, and – barring one or two notable lapses – it has been an effective presence on the islands ever since.

Such resourcefulness in the wake of disaster had become one of the recurring themes of the book, so it was all the more distressing that the Boxing Day tsunami had struck so many shorelines with no warning: even more distressing, perhaps, was the cruel irony that, only the previous year, governments from around the Indian Ocean had called a meeting to discuss the planned installation of their own tsunami warning system, only to vote against it on economic grounds. Since the last major tsunami in the region had occurred in 1833 (with a much smaller one fifty years later, precipitated by the eruption of Krakatau), the risk of another had seemed out of all proportion to the cost of installing the equipment. But even had they known what seismologists were discovering about the active nature of the Java Trench, would their decision have been any different? Governments are notoriously reluctant to spend money on speculative hazard mitigation, in spite of the memory of recent disasters, every one of which serves as an object lesson in how to behave when the next one arrives – though, as will be seen in the course of this book, on the rare occasions when such lessons have been heeded, they have seldom been heeded for long.

The true stories that make up *Terra* are based on eyewitness accounts of four historical disasters from around the world:

the Lisbon earthquake of 1755; the European weather panics of
1783; the eruption of Krakatau in 1883; and the Hilo tsunami
of 1946, episodes chosen for the light they shed on the intercon-
nected processes of the earth and its atmosphere, as well as for
the influence each of them had on the development of scientific
understanding.

The Lisbon earthquake was in many respects the first modern
disaster, establishing the protocols of international humanitarian
response, as well as ending the theological presumption that disasters are a judgement on the victims. It was also the first earthquake
to be methodically assessed, and, as will be seen in the course of
Part One, the new science of seismology emerged from the unprecedented outbreak of rational attention that was paid to the
earthquake and its aftermath.

The weather panics of 1783, meanwhile, revealed the vulnerability of our atmosphere to rapid and dangerous climate change,
and introduced a new area of scientific enquiry that has taken
centre stage over recent years, as the consequences of rising global
temperatures become ever more obvious – and ever more irreversible. The role of print media in the circulation of information
(and misinformation) was also defined during this summer of
strange weather, the Europe-wide coverage of which became the
first non-political rolling news story in newspaper history.

Part Three is an account of the catastrophic eruption of
Krakatau, still the most famous eruption in history, and the first to
be studied on a global scale, its impact felt by everyone on the
planet, whether they were aware of it or not. The recent invention
of telegraphy ensured that the story became an international
news event within hours of the eruption, directing the attention of
scientists all over the world to the severity of its local impact, as well
as to its long-range atmospheric effects.

Part Four describes the aftermath of the 1946 Hilo tsunami, the
first major post-war natural disaster, and the first tsunami to be
studied at first-hand, by a team of American oceanographers
who happened to be stationed on the Hawaiian islands during

the run-up to Operation Crossroads, the first of the Bikini Atoll bomb tests. It was their recommendations that led to the establishment of the Pacific Tsunami Warning System, a model of rational preparedness in the face of the violence of nature.

Four true stories, then, each of which bears historical witness to the earth's unimaginable powers and energies, and each one a turning point in the history of scientific understanding. But at the heart of all these tales of the earth are the voices of ordinary people caught up in a series of extraordinary circumstances; and it is their first-hand accounts of collective catastrophe and individual survival that allow us to see the tectonic crises endured by our suffering planet from an ultimately human perspective.

PART ONE

EARTH

THE LISBON EARTHQUAKE
1755

I

On a cloudless November morning in 1755 a diffident English army chaplain, newly arrived in Lisbon, was walking on the battlements of the Castelo de São Jorge, from where an unimpeded view of the entire surrounding city was spread out before him like an architectural plan. Churches, palaces and vast cloistered convents rose like barns through the sloping fields of red-tiled roofs, while boatyards and warehouses appeared to spill onto the teeming waterside below. It was Saturday, November 1st – All Saints' Day, one of the holiest days in the Portuguese year – and the sound of church bells hung in the air as the morning sun rose high over the city, its light reflecting from the tiled facades of the taller and more prosperous houses that faced one another over the riverside squares. It was an unforgettable sight, and the clergyman stood on the high limestone battlements, gazing across the sunlit city – 'straining Time to the utmost', as he was later to describe it, 'on account of the extreme fineness of the morning'.[1]

He was, in fact, late for an appointment at the house of the British Envoy, where he ought to have been making his way, since he had agreed to conduct the All Saints' Day service that was to be held in the envoy's chapel. The service was due to begin at ten, and it was now nearly a quarter to, but he had already decided that he would take his time and offer plausible excuses when he arrived. He had, after all, come to Lisbon principally for the sake of his health, and he was sure that the warm Atlantic air that swirled around the castle walls was already doing him some good. If he stayed where he was for another minute or two he wouldn't be all that late, and he could always claim that he had lost his way in the maze of unfamiliar streets.

But, as it turned out, he wouldn't have to explain anything to Envoy Castres and his guests, for as he was standing on the castle's south-facing platform, looking out over Lisbon and the hills beyond, a sudden noise like a peal of thunder seemed to shake the city from below. It sounded, up at the castle, like a long-drawn-out explosion echoing through the hills from a nearby quarry. In the town itself, according to a number of eyewitness accounts, it sounded more like heavy traffic being driven hard through the cobbled streets, but at that point no one was sure what it could be. 'I was discoursing with two Portuguese friends in the Compting-house', wrote an English merchant to his brother a few days later, when 'suddenly we found the House shake, and a great Noise like a Coach and Six driving by: We stared at each other: They said it was a Coach: I answered, none came through our Street.'[2] But there was no time for further discussion, for less than a minute after the first shock came a second, much greater, shock, and not just an isolated rumbling and shaking, but a sustained, deafening roar that bellowed through the city in waves. The ground began to heave so hard that it cracked, sending a network of dark fissures snaking through the city streets, as stone foundations were sheared from under violently toppling buildings, hurling them from one side of the street to the other, their walls and roofs crashing inwards under the force of the collision. It seemed as though the entire city was convulsing from below in wave after wave of erupting force, as it imploded into the heaving ground in a storm of broken masonry.

From his vantage point on the castle walls, the chaplain looked on in horror as the world went into reverse, as this ancient city unmade itself in a frenzy of upheaval and destruction. After two incomprehensible minutes the worst of the shaking stopped, but a large part of the city was already lying in ruins beneath a rapidly rising cloud of dust and smoke. As the dust cloud spread, plunging everything beneath it into a sudden choking darkness, buildings all around the city continued to fall, their walls and roofs collapsing noisily into the surrounding sea of rubble. A few minutes later a third shock came, finishing off some of the larger structures that had managed to remain upright. The entire sequence of tremors lasted less than ten minutes, but already thousands of people lay dead or dying in the ruins, among which a series of small fires had begun to break out, to the increasing panic and alarm of the survivors. 'It is not to be express'd by human tongue how dreadful and how awful it was', as a letter sent by a survivor to the *Gentleman's Magazine* in London described it: 'Terror in beholding frightful pyramids of ruined fronts, some inclining one way, some another; then horror in beholding dead bodies by six or seven in a heap, crush'd to death, half buried and half burnt; and if one went through the broad places or squares, nothing to be met with but people bewailing their misfortunes, wringing their hands, and crying: the world is at an end.'[3]

Lisbon, the richest and most beautiful city in Europe, with its gilded churches, its fountained courtyards, and its centuries of imperial gain, had been erased from the face of the earth, and there was nothing that anyone could do; but as an agitated crowd of dust-covered locals began to gather in the castle gardens, clutching salvaged crucifixes and images of St Anthony (that some of them had rescued instead of their own children, according to a number of horrified witnesses), our clergyman-tourist sank to his knees and offered up an English prayer.

II

Until the morning of 1 November 1755, eighteenth-century Lisbon had been a famously sensual and complex city with an atmosphere that verged on the oriental (see picture 1). Travellers from the north who stepped from their boats onto the marble quays of Lisbon docks were immediately surrounded by sights and sounds that made them wonder if they were still in Europe. 'Pre-earthquake

Lisbon', wrote the novelist Rose Macaulay, 'was a Lisbon of churches, convents, gold and jewelled ornaments, abject poverty, negro slaves, priests, friars, sumptuous processions, superstition, squalor, corruption, women eating sweets and playing guitars at windows, and rich galleys sailing in from Brazil.'⁴ It was a city unlike any other in Europe, with a long history of conquest and commerce that had soaked it in wealth and gain.

Lisbon was magnificent, due largely to the efforts of its merchants and its navigators, who by the sixteenth century had mapped two-thirds of the world, and established a global trading empire spanning eastwards from Madeira to Macau. Shiploads of gold and other precious metals made their way to Lisbon from the seaports of Africa and Asia, alongside other valuable cargoes of spices, jewels, textiles and timber. As more and more ships from more and more territories queued up to unload at the riverside docks, Lisbon blossomed into the undisputed capital of Europe's overseas trade. Hundreds of foreign merchants descended on the city, attracted by the proximity of such unparalleled wealth; chief among these were the British, keen to take advantage of a series of binding trade agreements that dated back to 1385, when five hundred English archers, stopping off in Lisbon on their way to the Crusades, helped overthrow the Castilian assault on the throne of João I. England had agreed to protect the vulnerable Portugal 'as though she were England herself', in return for the right to export and sell unlimited quantities of valuable homespun textiles. These agreements were to prove so favourable to British commercial interests that by the time the English king Charles II married the Portuguese princess Catherine of Braganza (whose legendary dowry included Bombay, Tangier and the Sri Lankan port of Galle – the starter-kit for Britain's first Empire in the East), the vast bulk of Portugal's import and export business was being handled by British merchants, whose offices and warehouses commanded the length of the Lisbon waterfront.

The relationship between the Lisbon locals and the growing community of foreign merchants was generally cordial, although each tended to harbour ambivalent feelings concerning the religious practices of the other. The Portuguese clergy had been fiercely opposed to the building of Protestant places of worship, and especially to the proposal for an English burial ground, which was eventually established in 1729 after a century of persistent diplomacy. Shielded behind a high wall and a row of cypresses on a hill at the edge of the city, the 'cemetery for heretics' soon began to fill, mainly with the increasing numbers of consumptive Brits who were dispatched to the warmth of Lisbon for the sake of their health, but who never made it home. The novelist Henry Fielding remains its most celebrated burial; he died in October 1754 after three painful and dispiriting months in the city, during which he quarrelled with most of the merchants he encountered there, 'a Set of People who are tearing one another's Souls out for Money', as he described them in his impressively bad-tempered journal.[5] The last sentence that he ever wrote, fittingly enough for an author, was a complaint about the quality of Portuguese paper, and the difficulty of getting hold of decent ink. To add insult to his final injury, services at the burial ground were usually conducted under cover of darkness in order to avoid trouble with the locals, but at least it was an improvement on the previous arrangement, which had seen the bodies of all non-Roman Catholics unceremoniously dumped into the sea.

For their part, the Protestant residents found the emotional intensity of Portuguese Catholicism to be the city's most unsettling feature. The Portuguese observed so many saints' days and festivals that there were only a hundred and twenty-two working days in the year, and the merchants often complained that their employees kept absenting themselves in order to gather in the public squares to watch columns of clerics and nobility pass in glorious procession from palace to church, and then back again from church to palace, while their precious stores and warehouses stood unmanned for the rest of the day.

The tourists, of course, loved all these colourful processions, especially the notorious Lenten procession, when a line of fasting penitents flayed themselves raw with all manner of home-made implements, while marching through the city streets chanting *'Ora pro Nobis'* under the indulgent gaze of the priests. Protestant onlookers found the whole thing repulsive and entertaining in equal measure, and many of them timed their trips specially to coincide with the flagellants' gruesome displays. The English Methodist minister George Whitefield, for example, was in Lisbon during April 1754, and wrote a series of scandalized letters home in which his growing fascination with the psychology of abasement was clear in every line. He went to see the penitents every day during his visit, and watched them for hours, 'sights of this Nature being quite a Novelty to me, I was fond of attending as many of them as I could', as he explained to his correspondent at home. One evening's parade apparently went on all night, with 'most of them whipping and lashing themselves, some with Cords, and others with flat Bits of Iron. It being a Moonshine Night, I could see quite well: the whole scene was horrible; so horrible, that, being informed it was to be continued till Morning, I was glad to return from whence I came, about Midnight'.[6] As Rose Macaulay pointed out, it was just as well that Whitefield's ship left Lisbon when it did, for had he stayed any longer watching the flagellants at work he may well have ended up joining in.

When Portugal's dominance of the Asian sea routes declined during the seventeenth and eighteenth centuries, with the rise of the Dutch and British East India Companies, the focus of its empire shifted west to Brazil, whose territories were vaster and richer by far than those of any other colony in the world. Since its annexation by Portugal in 1500, Brazil had been exploited as a slave-worked plantation, producing sugar and tobacco in industrial quantities, but when gold was discovered in the Brazilian highlands in 1697, the fortunes of both countries were transformed overnight. Mass emigration from rural Portugal during the early years of the Brazilian gold rush hastened the collapse of domestic industries such as textiles, fishing and agriculture, while labourers and overseers in the Brazilian plantations also fled to the highlands of the north in search of gold. Soon Lisbon was largely dependent for its income on the products of the Brazilian mines, supplemented by the British-run port-wine industry that was developing around Oporto in the north. Slowly but surely, Portugal was laying the foundations of its economic future, in which short-term prosperity would give way to long-term dependency, with most of its industries in terminal decline, and much of its trade in foreign hands. But as long as the supply of gold (and, later, diamonds) kept coming in from Brazil, the situation in Lisbon appeared sustainable.

The sheer scale of Portugal's income from the gold mines of Brazil is hard to comprehend, although it was quickly matched by the scale and enthusiasm of its expenditure by the crown. The first half of the eighteenth century saw at least a thousand tonnes of Brazilian gold make its way into Lisbon harbour. Compared with the annual yield of half a tonne that had been shipped from the West African gold coast during the first imperial boom years of the fifteenth and sixteenth centuries, these were unimaginable riches, and they drove the King of Portugal delirious with wealth.[7] Dom João V, who ascended to the throne at the age of seventeen in 1706, just as the gold rush began in earnest, did what any young monarch would have done in his place: he dispensed with parliament, surrounded himself with sycophants and mistresses, and embarked upon the creation of an absolutist regime that would be known throughout the world for the lavishness of its spending. He was, after all, the richest monarch in Christendom, and he was keen that all of Christendom should know it.

Dom João's programme of public expenditure began with the wholesale ornamentation of Lisbon's sixty-five medieval and baroque churches, along with the building of dozens of new ones in the modern neo-classical style. Although a tenth of the population of Lisbon remained homeless, the interiors of their city's churches – thanks to the bounty of the Brazilian mines – were soon swimming with gold from floor to ceiling, their walls draped with the costliest paintings, and their side-chapels studded with gems and precious stones collected from around the world. The Chapel

of St John the Baptist, for example, which was installed in the
ancient church of St Rock in 1750, after eight years' labour by a
team of Italian craftsmen, was the most expensive chapel the
world had ever seen. Constructed from the rarest marbles and
semiprecious stones, including lapis lazuli, porphyry, jade, agate
and amethyst, and heavily gilded and tiled throughout, the chapel
featured a series of exquisite mosaics depicting scenes from the life
of Christ and the Apostles, inlaid into carved surrounds of the
finest Carrara marble. Visitors to the church – once they had made
their way past the throng of beggars at the door – could hardly
believe what they saw, 'all was so magnificently, so superstitiously
grand', in the words of George Whitefield, the Methodist minister,
whose disapproval of Portuguese religious excess kept faltering
before its sensory allure.[8]

But the redecoration of Lisbon's churches was only the beginning of what would become Dom João's lifelong mission to fritter
away the revenues from his Brazilian possessions on works of ecclesiastical display. While a large proportion of the rural population
was choosing to emigrate to the colonies rather than starve at
home, their king pressed on with his ambition to see the world's
largest and costliest building erected on Portuguese soil: the vast
convent-palace of Mafra, which rose on a hilltop outside the capital
over a twenty-seven-year period, and which was destined to be the
most extravagant and expensive architectural gesture ever made by
a European monarch. Its scale dwarfed both Louis XIV's palace at
Versailles and Philip II's Escorial in Madrid, just as it was intended
to do, although its overall design was far less distinguished than
that of either of its illustrious rivals. It was so enormous that you
could walk through the palace for a week, it was said, without once
retracing your steps. 'This room, that room, room upon room
upon room', as the Portuguese novelist José Saramago lamented in
the wake of an exhausting tour of the building; 'the traveller
searches anxiously for a guide', he wrote, 'and clutches on to him
like a drowning man. The guides at Mafra must be very used to
this.'[9] Completed in 1744 at an estimated final cost of some forty

billion cruzados (£54 million in eighteenth-century money, a sum equivalent to at least twenty years' revenue from the gold mines of Brazil), the convent-palace of Mafra – Europe's largest building – came closer to bankrupting the Portuguese crown than had Catherine of Braganza's notorious dowry in 1661; closer, even, than the economically disastrous War of the Spanish Succession, which had drained Portugal of money and men between 1702 and 1714.

The whole of Europe grew captivated by tales of Dom João V's wealth and extravagance, and stories of his extraordinary conduct were circulated far and wide. One story told how the king's agents wrote to the managers of the famous bell foundry at Liège, in Belgium, for an estimate on an order for fifty enormous cast-iron bells that were destined for the bell towers of the convent. It was the largest order the foundry had ever received, and the estimated cost of the hand-cast bells added up to an unbelievable sum of money, which, in the embarrassed opinion of the foundry managers, no court in Europe could possibly have afforded. But when the price was agreed without a murmur from Lisbon, the foundry managers began to worry that the king or his agents must have misunderstood the bill, and would refuse to settle it once the work had been completed. They began to make discreet enquiries as to whether the Portuguese treasury really would be willing to pay, but when João got to hear of this, his response took the form of a carriage dispatched, unannounced, to the gates of the foundry at Liège, laden with *double* the amount requested in freshly minted gold.[10]

In the end, every skilled workman in the country was conscripted to work on the monastery at Mafra, and during the final stages of the building work an army of forty-five thousand labourers was employed on the site, which had grown into a kind of temporary city, complete with its own shops, farms, schools and graveyards: a sort of parallel Lisbon, desperate and ruinous, that had sprung from the mind of the king (see picture 2).

But throughout the long centuries of pageantry and wealth, there had been frequent rumblings underground. The years 1009, 1017,

1117 and 1146 were marked by damaging earthquakes in and around the Lisbon area, as were 1321, 1337 (which saw a particularly severe one that occurred on Christmas Day), 1344, a 'disastrous' event in which the century-old cathedral was almost totally destroyed, and 1356, during which the bells of all the churches rang out by themselves for a full fifteen minutes, to the terror of the assembled inhabitants.[11] One of the worst shocks of all occurred on 26 January 1531, in which most of the city's churches and some one and a half thousand of its houses collapsed, trapping hundreds of inhabitants in the ruins. Although no figures have survived (most of Lisbon's early records were destroyed in 1755), the death toll is likely to have been high. It had been the worst earthquake to shake the city in its three-thousand-year history, and the rebuilding took decades to complete. At least a dozen further earthquakes hit Lisbon during the following two centuries, including severe ones in 1597, 1598, 1699 and 1724, but nothing seems to have prepared the city for the grand event of 1755, an event that appears, in retrospect, to have been a matter not of *if* but of *when*.

Earthquakes have an ancient pedigree; in fact, they are nearly as ancient as the planet itself. When the earth was first formed, some four and a half billion years ago, it consisted mainly of hot gases that cooled over time, thickening into concentric layers surrounding a solid nickel and iron core. Wrapped around the solid core is a layer of molten metal, and wrapped around that is the 3,000-kilometre (1,860-mile) deep mantle, a hot, viscous region of molten rock and iron, the outer surface of which has cooled and hardened into a brittle crust of rock known as the lithosphere. As the young earth continued to cool, the lithosphere shattered into large segments, now known as tectonic plates,* which began slowly to migrate, their movement driven by thermal convection currents rising from the mantle below.

---

* From the Greek word *tekton*, meaning 'carpenter'.

The movements of these tectonic plates are varied, complex and unpredictable, with some rubbing alongside their neighbour, one ragged edge slowly grinding past another, while others collide head on, one subducting below the other and melting back into the mantle like the disappearing end of a conveyor belt. The lost plate material is replaced at the other end, where the sea floor spreads at the mid-ocean rifts, and new molten matter rises up from the mantle to cool and solidify into rock (see picture 3).

The earth's tectonic plates are forever on the move, travelling a few slow centimetres every year, but it is their constant jostling as they collide and grind that causes earthquakes to occur along their margins. Not all tectonic interaction gives rise to serious quakes. Often, two plates will manage to slip past one another with a minimum of interference; but sometimes a jam will occur along a particular region of the boundary, which leads over time to a build-up of strain as the locked-in plates attempt to continue their journey. Depending on the varying physical nature of the plates and their fault lines, these seizures can persist for months, years, or even for centuries, while the strain steadily increases along the join. When the blockage finally gives way, and the stuck sections of the plates jolt free, a huge amount of energy is suddenly released, which travels through the earth in seismic waves, causing quakes to occur on the surface.

As can be seen from the map overleaf, Lisbon sits near the meeting point of two major tectonic plates, the Eurasian and the African, which are moving steadily eastwards, away from the ever-spreading sea floor that diverges along the Mid-Atlantic Ridge. As the plates are pushed along their way, they travel in slightly different directions and at slightly different rates, leading to frequent collisions, seizures and slippages recurring at certain regions of the join. In the case of Lisbon, the major tremors seem to stem from the Azores–Gibraltar Fracture Zone, a particularly active region of the Eurasian and African plate boundary, where major earthquakes have occurred in the past with alarming regularity. At certain points along the fracture zone, the edges of the two plates have a regular

TERRA

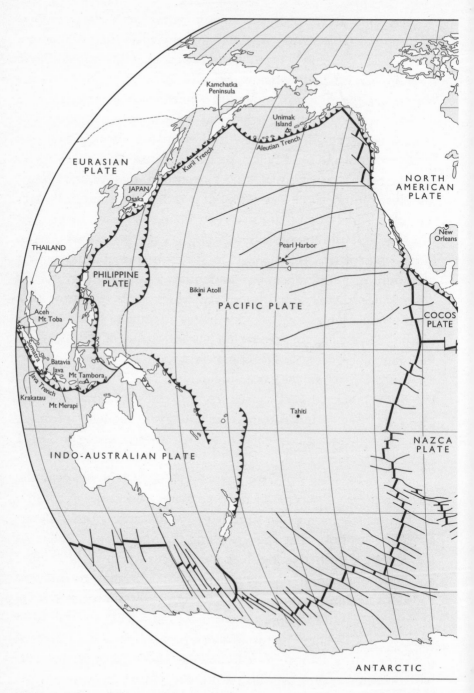

Figure i. Map of the earth's major tectonic plates, the movements of

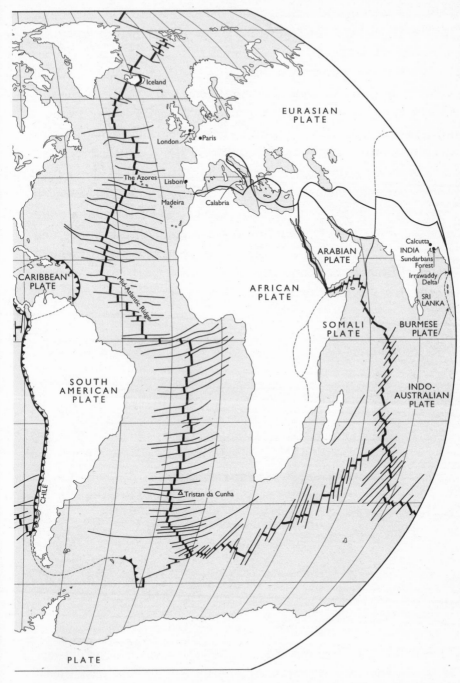

which give rise to earthquakes, volcanoes and the majority of tsunamis.

habit of colliding and sticking, until the force exerted by the rest of the plates dislodges the jam with a series of jolts that are known as an elastic rebound.

These jolts release two distinct kinds of body waves, which travel through the earth at different speeds, and so arrive at the surface in stages. Aristotle, writing in 340 BC, classified earth tremors into 'movers' and 'shakers', and he was not far off the mark, since the two kinds of body-wave motion give rise to noticeably different effects once they reach the surface of the earth.[12] The fastest waves, and thus the first to arrive at the surface, are the so-called P-waves (the 'primary' or 'pressure' waves), which travel at around six kilometres (nearly four miles) per second through the solid parts of the earth, and at around a third of that speed through water. P-waves are high-frequency longitudinal waves, which means that they propagate in the same direction as the displaced

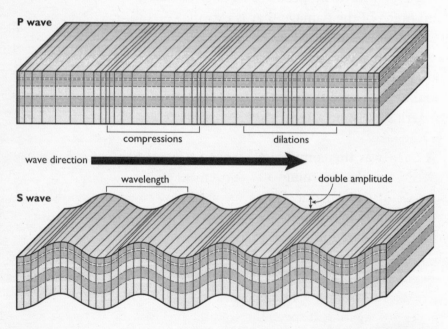

Figure ii. Primary ('P') waves and Secondary ('S') waves travel at different speeds through the solid earth, and propagate in different ways, giving rise to noticeably different effects on the ground.

material itself. Being so fast, they tend to cause less damage on the surface than do the slower S-waves (the 'secondary' or 'shear' waves). S-waves are transverse waves, which means that they travel in a direction perpendicular to that of the displaced material, and they move at around half the speed of the P-waves. Unlike longitudinal waves, they can only pass through the solid parts of the earth, but their slower speed and lower frequency give rise to higher amplitudes of motion, making them far more destructive than the P-waves.

When these two kinds of body wave hit the surface, they give rise in turn to two kinds of surface wave, known as Raleigh waves and Love waves, after the seismologists who identified their patterns. Raleigh waves are low-frequency longitudinal waves, which undulate slowly across the surface of the earth, doing relatively little in the way of damage, while the transverse Love waves, which are similar to S-waves in speed and direction, cause most of the shaking and much of the damage that is experienced during a tremor. All these various seismic waves – the 'movers' and the 'shakers' – travel at different speeds and in different directions, colliding, reflecting, bouncing and refracting as they pass through different materials on their way, with their interactions giving rise to an unpredictable pattern of seismic activity that is experienced on the surface as an earthquake.

Such was the complicated sequence of events that was set in motion on the morning of 1 November 1755. Deep below the surface of the Atlantic Ocean, at a point some one hundred to two hundred kilometres (sixty to one hundred miles) south-west of Lisbon, a section of seized-up plate margin was about to shift free, releasing massive waves of strain energy, and displacing a large area of sea floor in the process. The initial slippage seems to have occurred at around 9:40 a.m., sending a variety of seismic body waves propagating at speed through the intervening earth and sea, shaking the ground for a second or two and causing widespread panic and alarm. This was the initial shock that was felt throughout Lisbon and beyond, the tremors experienced at a number of places along the Portuguese, Spanish and North African coasts. Then, less than a minute later, as the slower but deadlier S-waves arrived, a staggered pair of longer slippages seems to have occurred along the same part of the fracture zone, sending further body waves of a far greater magnitude propagating outwards at a variety of frequencies. From that moment on, as the fast-moving shock-waves of violent energy hurtled and refracted along their way, distorting the bedrock under sea and land, percussing through surface rocks and buildings, and bringing much of what lay in their unstoppable path crashing to the ground, the ancient stone-built port of Lisbon never really stood a chance.

III

The earthquake came entirely without warning to a city that was wholly unprepared. Its timing, moreover, seemed particularly cruel, since by half-past nine on All Saints' Day morning most of the city's glittering churches would have been filled to capacity with worshippers. Candlelit masses had begun before dawn, and were to have continued throughout the rest of the morning, with the afternoon and evening taken up with a series of noisy processions and feasts. All Saints' was the high point of the Lisbon year, and it turned the whole city into a pageant of prayer, with the churches illuminated by long wax tapers whose flames danced bright amid the gilded interiors. Most of Lisbon's quarter-of-a-million-strong population would have aimed to pass at least some of the morning in one of the city's many churches, with the rest of their time spent preparing food and flowers for the coming feasts, or just milling around the crowded streets enjoying the holiday mood. Even some of the Protestant residents were keen to mark the occasion, including, of course, our clergyman-tourist on the castle walls, who was about to make his way down to the ten o'clock service at the British Envoy's private chapel when the earthquake struck.

There are dozens of other survivors' accounts that record
the moment of the earthquake's arrival, and from them we can
reconstruct the events of the morning in some detail. An assort-
ment of eyewitnesses worthy of Chaucer, including diplomats,
wine merchants, ship's captains, priests, journalists, labourers, nuns
and tourists, have left us their written impressions, and each one
tells a uniquely personal story of individual survival and loss
played out against a background of collective disaster. All in all, they
make for extraordinary reading, not least because, as the editor
of the *Gentleman's Magazine* pointed out in December 1755, in the
introduction to his own selection of earthquake letters, 'there is
something unspeakably striking in letters written on the spot,
describing scenes of distress which are still before them, and dangers
which they have themselves with difficulty escaped.'[13]

The following pages narrate some of the key episodes that
unfolded during the day of the disaster, selected from some of
the many first-person accounts that have survived the intervening
years. Not all of them were published at or near the time, but I
begin with one of the first that was – it appeared only a week or
so after the earthquake – and was written by a British merchant
who lived in a four-storey house to the east of the city centre. His
anonymously published pamphlet, entitled *An Account of the late
Dreadful Earthquake and Fire, which destroyed the City of Lisbon*, began
life in the form of a personal letter that he sent to a friend in
London. The friend, struck by the letter's immediacy and pace, as
well as by the newsworthiness of its contents, arranged to have it
published there and then by a bookseller in Paternoster Row. For
many of the readers who bought or borrowed the forty-five-page
booklet, it would have been their first encounter with an actual
eyewitness description of the event, and such was its circulation
that sections from it were later used by a number of journalists and
historical chroniclers in subsequent accounts of the disaster.

It starts with the merchant sitting in a chair in the third-floor
bedroom of his house, just before ten o'clock in the morning, 'the
Weather being serene, and the Sky without a Cloud in it':

When I felt the House begin gently to shake; which gradually increased with a rushing noise, like the Sound of heavy Carriages, driving hard at some Distance, and such I at first imagined the Cause of the Noise and Shaking I heard and felt. But both of them gradually increasing, and observing the Pictures in my Room to flap against the Walls, I started up, and immediately perceived it was an EARTHQUAKE; and having never been sensible of the Shaking of one before, I stood a good while very composedly remarking its Operations; till from waving and shaking, I thought the Room begin to roul, which made me run toward an inward one, more to the Centre of the house; but the Motion was then so extremely violent, that I with difficulty kept upon my Feet. Every part of the House cracked about me, the Tiles rattled on the Top of it; the Walls rent on every side; the Doors of a pretty large Book-case that stood in my Room, and which were locked, burst open, and the Books fell from the Shelves within it, but not till after I was got into the Room adjoining; and I heard, with Terror, the falling of Houses round about, and the Screams and Cries of People from every Quarter. At length, all beginning to settle into stillness again, I went into three or four Rooms of the Floor I was upon, to look for Servants, but finding none, concluded, with good reason, they had all left the House. So returning to my Room, I determined to change my Cloaths (for I was in a Night-Gown, Cap and Slippers,) and go out also. I had drest my Legs, and was putting on my Coat and Waistcoat, (having first put up my Books in their Case and locked the Doors of it) when I felt the second Shock begin: So I snatched up my Hat, and taking my Wig from a Sconce, ran down one pair of Stairs and half way another, when I stopt short, on hearing Tiles and large Stones falling from the Top of our own House and another into a small yard I must pass through. This made me reflect, that by flying from one falling House, I ran the risk of being buried under the Ruins of many others in the narrow Streets I must be obliged to pass before I could get to any Place of greater Safety, so I determined to

remain where I was, which was on a winding stone Staircase,
each step of which was an entire Stone, of about the length
of a Yard and a half; and this place I chose preferable to any
other on the Consideration, that if the House fell, the Stones
over my Head would put an immediate end to my Life, and
prevent the more miserable Fate of being buried alive under
the Ruins. Here, while I remained, the Steps I stood upon as
well as those over my Head, listed to a most shocking Degree,
and I expected every Moment to be crushed to Death. Here,
while I continued, I heard, from some part of the Yard below
me, a mournful Voice groaning, and calling out for Help, with
considerable intervening pauses, at least for a dozen Times
before the shaking of the House, and the falling of Stones
would permit my endeavour to offer any Assistance. Which
when I found an opportunity for doing, I did, and discovered
the Person in Distress was our own House-keeper, who in the
first Shock, had endeavoured to run out of our House, with
a Man Servant, but were met at the Street door by the Wall
of a House falling from the opposite side of the Way, which
wounded them both, but particularly the poor Woman, and
half buried them in its Rubbish.[14]

After pulling his two injured Portuguese employees from the ruins
of the fallen house, the merchant left them in the care of some Irish
neighbours who lived on the less badly damaged side of the street.
Then, ever curious, he decided to venture into the city itself in
order to gain a better idea of the extent of the destruction. He soon
ended up in the Terreiro do Paço ('Palace Terrace'), the large public
square that lay between the river and the now ruined royal palace,
and which, because of its size and situation, seemed to offer the
surest refuge from the danger of falling buildings:

There I found Numbers of People, of all Nations, collected
together; with such Signs of Terror and Distress in every
Countenance as can be much better imagined than described.
There were among them several Persons almost naked; one of

which was an English Surgeon, with nothing on him but a
Shirt, Cloak, and Pair of Slippers. I endeavoured to prevail on
him to go and visit the poor Woman I had left behind me, by
assuring him, that upon his asking for them, my Servant
would supply him with a whole Suit of my Cloaths, and every
thing else he was in need of (for he could get none of his own,
the House he lived in being fallen down) and he promised me
that he would go: But I believe the poor Man was terrified
from doing it, for he did not pay the Visit, as the poor Woman
has since told me, who fortunately escaped with her Life.

It was then that the merchant decided to make his way to a nearby
village, where a friend of his owned a country retreat, and from
where, at some point over the next few days, he wrote and dispatched his letter.

In another part of the city, meanwhile, a seventeen-year-old
English nun named Catherine Witham lay beneath a blanket in her
convent garden, alternately praying and weeping in shock. Half an
hour earlier she had been standing at the refectory sink, washing up
the breakfast things ('which is tea and bread and butter when 'tis
not fasting time'), and looking forward to attending the special
High Mass scheduled for ten o'clock. She had just added a newly
cleaned plate to the pile already on the draining board, when, as she
described in a long and wildly spelled letter which she sent to her
mother in England, 'the Dreadfull afair hapned':

itt began like the rattleing of Coaches, and the things befor me
danst up and downe upon the table, I look about me and see
the Walls a shakeing and a falling down then I up and took to
my heells, with Jesus in my mouth, and to the quire I run,
thinking to be safe there, but there was no Entranc but all
falling rownd us, and the lime and dust so thick there was no
seeing. I mett with some of the good Nuns they Cryed Outt
run to the low garden, I ask where the rest was, they sayde
there, so Blessed be his holy Name we all mett together, and
run no further, we was all as glad to see one another alive and

well as can be exprest. We spent the day in prayers, but with
a great deal of fear and apprehension, as we had shakes and
trembles all that day and night, and in fine ever since, only
God knows how and when itt will end.[15]

Despite the loss of their convent building ('poor Sion Houes', as
Catherine Witham lamented it), the community of English Bridgettine nuns all survived the disaster, just as they had survived their
difficult years of exile following the dissolution of the monasteries
in England. Founded in Isleworth on the north bank of the Thames
in 1415, the Bridgettine community fled newly Protestant England
in the late 1550s, only to spend the next thirty-five years drifting
through Catholic Europe in search of a permanent home. Eventually they found shelter in a comfortable Lisbon convent building in
1594, and there they remained for a century and a half until the All
Saints' Day earthquake rendered the sisterhood homeless once
again. But at least they had the shared comfort of sheltering in their
garden together. 'We have got a Wooden houes made in the
garden, where the two good fathers and aboute half of us lives and
lays', wrote Catherine, 'but we lye in our Cloes I have never lain
without my Cloes since All Saints. Which I find vere Uncomfortable but I beg God to accept it as a small Pennance.'

And it was a small penance for, as Catherine Witham was well
aware, there were many others whose situation was far less fortunate, since by this time most of the buildings in central Lisbon had
similarly collapsed, trapping thousands of people in their ruins.
Many already lay dead or dying in the maze of narrow streets, as
countless scenes of horror and distress played themselves out all
over the city.

The following sad account was written by Daniel Braddock,
another resident British merchant, who was either the younger
brother or the nephew of Major-General Edward Braddock, the
celebrated British officer who had died in action earlier that year
on the Monongahela River in Ohio. Daniel's letter describes what
happened when he tried to help a Portuguese neighbour and her

child make it through the ruined streets to the safety of the Terreiro do Paço:

> Finding the passage this way entirely blocked up with the fallen houses to the height of their second stories, I turned back to the other end which led into the main street, (the common thoroughfare to the Palace) and helped the woman over a vast heap of ruins, with no small hazard to my own life; just as we were going into this street, as there was one part I could not well climb over without the assistance of my hands, as well as feet, I desired her to let go her hold, which she did, remaining two or three feet behind me, at which instant there fell a vast stone, from a tottering wall, and crushed both her and the child in pieces; so dismal a spectacle at any other time would have affected me in the highest degree, but the dread I was in of sharing the same fate myself, and the many instances of the same kind which presented themselves all around, were too shocking to make me dwell a moment on this single object.[16]

Braddock continued his journey down to the riverside square, but he refused to answer any further cries for help, since, as is clear from his description, he scarcely had the energy to save himself. He was not alone in feeling a kind of dulled detachment to the terrible scenes that unfolded all around him – it is in fact a common reaction in the midst of sudden disasters – and most of the survivor accounts from Lisbon describe how the shouts of people who were buried in the ruins made little impression on the people hurrying past. According to one account, published in the December edition of the *Gentleman's Magazine*, 'as you passed along the streets you saw shops of goods with the shopkeepers buried with them, some alive crying out from under the ruins, others half buried, others with broken limbs, in vain begging for help, but they were passed by crouds without the least notice or sense of humanity.'[17]

But the growing numbers of survivors who had managed to make their way down to the riverside squares were not yet out

of danger, for another effect of the slippage along the Azores–
Gibraltar Fracture Zone was just about to make itself felt. As
described earlier, the earthquake's various seismic waves would
have travelled at great speed through the earth and sea, propagated by the elastic deformation of the materials through which
they passed. It was these that had been responsible for the sequence
of severe shakes that had brought down the buildings of the city.
But as Lisbon shook and collapsed beneath its rising cloud of
dust and smoke, a series of much slower shock waves was making
its way through the waters of the Atlantic, and was soon to make
landfall along the shores of the river Tagus. Such seismic sea
waves, known as tsunamis, can travel across the Atlantic at speeds
of 500 kilometres (310 miles) per hour – the speed of an airliner,
although fifteen times slower than seismic energy waves – and
are usually associated with sudden subsidences or slippages along
undersea faults. At the epicentre of the earthquake, perhaps a
region of the abyssal plain north of the Gorringe Bank, part of
the sea floor must have subsided or slipped during the violent
interaction of the plates, causing a massive quantity of displaced sea
water to surge suddenly downwards, only to rebound quickly outwards in a series of powerful waves. According to the Portuguese
seismologist João Duarte Fonseca, recent research has identified
an underwater geological structure between the Gorringe Bank and
Cape St Vincent (the exposed headland on Portugal's south-west
corner), which has been named 'the Marquis of Pombal Fault' in
honour of the rebuilder of Lisbon. Could this have been the exact
birthplace of the tsunamigenic quake?[18]

Whatever the precise location of the earthquake, some forty
to fifty minutes after its principal shocks were felt, the water in
Lisbon harbour was seen suddenly to recede, exposing a shipwreck-
studded sandbank at the mouth of the Tagus estuary. Hundreds
of people who had escaped the earthquake by clambering onto
boats that had been moored in the deceptively calm waters of
the harbour were the first to notice the strange drop in sea level,
just before they also became the first to notice the twelve-metre

(forty-foot) wave rapidly advancing towards them from the western mouth of the estuary. A surge of panic broke out among the people on the boats, and Daniel Braddock, who was still surrounded by the large crowds assembled at the Terreiro do Paço, turned towards the source of the noise, and was greeted by the sight of a mountainous wave making its way towards the shore:

> On a sudden I heard a general outcry, 'The sea is coming in; we shall all be lost.' Upon this, turning my eyes towards the river, which in that place is near four miles broad, I could perceive it heaving and swelling in a most unaccountable manner, for no wind was stirring; in an instant there appeared, at some small distance, a large body of water, rising as it were like a mountain, it came on foaming and roaring, and rushed towards the shore with such impetuosity, that we all immediately ran for our lives, as fast as possible; many were actually swept away, and the rest above their waist in water at a good distance from the banks. For my own part, I had the narrowest escape, and should certainly have been lost, had I not grasped a large beam that lay on the ground, till the water returned to its channel, which it did almost at the same instant, with equal rapidity. As there now appeared at least as much danger from the sea as the land, and I scarce knew whither to retire for shelter, I took a sudden resolution of returning back with my cloaths all dropping, to the area of St. Paul's: here I stood for some time, and observed the ships tumbling and tossing about, as in a violent storm; some had broken their cables, and were carried to the other side of the Tagus; others were whirled round with incredible swiftness; several large boats were turned keel upwards; and all this without any wind, which seemed the more astonishing. It was at the time of which I am now speaking, that the fine new quay, built entirely of rough marble, at an immense expense, was entirely swallowed up, with all the people on it, who had fled thither for safety, and had reason to think themselves out of danger in such a place: at the same time a great number of

boats and small vessels, anchored near it (all likewise full of people, who had retired thither for the same purpose) were all swallowed up, as in a whirlpool, and never more appeared.

A train of three vast waves had swept up the river, over the docks and into the already devastated city, before washing backwards into the estuary, dragging people and debris in its wake. As Daniel Braddock so vividly described, the tsunami indiscriminately smashed the boats as well as the Cais da Pedra – the costly and much-admired new marble quay – into pieces, drowning all who had congregated on them for safety.

The earthquake had been terrible enough by itself, but the coming of the tsunami added a new layer of horror to the crowded events of the morning. It was as though the city's gentle river, for so long the conduit of its wealth and good fortune, had risen up to strike it in its hour of greatest need. Some of the survivors in the square, who had witnessed the waves' destructive advance, suddenly abandoned all hope of rescue, and ran back into the burning ruins of the city. Others, meanwhile, believing that the day of judgement had finally come, gathered around the many priests who were among the survivors, and were soon 'falling on their Knees, kissing the Earth, beating their Breasts, slapping their cheeks, and crying out for Absolution, which was granted in general Terms to Hundreds of them at once.'[19] A rising mood of mass hysteria had begun to take hold.

This sequence of events on land had been observed from the water by a visiting sea captain, whose vessel was docked further out in the Tagus estuary, and so survived both earthquake and tsunami. In a letter that he sent to the *Gentleman's Magazine* in London, he described the proceedings of 'this dismal catastrophe' as he watched them unfolding from the deck of his ship:

Ten minutes before ten I felt the ship have an uncommon motion, and could not help thinking she was aground, although sure of the depth of water. As the motion encreased my amazement encreased also, and as I was looking round to

find out the meaning of the uncommon motion, I was immediately acquainted with the direful cause; when at that instant
looking towards the city, I beheld the tall and stately buildings
come tumbling down with great cracks and noise . . .

Almost all the palaces and large churches were rent down,
or part fallen, and scarce one house of this vast city is left
habitable. Every body that were not crushed to death ran out
into the large places, and those near the river ran down to save
themselves by boats, or any other floating conveniency, running, crying, and calling to the ships for assistance; but whilst
the multitude were gathered near the river side, the water
rose to such a height that it overcame and overflow'd the lower
part of the city, which so terrified the miserable and already
dismayed inhabitants, who ran to and fro with dreadful cries,
which we heard plainly on board, that it made them believe the
dissolution of the world was at hand; every one falling on his
knees, and intreating the Almighty for his assistance.[20]

There was now such panic and alarm among the crowds in the
square that 'the terrors of death were in all their countenances', as
Daniel Braddock memorably phrased it, and the priests were
having some difficulty keeping control of their agitated flocks,
whose 'shrieks and cries of *Misericordia* could distinctly be heard
from the top of St. Catherine's hill, at a considerable distance off.'

Braddock, still in fear of his life, began to worry about the
wisdom of remaining among the survivors at the riverside, for he
had begun to sense a darkening of their mood. He had also begun
to worry about the fate of a newly arrived English friend, with
whom he had arranged to have dinner that evening, and whose
lodgings were on the top floor of a house in the centre of town. He
decided, in a fit of bravery, to see if he could find out what had
become of his friend, and so he headed back towards the ruined city
centre:

but the new scenes of horror I met with here, exceed all
description; nothing could be heard but sighs and groans, I did

not meet with a soul in the passage who was not bewailing
the death of his nearest relations and dearest friends, or the
loss of all his substance; I could hardly take a single step without treading on the dead or the dying: in some places lay
coaches, with their masters, horses and riders, almost crushed
in pieces; here, mothers with infants in their arms; there,
ladies richly dressed, priests, friars, gentlemen, mechanics,
either in the same condition, or just expiring; some had their
backs or thighs broken, others vast stones on their breasts;
some lay almost buried in the rubbish, and crying out in vain
to the passengers for succour, were left to perish with the rest.

After struggling through the horror-laden city he eventually arrived
at the spot where his friend's house had once stood, but the house,
along with its neighbouring buildings, had collapsed in its entirety,
and there was no sign of life among the ruins. Giving up his friend
for dead, and now thinking 'of nothing else but saving my own life
in the best manner I could', Braddock – understandably wary of
ending up next to the river again – turned instead towards the hills
surrounding the city. He spent the rest of that terrible afternoon
trying to navigate his way towards them, but it was not an easy
task, for by this time there were thousands of panic-stricken people
swarming through the ruined streets, not one of whom had a clear
idea of what to do or where to go. Large areas of the city, moreover,
were now entirely impassable, with the rubble from rows of fallen
buildings blocking what had once been narrow streets. Hundreds
of people, as Braddock reported, were clambering over piles of
masonry in an attempt to make their way towards the safety of
open spaces, yet many of them had also laden themselves down
with whatever household possessions they had been unwilling to
leave behind; not only bags of money and jewels, but larger objects
such as dresses, carpets, paintings and candelabra, salvaged from
fallen or burning houses, dragged through the chaos of the city
streets and then dumped in great piles in the riverside squares as
though ready for the auctioneer's hammer.

Lisbon, or what was left of it, appeared to have gone mad with grief and terror, but even after the twin shocks of earthquake and tsunami had wrought such devastation upon the suffering city, worse was still to come. The series of small fires, which had broken out all over the city, mostly from the fall of roof timbers onto the thousands of lit church and household candles, as well as from the many kitchen ranges that were primed for the All Saints' Day feasts, had gained in intensity as the day wore on. Fanned by a fresh north-easterly breeze that had slowly picked up over the course of the morning, the flames had coalesced into a single large fire that had spread across the ruined metropolis and was advancing towards the crowded riverside squares.

The best account we have of the fire's progress was written by a young English wine merchant named Thomas Chase, who had been born and brought up in the Lisbon trade, and whose birthday – 'the day that made me twenty-six years of age' – happened to fall that very morning. He had been in the fourth-floor bedroom of his city-centre house when the first groundswells of the earthquake arrived. Just as he had decided to try to make it down the stairs and into the street, however, the entire building, 'which was so old and weak, that any heavy carriage passing made it shake all over', suddenly collapsed beneath him. 'I thought the whole city was sinking into the earth', he wrote in a long and vivid letter to his mother in England, 'for immediately I felt myself falling.'[21]

Waking in darkness amid piles of dust and rubble, it took him a few seconds to realize where he was and what had happened: he had fallen to the ground along with all four storeys of his now flattened house, but, against the odds, he had survived the sudden demolition. His injuries, however, were terrible:

My right arm hung down before me motionless, like a great dead weight, the shoulder being out, and the bone broken: my stockings were cut to pieces, and my legs covered with wounds, the right ancle swelled to a prodigious size, with a fountain of blood spouting upwards from it: the knee also was much bruised, my left side felt as if beat in, so that I could hardly breathe: all the left side of my face was swelled, the skin beaten off, the blood streaming from it, with a great wound above, and a small one below the eye, and several bruises on my back and head.

In spite of his mangled condition, Chase survived an eventful journey through the smoke and ruins of the city, arriving eventually at the crowded Terreiro do Paço, where he was tended – though in a somewhat distracted manner – by the wife of a family friend.

After the waves of the tsunami had come and gone, he assumed that the worst of the danger had passed, but he had begun to notice the wind picking up, and flames from the burning parts of the city beginning to approach the square. They had already reached the docksides to the north-east of the Terreiro do Paço, and had ignited the extensive sugar and tobacco warehouses that lined that part of the river. Within minutes, the unmistakable aromas of burning tobacco and caramelized sugar were drifting surreally over the ruins.

But the flames were getting nearer with every minute that passed, and they now appeared to be approaching from all directions. They had just begun to set fire to some of the larger bundles of clothing and possessions that people had brought to the square and then abandoned, when suddenly Chase heard a stranger cry out to him: ' "You are on fire!" ':

and feeling my quilt snatched away, saw it thrown upon the ground; the fire was then stamped out, and the quilt returned to me again. I then told Mrs. Graves, if she did not remove, we should be on fire again; that it were better to go into the corner of the Square, where the entrance to the Palace had been, as the only place free from bundles, and where the wind did not blow the flames; in short, rather to run the risque of the falling of the walls, than to remain thus certainly exposed to the fire: but Mrs. Graves, whose spirits were now quite exhausted, replied, it was impossible to go anywhere to avoid

the evil; and having already removed several times to no purpose, she would stir no farther. Soon after I heard several
Portuguese men and women animate each other to attempt
an escape, notwithstanding the flames, through the ruins of
the Palace; they in consequence mounted over the rubbish,
and soon disappeared: when part of an arch, through which
they were to pass, falling in, it caused a kind of compassionate
cry among the people near us; but as none of the adventurers
returned, I would hope they were successful.

Chase and his companions spent the following hour continually
shifting their positions as the flames passed from one side of the
square to the other, 'bursting out all at once with violent heat', as
he described their terrifying appearances. At one stage the flames
seemed to have finally run their course, and for a few minutes the
exhausted Chase was able to lie back down on the pavement in an
attempt to gain some respite from the pain of his wounds, until he
heard a collective scream rise up from the assembled crowd, and,
looking up from inside his blanket:

I saw every one kneeling down, and the great Square full of
flames; for the people from the adjoining streets had by this
time filled it with bundles, and, as the fire increased, had taken
themselves only away; these were now all in flames, except
just at our corner, and under the Palace-walls, where Mr.
Graves's family had retired; but as the wind blew very fresh,
and drove the flames in sheets of fire close slanting over our
heads, expecting them every minute to sieze upon us, I again
lost all my spirits, and abandoning myself to despair, thought
it still impossible, after so many escapes, to avoid the sort of
death I so much dreaded. Passing away some time in these
horrid apprehensions, the wind suddenly abated, and the fire
burning upright, made no further progress. This restoring
hope to us again, hunger obliged those who had provisions to
think of eating, when an Irish Roman Catholic gentlewoman,
sitting near me, asked if my name was not Chase. She said, she

knew my father many years, and gave me a large piece of water melon.

Chase and his friends had had a lucky escape, for there were many others in the crowded square who had been horribly burned by the fire, in what must have seemed a gruesome parody of the annual *autos da fé*, in which – on platforms erected in the centre of that same square – the officers of the Portuguese Inquisition had consigned dozens of their victims to the flames (picture 4).

But the fire that had taken hold of the rest of the city was now completely out of control, and was fast devouring whatever remained, whether ruins or standing buildings. At one point a burning mule ran out of the inferno and into the north side of the Terreiro do Paço, before collapsing to the ground in obvious pain and terror. For many of the survivors who witnessed such scenes, it must have seemed beyond the realms of possibility that their ancient and magical city, which had woken that morning to sunshine and prayers, had, in the course of a few short hours, been destroyed by a trinity of natural disasters: earthquake, deluge and now this raging firestorm, as though the elements themselves had somehow declared war upon the city (picture 5).

It was, quite simply, a vision of hell on earth: the city of Lisbon burning in ruins, an entire urban civilization, with its centuries of accumulated treasure held in libraries, galleries, churches and convents, fallen in a single day. Nothing in the city would ever be the same again; even up in the castle gardens, some distance from the worst of the carnage below, our visiting army chaplain had suffered a strange reversal, after his English prayers had served to attract the attention of the growing crowd. As the morning wore on, their ranks had been swelled by a number of friars who had escaped from a fallen monastery nearby, and who paid particular attention to the ecclesiastical stranger among them. Having only just arrived in Lisbon, the chaplain spoke not a word of Portuguese, and, as he soon discovered, was also unable to make himself understood in Latin, since his English pronunciation was entirely incomprehensible to the ears of the Portuguese friars. He soon found himself surrounded by a large and vocal crowd, which, at the friars' instigation, began to chant in what he took at first to be a hostile and threatening manner. He began to panic, fearing that the distressed survivors might take the view that the presence of this 'solitary Clergyman, whose Function and Religion he had reason to conclude were particularly obnoxious' might somehow be responsible for the crisis befalling their city. But, as was described in the merchant's letter from which this account of the episode derives, it seems that the clergyman had entirely mistaken the motives of the Portuguese crowd:

> for it was from good Will to save his Soul, for the Priests that were with him fairly Baptised him, without his knowing what they were about, 'till they came to the Use of the Water in the Ceremony, and then it was in vain to resist. After they had accomplished their Work, the poor misguided Zealots expressed so wonderful a Regard and Fondness for their fan-cy'd Proselyte, that the Priests even proceeded to kneeling down before him and embracing his Knees, nay to the very kissing of his Feet.[22]

What an extraordinary morning it had been for our clergyman up at the castle, for within the space of a couple of hours on a sunny Saturday morning he had witnessed the destruction of an ancient city, been forcibly received into the Church of Rome, and then hailed as a beacon of much-needed hope by a crowd of post-apocalyptic survivors who, moved to perform a merciful deed in an attempt to mitigate the sins of their city, had stripped him of his heretical religion and clothed him in the garments of their own.

*

'Of all Temporal Judgements', asked the New England theologian Thomas Prince in an excitable sermon written in 1755, 'what is more *Terrible* than a sudden and destroying Earthquake? Famines,

Plagues, and Wars are wasting and dreadful Calamities. But these destroy in a gradual manner, and give the Inhabitants Time to escape or prepare to meet them. But an *Earthquake* comes on a sudden, and frequently does it's destructive Work in a Moment, and there is no resisting or flying away.'[23] He was right: it had only taken a minute or two for the fate of Lisbon to be sealed, and by the early afternoon, once the dust cloud had lifted, the extent of the morning's devastation was clear for all to see. The city centre had been flattened by the earthquake, the docks and warehouses that ranged along the riverside had been destroyed by the tsunami and its accompanying flood, and most of what was left was now on fire, including all those piles of personal possessions that had been rescued from the fallen houses. 'Them that has seen Lisbon before this dreadful Calammity and to see itt now would be greatly shokt', wrote sister Catherine Witham from the refuge of her convent garden; 'the Citty is Nothing but a heep of Stones caused by the Great fier tis Callculated above forty thousand was destroyed and one of the most terrible things that hapened was this, that many poor Souls Inclosed in the Ruings not Killd, but Could not gett out so some was burnt alive and Others dyed of hunger.'[24]

For her, as for many others, the stricken city had been transformed into something resembling an outpost of hell, and with a continuing north-east wind, the absence of rain, and the impossibility of organizing any form of fire resistance, Lisbon went on burning for a week, in a wide crescent of flame that stretched from the lower slopes of the castle hill, right through the ruined shell of the city itself and on to the low-lying São Paulo district, beyond the Cais do Sodre to the west. What had once been a crowded, vibrant city was now a vast funeral pyre, from which 'dwellings, friends and treasures all were gone', in the words of the soldier-poet Lieutenant John Biddulph, who, stationed in Portugal when the earthquake struck, wrote and published a 260-line poem on the disaster in December 1755, in which he described how Lisbon, 'that once fair Town with all her Store . . . now heaving in Death like one vast Body lay', and how, at the end:

The Fires, that glimm'ring still with pale'y Red,
Like Burial Tapers, nodded o'er the Dead,
Performing the last Office, as they wave,
Add Dust and Ashes to the gen'ral Grave.[25]

IV

The fire in the city eventually died down, although aftershocks continued for several weeks, as rocks and other crustal materials shifted
by the earthquake settled into their new alignments. A couple of
major shocks, one on 11 December and the other on 21 December
1755, caused fresh waves of panic to erupt throughout the Lisbon
area, but for the most part the survivors and the bereaved of the
earthquake remained in a state of listless incredulity. Some began to
search the ruins for the bodies of their relatives and friends, or tried
to salvage whatever they could in the way of personal possessions
and money, but on the whole the city and its people appeared devastated beyond hope of recovery. 'I have seen hundreds of people in
the same melancholy situation with myself,' wrote a seventy-two-
year-old Lisbon merchant in a letter to *Read's Weekly Journal* in
December 1755; 'they have nothing left but the sad remembrance of
their former fortunes. Lisbon is now no more; and if it should ever
be rebuilt, who would venture to settle there?'
     Not the king, for one, if his proclamations were to be believed.
He and his family had had a remarkable deliverance, having left
their riverside palace after attending Mass at dawn, for an All
Saints' Day coach trip to the countryside – the jaunt being made,
apparently, at his youngest daughter's insistence. They had ridden
as far as the neighbouring town of Belém, some five kilometres
(three miles) along the riverside road, when the earthquake arrived
in Lisbon. Their sixteenth-century palace had been among the
first of the city-centre buildings to collapse, and had the family
stayed at home that morning, as was their usual custom on major
festivals, when they liked to watch the comings and goings from

the balconies overlooking the square, it is doubtful that any of them would have survived. Taking this preservation as a sign from God, the king refused to abandon the safety of the countryside, and for several months after the Lisbon disaster the entire royal family lodged in a collection of marquees, declining to venture indoors even during the day. When the British Envoy, Abraham Castres, paid them an official visit on the second day after the earthquake, the queen and the princesses declined to make an appearance, being, as they put it, 'under their tents, and in a dress not fit to appear in.'[26]

The distressed king began to make plans for relocating his capital city to the ancient university town of Coimbra, some 240 kilometres (150 miles) to the north, and then for transferring his court and family across the Atlantic to Brazil, swearing never to set foot in Lisbon again. Many of his poorer subjects felt the same way, and the outskirts of the capital became a city of tents, a vast refugee camp that ranged over the hills outside the ruined metropolis, filled with thousands of people who were determined to leave, but who had nowhere else to go. Central Lisbon itself, meanwhile, was virtually abandoned, while the outlying parishes continued to fill with increasing numbers of the homeless and dispossessed. The parish of Santa Isabel, for example, to the north-west of the city, was said to have had a refugee population of more than twenty-five thousand, 'and if you go out of the city', wrote a correspondent to the Gentleman's Magazine, 'you behold nothing but barracks or tents made with canvas or ship's sails, where the poor inhabitants lye'[27] (see picture 6).

Eighty-five per cent of Lisbon's twenty-four thousand houses had either been destroyed outright or left unfit for habitation. But even some of the buildings that had survived remained empty during the following weeks, the frequent aftershocks rendering their owners too nervous to sleep indoors. 'Will your Earth never be quiet?' asked the Spanish Ambassador in a letter to the British Envoy, Abraham Castres – and the beleaguered Castres, who had survived the earthquake by jumping out of a second-floor window, may well have asked himself the same question.[28] His large house in the Lisbon suburbs (to where our chaplain on the castle had been heading) had withstood the shocks, 'tho' greatly damaged', and was now inundated with people seeking help. Few of the petitioners, however, were brave enough to step inside, fearing that the badly leaning house might collapse at any moment. Their fear was understandable, although it did nothing to help the work of Envoy Castres, who described the situation in a letter written on 6 November to his official London contact, Thomas Robinson, Secretary of State for the Southern Department:

> Several of my friends, burnt out of their houses, have taken refuge with me, where I have accommodated them, as well as I could, under tents in my large garden; nobody but Lord Charles Douglas, who is actually on board the packet, besides our chaplain and myself, having dared hitherto to sleep in my house since the day of our disaster . . . The dismal accounts brought to us every instant of the accidents befallen one or another of our acquaintance among the nobility, who, for the most part, are quite undone, has greatly affected me; but in particular the miserable objects among the lower sort of his majesty's subjects, who all fly to me for bread, and lie scattered up and down in my garden, with their wives and children. I have helped them all hitherto, and shall continue to do so as long as provisions do not fail us, which I hope will not be the case, by the good orders M. de Carvalho has issued in that respect. I must humbly beg your pardon, Sir, for the disorder of this letter, surrounded as I am by the many in distress, who, from one instant to another, are applying to me either for advice or shelter.[29]

Fortunately for the petitioners in the Envoy's garden, as well as for the Bridgettine nuns in theirs – 'we layde under a pair tree, covered with a Carpett, for Eight days', according to the stoical Catherine Witham – the weather stayed fine for the next few weeks, but the overall outlook for the people of Lisbon remained desperate. Most of the dead still lay unburied, not that there was room for all of them anyway, since the burial grounds of the city's churches were already woefully overcrowded. The precise death toll of the Lisbon earthquake has never been securely established, although estimates range between twenty thousand and ninety thousand dead, from a population of a quarter of a million. Every day saw more bodies recovered from the ruins, though all that could be done with them was lay them out in the abandoned squares, alongside the badly burned carcasses of the hundreds of horses, dogs and mules that had also perished in the fire. 'Oh! dreadful sight', wrote an eyewitness in a letter published in the *Whitehall Evening Post* on 21 November: 'I believe I saw 8 or 9,000 dead bodies, some upon the rubbish, others half way up their bodies in the rubbish, standing like statues; and at this time the stench was so great that it was impossible to stay long among the ruins.'

The king was inconsolable at the scale of the devastation, and wrote a letter to his sister, Bárbara de Braganza, in which he described himself sorrowfully as 'a king without a kingdom, in a country without a capital.'[30] Incapacitated by grief, he remained in his tent, unable to act or make rational decisions; but instead of recalling parliament and charging its members to take control of the situation, he simply delegated all power and responsibility to his ambitious First Minister, Sebastião José de Carvalho e Mello, the future Marquis of Pombal, whose house in the Rua Formosa had been one of the few buildings in the city centre to survive the day unscathed – a fact that the king apparently interpreted as another signal from God. Legend has it that Pombal had been the first to arrive at the king's encampment and, when asked by the monarch: 'What is to be done to meet this infliction of divine justice?', replied with the words that would make him famous: 'Bury the dead, Sire, and take care of the living.'[31] Whether or not these words were actually exchanged during the meeting, Pombal's rational calmness in the face of the disaster so impressed the irresolute king that he handed over all powers of state to his fifty-six-year-old First Minister, and from that day forward the Marquis of Pombal was in charge of the city's destiny.

His first achievement was to persuade the king to abandon his
planned relocation to Brazil, and to accept the idea that this was
not the time to go breaking the bonds with his people; on the con-
trary, as Pombal and his advisers urged, it was essential for Lisbon
to be rebuilt and reinstated as Portugal's capital. Once this guiding
principle had been agreed, the imposing Pombal, who was well
over two metres (six feet) tall (and known among the British as 'the
Lisbon Oak'), installed himself in a coach borrowed from the royal
residence at Belém, in which he travelled back into the ruins of
Lisbon, issuing decree after decree governing every aspect of the
city's reconstruction. His energy was phenomenal, and within a
week he had issued over two hundred orders from his itinerant
horse-drawn headquarters governing the burial of the dead, the
clearing of ruins, the collection of provisions and medical supplies,
the feeding of refugees, the calling up of troops, the appointment
of magistrates, the maintenance of discipline, the gagging of the
press, the fixing of prices, the movement of shipping and the protection of the now vulnerable Portuguese coast against marauding
North African pirates. He took sole responsibility for all decisions
made in the aftermath of the disaster, and sought to offer encouragement to his dispirited fellow subjects, not least through the
example of his own great courage and common sense. According
to one admiring account that was published at the time, 'during
twenty-four hours on end he took no nourishment except a bowl of
broth, which was brought to him by his wife, who picked her way
to his carriage over the débris in the streets.'[32]

Pombal, however, soon began to display the frightening zeal of
someone who had found his cause in life, and who was prepared to
impose it on others by force. Lisbon would rise again, he declared,
whatever the feelings of its surviving inhabitants. To this end,
martial law was declared, and troops were called in from neighbouring provinces and stationed around the perimeters of the city
with orders to turn back the tide of exiles who were still flowing
into the countryside. All able-bodied men were made to return to
the ruins under military supervision, where they were conscripted

into work-teams assigned to various specific tasks such as clearance, demolition, rescue and burial. Thieves and looters, of which there were many, were hanged on the spot on seven large gallows, conspicuously erected for the purpose, their bodies added to the piles of dead already awaiting disposal. It soon became evident that the rapid burial of such vast numbers was an impossible undertaking, and so, once he had gained the permission of the Lisbon Patriarch, Pombal arranged for the majority of the bodies to be taken out in barges to the mouth of the Tagus estuary, where they were weighted down with rubble and thrown into the sea. Despite the fact that it was an emergency measure, designed to prevent the spread of disease, many among the Lisbon clergy protested at the sacrilege, but Pombal, whose frustration with the priesthood had been increasing by the day, dismissed their protestations out of hand.

Historians have often portrayed Pombal as an anti-clerical tyrant who took advantage of the earthquake to impose his vision of secular modernity on the reluctant people of Lisbon. But this was only partly true, for it is also clear that he was sympathetic towards the survivors' need for spiritual support, and was genuinely grateful for the churches' efforts on behalf of the earthquake's victims. But at the same time he resented the sense of despondency and alarm that some of the priests sought to encourage among their desolate congregations. The Jesuits in particular had been active in spreading a rumour that the first anniversary of the earthquake would herald the final judgement, and one leading Jesuit theologian, Gabriel Malagrida, published an inflammatory sermon entitled *The Real Cause of the Earthquake*, a copy of which he foolishly sent to Pombal. In it, he declared that the only activity in which the people of Lisbon ought to be engaged was meditating upon their sins under Jesuit guidance, not working alongside the civil authorities in their blasphemous rebuilding of a city destroyed by God. 'Learn, O Lisbon,' wrote the Italian-born preacher, 'that the destroyers of our houses, palaces, churches, and convents, the cause of the death of so many people and of the flames that devoured such vast treasures, are your abominable sins, and not comets, stars, vapours and exhalations, and similar natural phenomena: Tragic Lisbon is now a mound of ruins [and] it is scandalous to pretend that the earthquake was just a natural event.'[33] The more secular-minded Pombal was unimpressed by the pamphlet and, interpreting its argument as a challenge to his authority, he ordered Malagrida's immediate banishment from Lisbon. But when Malagrida continued to preach from exile against the 'worldly' reconstruction, Pombal had him arrested for blasphemy and sedition and, following a lengthy period of imprisonment and torture, he was executed along with forty others in a show of public might.

The Malagrida episode, complete with its barbarous conclusion, exemplified the painful struggle between civil and religious authority that was such a shaping characteristic of the European Enlightenment. Pombal's vision for post-earthquake Lisbon was of a city that would rise from the ruins to become a modern European centre of learning and enlightenment, having thrown off the bigotry of its priest-haunted past. But as long as opinions such as the Jesuits' were allowed to circulate freely, Portugal would remain, in Pombal's view, a decadent and benighted backwater. So he cracked down hard on religious dissent, especially where the causes of the earthquake were concerned – a subject to which he would give increasing attention the more the rebuilding went on.

Pombal's secular and scientific views had been strengthened during the six years he spent in London from 1739 to 1745 as the Portuguese Ambassador, where he had grown to admire the rational spirit behind Britain's burgeoning mercantilist economy. Influenced by the tone of sceptical enquiry that permeated British attitudes to natural knowledge, he took the line that phenomena such as earthquakes were naturally occurring rather than divinely ordained events, and that the only way for Lisbon to overcome the tragedy would be through human ingenuity rather than prayer. There were many among the clergy who thought differently, of course, and who continued to preach on behalf of moral reform, but Pombal's thoughts on the subject remained fixed: the destruction of the city had been an earthly event, and its safe rebuilding for

its future inhabitants – the rising of Pombal's rational phoenix –
would be a matter for engineers rather than priests.

But even as the ruins began to be cleared away, and plans for
constructing an antiseismic city were drawn up and discussed,
morale among many of the poorer survivors remained low. For one
thing, the spell of mild weather had not lasted long, and the weeks
and months that followed the disaster turned increasingly cold and
wet. Although international aid had been requested and supplied
(most generously by the governments of Britain and Germany;
France, however, refused to contribute so much as a centime),*
life in the outlying camps remained hard, with foreign observers
reporting that 'the unhappy fugitives from Lisbon are now perish-
ing in great numbers by diseases which have been contracted partly
by fatigue, watching, and terror, and partly by scarcity of provision,
and want of shelter from the weather.'[34] Pombal's leadership had
been highly effective in the immediate aftermath of the disaster, but
as the months went by his attention became increasingly drawn to
the design of the replacement city, leaving much of the day-to-day
welfare provision in the hands of parish priests. Many of these
priests worked tirelessly, distributing whatever food and clothing
they could find from makeshift headquarters, while some of them
even managed to salvage enough material to construct temporary
wooden churches in an attempt to maintain normal religious
life. But the near-continuous aftershocks – five hundred had been

---

*   The British sent aid in the following form:

Beef, 6,000 barrels	estimated value:	£10,000
Butter, 4,000 firkins	—	£3,000
Flour, 10,000 quarters	—	£15,000
Wheat, 10,000 ditto	—	£15,000
Biscuit, 1,000 bags	—	£1,200
Rice, 1,200 barrels	—	£1,000
Pickaxes, Spades, Crows, Screws, &c	—	£1,000
In Portugal Gold	—	£30,000
In Pieces of Eight	—	£20,000
Shoes	—	£1,000
Total:		£97,200

registered within six months of the earthquake itself – did nothing to lift the mood among the grieving survivors, who remained far more receptive to what their priests had to say than they had ever been to Pombal's bullying proclamations. And in spite of his suppression of the Jesuit-sponsored rumours, many people continued to believe that Lisbon had been punished by an angry God, although the reasons for the punishment varied wildly, with some blaming the city's idolatrous love of gold, some blaming the sexual licence that famously prevailed at court and others claiming that the unchecked presence of so many Protestant heretics had drawn down his jealous wrath.

Protestant commentators from outside, meanwhile, naturally declared that Popish idolatry had been the sole target of God's righteous anger, with George Whitefield, the Methodist preacher who had visited Lisbon only eighteen months before, happily delivering an I-told-you-so sermon that ended with the words 'I know that my Redeemer liveth':

> But O that all who were lately swallowed up in Portugal had known it! Then an earthquake would only be a rumbling chariot to carry the soul to God. Poor Lisbon! how soon are all thy riches and superstitious pageantry swallowed up![35]

Whatever the reasons for its destruction by God, Lisbon had clearly paid a heavy price. But the inescapable implication, that God the father was merciless rather than merciful, was a problematic issue for many theologians, who struggled with the realization that thousands of the city's most God-fearing residents, the majority of whom were women and children, had been killed while at their prayers. If God had indeed been responsible for this earthquake, then why did he punish the innocent so severely, when – as it soon emerged – hundreds of criminals had made their escape from the fallen prisons unharmed? And why had most of the churches been destroyed when the row of brothels along the Rua Suja had survived the day unscathed? Did any of this have any wider meaning; was it all part of God's mysterious plan; or was it merely the result of a natural event that had centred on Lisbon at random? Although the theology surrounding the Lisbon earthquake soon became complex and, frankly, incoherent, dividing along predictably sectarian lines of blame, much of it fixated on a single, overriding question that continues to be asked to this day: Why does God allow bad things to happen to good people?

This question proved so difficult to answer that, in one sense, the earthquake was easier to bear if one did consider it to be a random and meaningless event. But many people, even today, find it impossible to accept the idea that natural disasters, no matter how striking or memorable they are, might nevertheless have no intrinsic meaning. There is such a strong desire to attribute significance to our surroundings that the randomness of random events is denied in favour of the idea of a controlling will. But, as was also the case during the weeks following the Indian Ocean earthquake and tsunami, there was something about the severity of the Lisbon tragedy, in which so many innocent people had died, that made it hard to sustain the once-prevalent view that God was directly in command of such events. For what sort of God would condemn to death thousands of church-going women and children, while destroying an ancient and elegant city upon which so much of the Christian world was economically dependent?

As has often been observed, the Lisbon earthquake occurred in the middle of the Enlightenment era, a phase of intellectual history in which natural philosophy, a new kind of sceptical, materialist outlook, was spreading across much of the world. The work of early eighteenth-century natural philosophers, who were essentially the precursors of modern-day scientists, had done much to promote the Newtonian conception of a universe in which natural causes were free to operate within a mechanical order laid down by the creator – God the architect – although not directly controlled by him on a day-to-day basis. God, in other words, had designed a world in which events such as earthquakes and cyclones could and would occur, while not actually being in charge of them when they struck.

The Lisbon earthquake turned out to be the first great test of this new materialist outlook, from which the idea of divine causation had not been banished entirely, merely relegated to the sidelines at a respectful distance. But proponents of this outlook were to have a struggle on their hands, for as we have already seen, there were plenty of voices raised against it, particularly among the more traditionally minded clergy, who worried about its challenge to their interpretive authority. The Methodist minister John Wesley, for example, had been made very uneasy by the rise of natural philosophy, and sought to undermine its claims whenever opportunity arose. His journals, much of which were written on horseback as he toured the British Isles as an open-air preacher, show how fully he immersed himself in the latest works of astronomy, cosmology and the geological sciences, principally in order to dispute their rational conclusions. For Wesley, everything that happened on earth was under the direct control of the will of God, so events such as major earthquakes were signs to be interpreted by theologians, not problems to be solved by natural philosophers. His response to the Lisbon earthquake was a typical production, a long and energetic sermon entitled *Serious Thoughts Occasioned by the late Earthquake at Lisbon*, in which he welcomed the earthquake as both a warning to sinners and a challenge to natural philosophers. 'Why should we not now, before *London* is as *Lisbon, Lima,* or *Catanea,* acknowledge the Hand of the Almighty arising to maintain his own Cause?', he asked: 'Why, we have a general Answer always ready, to screen us from any such Conviction: "All these Things are purely natural and accidental; the Result of natural Causes." ' He then went through a number of competing hypotheses, dismissing each one in turn, while reserving particular scorn for the imprisoned-air hypothesis, which, as we will shortly see, was the most popular earthquake explanation then around: 'as to the fashionable Opinion, that the exterior Air is the grand Agent in Earthquakes', he wrote, 'it is so senseless, unmechanical, unphilosophical a Dream, as deserves not to be named, but to be exploded.'[36]

Such theological attacks on the views of natural philosophers were a matter of course in the mid-eighteenth century, as were the repeated demands for wholesale repentance and woe; but the callousness with which religious enthusiasts such as Whitefield, Wesley and Malagrida denounced the dead of Lisbon came as a shock to many among the moderate clergy, who were uncomfortable with the idea of offering praise to such a cruel form of vengeance. Surely it was better to offer prayerful thanks that cities such as London and Leipzig had been spared destruction, than to revel in the misfortunes of Lisbon? Wesley's 'malevolent enthusiasm', as the Lincolnshire clergyman Peter Peckard described it in his *Dissertation on Revelation 11:13* (1756), clearly owed more to fanaticism than to any form of benevolence, and it ran counter to what he and many others regarded as the essentially amiable spirit of enlightened Christianity. The Archbishop of Canterbury, Dr Thomas Herring, agreed, describing Wesley as 'a most dark and saturnine creature' in the course of a private letter to a friend. 'I have read his *Serious Thoughts*', he wrote, 'but, for my own part, I think the rising and setting of the sun is a more durable argument for religion than all the extraordinary convulsions of nature put together . . . I own I have no constitution for these frights and fervors.'[37]

The archbishop was not alone in articulating such doubts, not just about the misanthropic character of Wesley, but about the wider moral significance of the earthquake itself, which became the first major tragedy in European history whose meaninglessness could be publicly debated, even among senior clerics. William Warburton, for example, who was then the royal chaplain, wrote to Richard Hurd, the Bishop of Worcester, pointing out that human vanity had wildly overestimated the significance of the event:

A drunken man shall work as horrid a desolation with the kick of his foot against an ant-hill, as subterraneous air and fermented minerals to a populous city. And if we take in the universe of things, rather with a philosophic than a religious eye, where is the difference in point of real importance between them?[38]

The city of Lisbon, in other words, was of scant significance in the great scheme of things, and its destruction, although terrible for the victims, was a passing event that carried no hidden message for the rest of the world. Even today it would be hard to voice such pragmatism in public, just as it was in the 1750s, but note Dr Warburton's careful distinction between 'philosophic' and 'religious', as well as his assumption that the earthquake had been the work of 'subterraneous air and fermented minerals' rather than the action of an angry God. When it came to the real causes of the Lisbon earthquake, his views, along with the views of many other moderate churchmen throughout Europe and North America, were far closer to those of natural philosophers than they were to those of noisy extremists such as Whitefield and Wesley, from whom the majority of quiet Anglicans recoiled.

Natural philosophers themselves, meanwhile, were busy getting on with the difficult task of interpreting the causes of the earthquake. Pombal did a great deal to encourage such researches, and was particularly keen for his own countrymen to participate in them first-hand, with the aim of establishing Portuguese seismology as an integral part of the wider advances being made within European science.

Among the first to answer Pombal's call was a Lisbon physician named José Alvares da Silva, who prefaced his treatise, entitled *Investigations into the Proximate Causes of the Lisbon Earthquake of 1755*, with the observation that mankind has a religious duty to investigate the operations of God-given nature. He then outlined some of the current hypotheses concerning the natural causes of earthquakes, including the sudden release of compressed air, the outbreak of subterraneous fires, and the operations of electrical forces within the solid parts of the earth, each of which he discussed in turn, before reiterating Pombal's initial request for further on-the-spot research. But da Silva had taken a significant first step, and within a few months of the Lisbon disaster, Portuguese seismology had become a distinct field of enquiry within European earth science, a situation that would have been completely unimaginable in pre-quake, priest-run Portugal. Soon, Portuguese researchers were confident enough to begin framing their own hypotheses, which included speculations on the seismic influence of the moon and sun, the gradual contracting of the Earth's circumference, the building up of combustible gases in caverns below the sea, and even on the beneficial effects of seismic waves, which, according to the claims of some adherents, served to loosen up the earth and open its pores so that noxious vapours might be exhaled into the air.

Similar ideas had been in circulation for some time, stimulated by other earthquakes elsewhere in the world, such as the one that struck Lima, Peru, in October 1746, claiming over four thousand lives. But the Lisbon earthquake, due partly to its severity and partly to its location – on a wealthy continent where large-scale natural disasters were not supposed to happen – commanded an unprecedented level of attention from scientists all over Europe. The last two months of 1755, for instance, saw no fewer than forty-seven papers on the Lisbon earthquake read out at meetings of the Royal Society of London, with many more to come over the following few years. The interests of an entire generation of natural philosophers had been suddenly, and fruitfully, diverted into the new and growing field of earthquake studies (it would only be known as 'seismology' from the 1850s onwards); among them was an enterprising young academic named John Michell, who had been admitted to Queens' College, Cambridge, as a Bible clerk in 1742. During his early years at Cambridge, Michell (who shared Isaac Newton's birthday: 25 December) distinguished himself in the study of magnetism and geometry, and later went on to propose the existence of black holes in 1783, but his most significant work, on seismic waves, was prompted by the destruction of Lisbon in 1755. His now celebrated paper, *Conjectures concerning the Cause, and Observations upon the Phænomena, of Earthquakes* (1760), began with a synthesis of the wealth of eyewitness material that had been generated by earthquakes throughout history. From this, he observed that certain regions of the earth are 'subject to the returns of earthquakes', that is, they are more seismically active than others, which might seem obvious to us today, but at the time represented a crucial advance in seismic understanding.[39] Earthquakes are not subject to random distribution, but are clustered in known areas of repeat activity, which meant that the task facing natural philosophy was not that of guessing where the next quake might occur, but of discovering the nature of what goes on in the strata beneath earthquake-prone regions. Michell's application of recent ideas on the uniformity of strata to the problem of earthquake production led to his suggestion that subterranean steam, generated from seawater vaporized by molten rock, made its way between the strata until it reached a discontinuity near the surface. The steam would then rush towards that area, its movements sending powerful waves hurtling through the earth's crust, which would then reach the surface as an earthquake.

It hardly matters that later research dispensed with Michell's subterranean steam, for it was his emphasis on the elastic propagation of waves that transformed the understanding of earthquakes. His cloth analogy expressed it brilliantly:

> Suppose a large cloth, or carpet, (spread upon a floor) to be raised at one edge, and then suddenly brought down again on to the floor, the air under it, being by this means propelled, will pass along, till it escapes at the opposite side, raising the cloth in a wave all the way as it goes. In like manner, a large quantity of vapour may be conceived to raise the earth in a wave, as it passes along between the strata . . . The part of the earth that is first raised, being bent from its natural form, will endeavour to restore itself by its elasticity.[40]

Since such waves, as Michell argued, 'might rise the higher, the nearer they are to the place from whence they have their source', while gradually diminishing with distance, it would be possible to determine the precise source of the earthquake (its underground 'focus' or 'hypocentre') by measuring the waves' direction and arrival time from a series of different locations. By applying this method to a set of eyewitness accounts from Lisbon, Michell was able to estimate the depth of the earthquake's focus to be somewhere in the region of one to three miles (1.6 to 4.8 kilometres) below the Atlantic Ocean, just off the Portuguese coast. This was an extraordinary insight, through which, only five years after the fall of Lisbon, and long before the city itself had risen from its ruins, seismology established itself as one of the most promising areas for original scientific research. Two years later, in recognition of his *Conjectures* (which, as one historian of science has observed, 'contains most of the ingredients of the presently accepted explanation of earthquakes'), Michell was appointed Woodwardian Professor of Geology at the University of Cambridge, a highly prestigious post, though one that required its holders to remain celibate.[41] In August 1764, having held the professorship for less than two years, Michell abandoned his glittering academic career in order to get married in the Midlands.

Alongside its impact on religion and science, the Lisbon earthquake also exerted an influence on European literary culture, although the questions that the disaster raised were not to do with faith so much as optimism. The profoundly pessimistic French novelist Voltaire, for example, composed a bleak 240-line *Poème sur le désastre de Lisbonne*, which was published only a few weeks after the event, in which he invited optimists and moralists alike to gather round and contemplate 'this ruin of a world':

> Behold these shreds and cinders of your race,
> This child and mother heaped in common wreck,
> These scattered limbs beneath the marble shafts —
> A hundred thousand whom the earth devours,
> Who, torn and bloody, palpitating yet,
> Entombed beneath their hospitable roofs,
> In racking torment end their stricken lives.
> To those expiring murmurs of distress,
> To that appalling spectacle of woe,
> Will ye reply: "You do but illustrate

The iron laws that chain the will of God"?
Say ye, o'er that yet quivering mass of flesh:
"God is avenged: the wages of sin is death"?
What crime, what sin, had those young hearts conceived
That lie, bleeding and torn, on mother's breast?
Did fallen Lisbon deeper drink of vice
Than London, Paris, or sunlit Madrid?
In these men dance; at Lisbon yawns the abyss.[42]

Voltaire's purpose in writing the poem, as he announced in a pungent two-page preface, was to remind his readers of 'the sad and ancient truth, recognized by all men, that evil walks the earth.' Optimism, he declared, along with the belief in a benign providence, was the most foolish possible response to the pain of human existence. In the face of the destruction of Lisbon, he asked, 'What may the most exalted spirit do?: Nothing. The book of fate is closed to view':

> Man, self-estranged, is enemy to man,
> Knows not his origin, his place or plan,
> Is a tormented atom, which at last
> Must condescend to be the earth's repast.

Although such views might well have been shared by many at the time, it was nonetheless shocking to see them written down, and Voltaire was roundly attacked from every quarter, both secular and religious, but of all the objections hurled at the poem, it was Jean-Jacques Rousseau's that irritated Voltaire the most. Voltaire's position was entirely wrong, declared the great philosopher of nature: optimism is the only means by which mankind can endure the unendurable, and Voltaire's assault on it was nothing short of an assault on life itself. 'You revel, but I hope,' as Rousseau wrote to his erstwhile friend in a letter dated 18 August 1756, 'and hope beautifies everything.'[43] Voltaire's response was entirely characteristic: an even more extreme rebuttal of the doctrine of optimism, in the form of his caustic satire *Candide; ou, l'Optimiste*, which was first published in Paris in 1759. Continuing from where the poem left off, the novel's bleakest and best-known episode takes place in Lisbon on the day of the disaster. Candide and his travelling companion, the ever-optimistic Dr Pangloss, have stepped ashore just in time to be horribly injured in the quake. As Candide lies on the ground in pain, his friend starts musing on the likely geophysical causes: 'what can be the *sufficient reason* of this phænomenon?' he asks:

> For God's sake, said he to Pangloss, get me a little wine and oil, I am a dying. This concussion of the earth is no new thing, answered Pangloss: the city of Lima, in America, experienced the same convulsions last year; the same cause, the same effects; there is certainly a train of sulphur underground from Lima to Lisbon. Nothing more probable, said Candid, but for the love of God, a little oil and wine. Probable? replied the philosopher, I maintain that the point is capable of being demonstrated.[44]

Voltaire was not alone in making dark little jokes about the casualties (and causalities) of the Lisbon earthquake. The Comte de Baschi, the French Ambassador to Lisbon, kept the court in Versailles in fits of laughter with his impressions of the violent death of his Spanish counterpart, who had been killed by the collapse of the Spanish royal arms from the porch of his official residence. 'Have you heard Baschi on the earthquake?' asked Madame de Pompadour in the course of a letter to a friend; apparently the Spaniard had had his young son in his arms, and Baschi's re-enactment of the ambassador's efforts to save him was one of the funniest things she had ever seen.[45]

The reaction of the French to the Lisbon disaster – including, as we have seen, their refusal to contribute to the international relief fund – gives some indication of the strength of the background hostility that would soon erupt into the Seven Years War (1756–63), during which Portugal would offer full support to British forces as they pursued their global campaigns of empire against the armies of France and Spain. So it was hardly surprising that the French

were left unmoved by the misfortunes of a hostile power, but even
in Britain – Portugal's oldest ally – signs of compassion fatigue
soon began to appear, and when a masked ball due to be held in
London at the end of January 1756 was cancelled after consulta-
tion with senior clergy, many of the ticket holders were openly
annoyed, including the novelist Horace Walpole, who had detested
the spectacle of wholesale public piety: 'you have no notion how
good we are grown', as he wrote to his cousin, Henry Seymour
Conway, following the declaration that a public fast-day had been
set for Friday 6 February; 'nobody makes a suit now but of sack-
cloth turned up with ashes.' But Walpole needn't have worried,
for the sanctimoniousness didn't last long, and as the diarist and
botanist Mary Delany wrote on 1 April 1756, five months to the day
after the destruction of Lisbon, 'earthquakes are forgotten, assem-
blies and balls go on as briskly as if no such warning had been
given; indeed, if we stop there it might be innocent, but luxury of
all kinds and gaming run higher than ever.'[46]

And besides, all such moral considerations were soon eclipsed
by the news that the gold was finally running out in Brazil. For
years this had seemed an unimaginable possibility to the merchants
who crowded the Lisbon docks, especially since there had recently
been a second surge in production. The first had occurred in the
1720s, and paid for the cast-iron bells of Mafra, while the second
had come in the early 1750s, and paid for the building of Lisbon's
sparkling Royal Opera House, which had only been in business for
a couple of months before it was completely destroyed by the
earthquake. It had, during its brief existence, been the most lavish
theatre in Europe, and had managed to attract the biggest names in
Italian opera with the promise of unprecedented rewards: the cas-
trato who had opened the opera's first and only season had been
offered the truly astonishing fee of three thousand gold moidores,
freshly minted from what would turn out to be one of the city's last
consignments (see picture 7).

So here, it seemed, was a strange kind of poetic justice at work,
in which a city built on unearned wealth is destroyed at the moment

when the wealth runs out. Not surprisingly, the idea that Lisbon had been punished by a vengeful God was briefly strengthened by the news from Brazil: 'Think O Spain, O Portugal, of the millions of poor Indians that your forefathers butcher'd for the sake of gold', as one theologian expressed it, and like so much about Lisbon's rise and fall, the timing of the end of its golden age was like something from a cautionary tale.[47] As for the large community of foreign merchants whose livelihoods depended on the bullion from Brazil, many of those who elected to stay moved into the Portuguese building trade. The commercial agent William Stephens was a typical example. He had lost everything in the Lisbon fire, but, thanks to his friendship with the Marquis of Pombal, he managed to secure the state monopoly on the manufacture of replacement glass. No new building rose in post-earthquake Lisbon without some of William Stephens's glass, and by the time he died in 1803 he was the richest man in the city, his spectacular reversal of fortune serving to bear out one of Voltaire's more sardonic observations, that the people who stood to gain most from Lisbon's fall was the gang of British merchants who had been running the place for years.[48]

Pombal, meanwhile, was proceeding with his plans, although the loss of revenue from the gold mines of Brazil, as well as the aftershocks that continued during the following year, caused a significant scaling down of his vision for the replacement city. But he was also pursuing his investigations into the likely causes of the earthquake, and, in collaboration with General Manuel de Maia, his chief military engineer, Pombal devised a questionnaire that was sent to every parish priest in the country, seeking first-hand information about the tremors and their effects. The sending of this questionnaire was a landmark moment in modern seismology, for it represented the world's first organized attempt to compile an objective account of an earthquake; questions such as 'How long did the earthquake last?'; 'How many aftershocks were felt?'; 'What kind of damage was caused?'; 'Were animals seen behaving strangely?' and 'Did anything happen to the water in the wells?' yielded hundreds of responses from the now cooperative parish priests (there was in fact a hefty fine for non-cooperation), which, when collated and cross-referenced by Pombal's engineers, revealed a great deal of new information about the earthquake and its associated tsunami, including the geographical extent of both phenomena.[49] The earthquake itself had been felt over a large area of western Europe, and caused widespread damage and loss of life throughout the maritime regions of Portugal, Spain and Morocco. Apart from Lisbon, the city nearest the epicentre, where the worst of the effects had been concentrated, Cadiz, Fez and Mequinez were severely affected, as were Casablanca and Agadir further down the North African coast. The tsunami, too, had a widespread reach, radiating out from the waters off Lisbon, making landfall along much of the Portuguese coastline, where in a number of low-lying areas the waves ran up to three kilometres inland. Madeira, south-west Spain and the west coast of Morocco also suffered severe inundations, and several hundred people were swept to their deaths along their shores. The tsunami, meanwhile, continued to make its way across the wide sweep of the Atlantic Ocean, until, some five and a half hours and 5,700 kilometres (3,500 miles) later, it swept into the Caribbean, causing localized flooding along the eastern shores of the Leeward and Windward islands. 'On the 1st November, about two in the afternoon the sea ebbed and flowed in a most surprising manner', as a correspondent from Barbados wrote in a letter to the *Gentleman's Magazine*; 'it ran over the wharfs into the houses, and at the old bridge brought up numbers of fish of several sorts.'[50]

Another, and more unusual, effect of the quake was observed in locations all over Europe, in the form of a series of seismic seiches,* in which land-locked bodies of water, such as lakes, ponds, wells and canals, are seen to oscillate with sudden violence. On Loch Ness, for example, in Highland Scotland, some 2,100 kilometres (1,300 miles) north of Lisbon, 'a great agitation' began just before

* The term was coined in the late nineteenth century by the Swiss seismologist F. A. Forel.

10 a.m. on 1 November, creating a series of metre-high waves that took more than an hour to die down; numerous similar sightings were reported elsewhere in Europe, all of which recorded a similar duration of the strange long-distance seismic phenomenon that ended just as abruptly as it began.[51]

Back in Lisbon, Pombal's questionnaire was continuing to yield crucial information, casting particular light on the varying ways in which man-made structures had been affected by the quake. Many of the respondents had noticed how some of the larger and more solid-seeming civic and religious buildings had been among the first to fall, while some of the flimsier wood-built structures, such as the infamous row of brothels on the Rua Suja, survived the day undamaged. Aside from the puzzling moral scheme that such random variations suggested, it became clear that different parts of the city had been affected in noticeably different ways, and that certain buildings had stood up to the shocks far better than some of their neighbours.

It soon became apparent that their varying fates had depended partly on the types of rocks and soils that underlay their foundations, and partly on their materials and design. Many of the city's heavier stone-built structures, such as the public buildings of the riverside areas, had been built on the sandy alluvial soils that lie beneath those parts of the city. But, given the *thixotropic* nature of sandy soils (they behave like a liquid when vigorously shaken), combined with the inflexibility of large stone structures, it would be Lisbon's historic public edifices that proved most vulnerable to the earthquake. The liquefaction had been clearly visible during the initial stages of the earthquake, with the layers of alluvial soil deposits actually serving to amplify the effects of the seismic waves, and many eyewitnesses reported seeing what looked like dry waves and dust spouts moving through the lower parts of the city, as the buildings all around them swayed like heads of corn. Elsewhere, by contrast, especially on the slopes of the limestone hills surrounding the city centre, the buildings tended to fare much better, particularly the lighter wood-framed houses, many of which were seen to pitch and roll under the stresses of the earthquake's energy waves, but which went on to survive the shocks intact.*

While Pombal and his engineers studied the results of the questionnaire, no new building work was allowed to begin, only the ongoing demolition of burnt-out structures, and the clearing away of millions of tonnes of rubble. It was a massive task, requiring complex organization as well as significant levels of outside help. Boatloads of picks, shovels and workboots were despatched from Portsmouth and Hamburg, along with rice and grain to feed the conscripted labourers, but, as one Italian visitor to the city noted, 'if half the people that have escaped the earthquake were to be employed in nothing else but in the removal of that immense rubbish, it is not very clear that they would be able to remove it in ten years.'[52] There was some truth in the observation, and most of the official rebuilding efforts ended up concentrating on the immediate city centre, leaving much of the work in the surrounding areas in the hands of private householders, who were left to get on with re-establishing their properties on their own. This was not how it was intended to be, for Pombal's wish had been for the entire city to be rebuilt along new, antiseismic lines, and he had called for strict building regulations to be applied and enforced across the whole of the Lisbon area. His engineers had even been instructed to compile detailed inventories of property rights and claims, which turned out to be an impossible task given that most of the relevant records had been destroyed in the fire. As a consequence, the new regulations were ignored in most of the outlying parts of the city, while in the city centre and riverside areas, the engineers continued with their ambitious plans for the world's first earthquake-resistant urban space.

The work proceeded apace, and within seven months most of central Lisbon had been cleared and levelled, with the steeper

---

* Most of them, however, would be claimed by the firestorm later that afternoon, or the following day, and the need for a city-wide fire-prevention programme became the first of the surveyors' recommendations.

western slopes reduced to a flat central area measuring some 200,000 square metres (2,100,000 square feet): Lisbon's ground zero. Because much of this low-lying area had been churned into unstable mud by the actions of the earthquake and its accompanying tsunami, thousands of timber pylons were shipped from Hamburg to be sunk as foundations. The new streets and buildings of the entire downtown and riverside areas were then constructed on top of these buried timber posts, which were designed to act as antiseismic stabilizers.

The new city centre was laid out on a strict grid pattern, a design chosen with future shocks and tremors in mind. Grid-pattern towns were already familiar from Spanish-built cities in South America, but this had been amended specifically to cope with the observed effects of earthquakes, as revealed in the answers to Pombal's questionnaire. So in contrast to the earlier maze-like arrangement, the rows of facing houses were kept unusually far apart, in order to allow safe passage in case of collapse – many of the earthquake's first wave of victims had been killed by falling masonry while fleeing the narrow streets. The seven new avenues running north to south were laid out at a width of eighteen metres (sixty feet), while the width of the cross-streets running east to west was set at a minimum of twelve metres (forty feet); so even if every building in the city collapsed due to another earthquake, there would still be room for refugees to pass through the middle of the streets.

The buildings themselves, meanwhile – none of which was permitted to be more than four storeys high – were constructed around a unique wooden frame, known as a *gaiola* (Portuguese for 'cage'), that was infilled with brick, stone and plaster to form the walls. The effectiveness of the frame's design had been tested and confirmed by Pombal's military engineers, who had a column of soldiers jump up and down around a half-scale model in an attempted simulation of an earthquake. The experiment – the first of its kind – showed that a flexible wooden frame could withstand prolonged vibrations far better than stone-built houses, which had been the first to fall during the earthquake.[53]

Once the antiseismic frames had been approved, they were installed throughout the downtown area, with high brick walls erected between each property as a precaution against the spread of fire. The corners of the wooden frames were then reinforced with stone, and a set of uniform exteriors – consisting of prefabricated tile and stucco claddings in a simple neo-classical design – were fitted along the lengths of the rows. The end result was a sizeable district of what looked like conventional stone-built houses but which were, in fact, nothing of the kind. And there they stand to this day, the wood-framed prefabs of the Baixa Pombalina (as the area is still known), floating on their twenty thousand timber pylons, a testament to the effectiveness of the world's first antiseismic urban design, as well as to the Marquis of Pombal's overarching belief in the application of science to society (see picture 8).

By the end of the century the rest of the city had mostly been rebuilt, although not everyone was pleased by its somewhat utilitarian appearance. The English Romantic poet Robert Southey visited Lisbon during the last week of January 1796, staying in a dingy guesthouse in one of the reconstructed suburbs. After walking around the city for a day or two, and comparing it with images of its pre-quake self, he concluded that the skyline had been spoiled by the decision to rebuild the ruined churches squat and low: 'Pombal ordered all the churches here to be built like houses, that they might not spoil the uniformity of the streets', he complained, 'and this villainous taste has necessarily injured the appearance of the city.' It was true that the once gilded city of the South was no longer an architectural treasure-trove, but Southey, in fact, had reason to be grateful to the long-dead marquis and his team of surveyors, since he had only been in Lisbon a matter of hours before one of its regular earth tremors struck. 'This is the seventh shock that has been felt since the first of November', as he wrote in his journal the following day. 'They had a smart shock on the 17th of this month, but the connoisseurs in earthquakes say that this last, though of shorter duration, was the most dangerous, for this was the perpendicular shake, whereas the other was the undulatory motion.'[54] Young Robert had been in town for less than twenty-four hours, but he was already smitten with the language of seismology, and pleased to have experienced a minor Lisbon earthquake for himself. He noticed, too, that when the Lisboetans felt the tremor they immediately extinguished all their candles, 'because the fire does more mischief than the earthquake', an encouraging example of civil defence in action that would have pleased the late marquis enormously – though he would have been less pleased to learn that a number of families had fled the city overnight, after a prominent cleric had 'gone about prophesying a severer one at the same hour ten days hence'. The architectural fabric of Lisbon might have been transformed beyond all recognition, but some things never change, and plenty of residents and visitors alike remained understandably preoccupied by the threat of future ruin. When the travelling invalid Henry Matthews visited the city for the sake of his health in the summer of 1817, he was struck by 'something in the appearance of Lisbon that seems to portend an earthquake; and instead of wondering that it was once visited by such a calamity, I am rather disposed to consider its daily preservation as a standing miracle. Repeated shocks have been felt of late years, and to an earthquake it may look, as its natural death.'[55]

Although Matthews's premonition may one day come true, so far Pombal's antiseismic designs have done much to preserve the city over the past two hundred and fifty years, during the course of which, according to the assessment of José Saramago, 'a historic town centre was lost, and another gained, which with the passage of time has also become historical. There is no point arguing with earthquakes.'[56] And Saramago is right: post-earthquake Lisbon still has the air of an ancient, elegant, riverside resort, and few visitors today can resist the view over the rooftops from the limestone battlements of the Castelo de São Jorge, the spot on which this story begins and ends, and from where you look out over a scene of resurrection, over a city that has risen from the dead.

PART TWO

AIR

EUROPEAN WEATHER PANIC

1783

I

Enthroned amid the splendours of a country house in Passy, a Parisian village-suburb on the road to Versailles, Benjamin Franklin passed an enviable few years as commissioner to the court of France. As befitted such a celebrated overseas ambassador, he had been granted free use of the Hôtel Valentinois – a well-appointed mansion on a hill above the Seine, on the roof of which he had, within a few weeks of his arrival, installed an iron lightning rod – and there he basked in the adoration of a country that had taken him to its heart.

He had originally come to France on the delicate mission of raising support for the American rebels in their war of independence from Britain, but in spite of the discretion required (given that the British and the French were still officially at peace), Franklin's arrival in Paris in December 1776 caused an unexpected stir throughout the country. To his genuine surprise, this long-haired seventy-year-old American philosopher, with his crabtree stick, bifocal spectacles (like the lightning conductor, they were his own invention), and his backwoodsman's fur hat complete with tail – 'think how this must appear among the Powder'd Heads of Paris', as he wrote to his friend Mrs Thompson at Lille – attracted waves of affection wherever he went.[1] He was already world famous as a scientist, an inventor and a leading revolutionary campaigner (it was only six months earlier that he had helped to draft the American Declaration of Independence), but once in France Franklin discovered that he had somehow been transfigured into the living personification of freedom, sagacity and natural grace. 'His clothing was rustic, his bearing simple but dignified, his language direct, his hair unpowdered,' wrote the Comte de Ségur, an admiring aristocrat who bore witness to the effects of Franklin's arrival upon the imagination of the people of Paris: 'it was as though classic simplicity, the figure of a thinker of the time of Plato, or a republican of the age of Cato or Fabius had suddenly been brought by magic into our effeminate and slavish age, the eighteenth century. This unexpected visitor charmed us all the more as he was not only a novelty but appeared when literature and philosophy were astir with demands for reform, for change, and for a universal love of liberty' (see picture 9).[2]

Six and a half years later, however, the American rebels had won their war and Franklin was preparing to leave Passy. 'The French are an amiable People to live with', he wrote to a friend in July 1783: 'They love me, & I love them. Yet I do not feel myself at home, & I wish to die in my own Country.'[3] He appealed to Congress to be allowed to retire – he was now seventy-seven years old, after all – but before being granted permission to return to Philadelphia his skills were needed for one last job, that of hammering out the peace accord with Britain. It was to prove a slow and frustrating business, and even though the British army under General Cornwallis had surrendered at Yorktown in October 1781, and the House of Commons had declared the war over in February 1782, the peace negotiations dragged on until September the following year, by which time Britain, France and America itself, after six years of ruinous war, were sliding deeper into economic malaise. Franklin, too, was exhausted and unwell, and wanted more than anything else to go home.

But as the summer of 1783 wore on, and the peace agreement started to assume its final shape, Franklin had been growing increasingly puzzled by a strange alteration in the weather. At first it was hard to describe exactly, even for someone as weather-wise as him, and for a day or so he gave it little thought beyond noting that the air seemed hazy. Certainly, nothing had happened during the first

half of the year that might have hinted at a seasonal anomaly.
January to March had been typically cold and blustery, followed
by an equally typical rain-soaked April, during which several inches
of rainfall were recorded at a number of European observatories.
Then, as the spring advanced, the air grew mild and the lengthening
days were filled with warming sunshine. Much to his regret, for he
had always loved spending time outdoors, Franklin had been kept
too busy by diplomacy to take advantage of the fine spring weather,
but during his earlier years in France he had made regular May
outings to the Bois de Boulogne, taken boat-trips down the Seine
to visit neighbouring villages, and declared, as many have done
before and since, that Paris is at its loveliest during the springtime.

But by the middle of June something decidedly unusual was
happening in the wide Parisian sky. A kind of opalescent haze, red-
dish and dry, was suspended like a dirty fog as far as the eye could
see. It showed no signs of dispersing, for 'this fog was of a permanent nature', wrote Franklin, who had started to pay much closer
attention to the state of the summer sky; 'it was dry, and the rays of
the sun seemed to have little effect towards dissipating it, as they
easily do a moist fog, arising from water.' During daylight hours, he
noted, the sun turned red and sickly, and its power seemed weakened by the layer of obscuring haze. The sun's rays were 'rendered
so faint in passing through it, that when collected in the focus of a
burning glass, they would scarce kindle brown paper.'[4] Similarly, at
night, even the brightest of stars appeared pale and dull, while the
moon was reduced to little more than a faint and bluish smear.
By the end of June a bitter, sulphurous smell had developed into
an additional nuisance, stinging the eyes and throats of those who
spent more than a few hours outdoors. It was horrible, as though a
thick blanket of bad air had draped itself over the city, and as the
weeks went by, the atmosphere continued to deteriorate, growing
dryer, hotter and steadily more corrosive until it seemed as if the
whole of Paris was about to be smothered by its sky.

It was all very disturbing, and the worsening weather made many
Parisians feel understandably nervous, especially since accounts of

identical developments had started coming in from other parts of
France. The haze, it was reported, had covered Dijon to the east,
Le Havre to the north and Provence to the south, where, according
to an article in the *Journal de Physique*, the fog exuded 'une odeur
fétide, sulfureuse, & picotoient les yeux' ('a fetid, sulphurous and
eye-watering smell'). Those 'whose lungs were weak, found dis-
agreeable effects from it', and many others apparently complained
of 'violent pains in the head; and that in general they had partly
lost their appetite.'[5]

Other accounts described how the opalescent haze shed strange
blue shadows on the ground below, and had the effect of tarnishing
any copper objects, such as overcoat buttons and weathervanes,
turning their surfaces green overnight. At times, too, the haze
appeared to glow with a kind of rich, embodied light, as if it was
somehow a living presence, or 'an electric fog', as the naturalist
Robert Paul de Lamanon described it in the *Journal de Physique*.[6]
'The most distinguishing property it had from ordinary fogs was its
dryness', added the physicist Dominique François Arago, 'and it
seemed to be endowed with a kind of phosphoric virtue, with an
inherent light', while the great Italian naturalist Giuseppe Toaldo
recorded in his observations made at the University of Padua that
'people could look at the sun without being incommoded, and
without using coloured or smoked glass':

> It appeared of different colours, according to the kind of rays
> which the difference in the density of the fog suffered to pass.
> As the yellow and red, being the strongest, were those which
> pierced it oftenest, the sun appeared like a ball on fire, or of a
> blood colour; which gave occasion to many whimsical people,
> whose imaginations were heated, to see there, as in the clouds,
> the figures of men and animals.[7]

Stranger still, as some of the regional newspapers reported, 'the fog
has turned the corn rusty', an event that prompted the Bishop of
Pas-de-Calais to call for three days of public prayer.[8]

Whatever had happened to the skies above France was worrying enough in itself, but it soon became apparent that the whole of Europe had been afflicted in a similar way. 'The fog is not peculiar to Paris', explained a French correspondent to the London *Evening Post*: 'those who come lately from Rome say it is as thick and hot in Italy, and even the top of the Alps is covered with it, and many travellers from Spain affirm the same of that kingdom', while a letter from Naples published in the *Morning Herald* also reported that 'the fogs continue, and are accompanied with so alarming an increase of obscurity that our bargemen do not dare venture on the waters without a compass.'[9] Further north, meanwhile, a weather observer in Turku, on the southern coast of Finland, noted in his summary for the end of June that 'the wind has been strange the whole month, but did not blow away the dry fog',[10] while in Britain, a character described as 'the oldest man living' was interviewed in Dover by the *Gentleman's Magazine*, and quoted as saying that he 'can scarce remember any fog of so long continuance as the present, not being able to descry the opposite shore for almost three weeks.'[11] With the opposing coastlines of England and France finally erased from one another's view, it must have seemed, for some at least, as if the weather itself had started to reflect the aims of the political negotiations.

On the morning of Friday 13 June 1783 the Buckinghamshire poet and recluse William Cowper wrote a disconsolate letter to the Revd John Newton, his friend and literary agent in London, in which he shared his unease over the strange complexion of the sky. 'I am and always have been a great Observer of natural appearances', he began, 'but I think not a superstitious one':

> It is impossible however for an Observer of natural phænom-
> ena not to be struck with the singularity of the present season.
> The fogs I mention'd in my last still continue, though 'till yes-
> terday the Earth was as dry as intense heat could make it. The
> Sun continues to rise and set without his rays, and hardly
> shines at noon even in a cloudless sky. At Eleven last night the
> moon was of a dull red, she was nearly at her highest elevation
> and had the colour of a heated Brick. She would naturally I

know have such an appearance looking through a misty
atmosphere, but that such an atmosphere should obtain for
so long a time and in a Country where it has not happen'd in
my remembrance, even in the Winter, is rather remarkable.[12]

Cowper, in common with the rest of the population of Europe, was
disturbed by the deteriorating weather conditions and kept returning to the subject throughout a long series of letters that he wrote
to Newton over the following few weeks. On 17 June, for example,
he complained to his friend that 'the Summer is passing away, and
hitherto has hardly been either seen or felt. Perpetual Clouds inter-
cept the influences of the Sun, and for the most part here is an
Autumnal coldness in the weather, though we are almost upon the
Eve of the longest day.'[13]

When the longest day (21 June) had come and gone with no
sign of improvement, Cowper's worry increased, and he wrote to
Newton the following Sunday to complain about 'the Bœotian
atmosphere I have breathed these six days past.' Judging from the
contents of the rest of the letter, he had evidently been discussing
'the disease that nature feels' with his equally worried neighbours
in Olney:

> So long, in a country not subject to fogs, we have been cover'd
> with one of the thickest I remember. We never see the Sun but
> shorn of his beams, the trees are scarce discernable at a mile's
> distance, he sets with the face of a red hot salamander, and
> rises (as I learn from report) with the same complexion. Such
> a Phænomenon at the end of June, has occasioned much spec-
> ulation among the Connoscenti at this place. Some fear to go
> to bed, expecting an Earthquake, some declare that he neither
> rises nor sets where he did, and assert with great confidence
> that the day of Judgement is at hand. This is probable, and I
> believe it myself, but for other reasons.[14]

Although Cowper's 'other reasons' for fearing that the end of the
world was nigh were moral rather than meteorological, stemming
from his evangelical Christian faith, as well as from the depressive

illness that had plagued him all his life, there was no mistaking his
growing unease over the strange appearance of the sky. 'Signs in
the heavens are predicted characters of the last times', he wrote,
'and in the course of the last 15 years I have been a witness of many;
but the present obfuscation (if I may call it so) of all nature may be
rank'd perhaps among the most remarkable.' The melancholy
Cowper (whose final poem, 'The Castaway', is among the most
powerful invocations of depression ever written) was evidently feeling more than usually under the weather, but he did make an effort
to end his letter on an optimistic note: 'But possibly it may not be
universal', he wrote; 'in London at least, where a dingy atmosphere
is frequent, it may be less observable.'[15]

Unfortunately for the habitually smog-bound Londoners,
Cowper's guess was wrong, and they, too, had suffered the same
contamination of the sky. It was now just as bad in London as it had
been in Paris, and the metropolitan papers, glad of the opportunity
to cover something other than crime, bankruptcy and the troublesome progress of the American peace talks, filled themselves
instead with meteorological woe. 'We have had the most shocking
weather here ever remembered in the memory of man', declared
the *London Recorder* on 27 July; 'the state of the atmosphere for this
past week has been more remarkably close and thick than was ever
observed at this season.' Even the imperturbable Horace Walpole,
ensconced in the study of his Thames-side pile, was beginning to
feel unnerved. 'I am tired of this weather', as he wrote in a letter on
15 July, to the Countess of Upper Ossory:

> It parches the leaves, makes the turf crisp, claps the doors,
> blows the papers about, and keeps one in a constant mist that
> gives no dew but might as well be smoke. The sun sets like a
> pewter plate red hot, and then in a moment appears the moon
> at a distance of the same complexion, just as the same orb in a
> moving picture serves for both.[16]

June 1783, he went on, 'has been as abominable as any one of its
ancestors in all the pedigree of the Junes . . . we have exchanged

spring and summer for autumn and winter, as well as day for night.'
He wondered, too, whether the hazy sky was merely a passing phenomenon, or whether it would prove to be an airborne herald of
more serious things to come. In other words, was 'a sun shorn of
his beams, and a moon that only serves to make darkness visible' a
sign that something terrible was about to happen?

If so, it was not only Britain and France that were on the
receiving end: by the end of June reports of the troublesome haze
had been carried by every newspaper in Europe. By the end of July
similar conditions had been observed in a number of countries
much further afield, including Russia, Turkey, Syria, Persia and
even (later) the eastern provinces of China, confirming the growing
suspicion that the same atmospheric deterioration was affecting
every corner of the known world. 'Severe dry fog. Sky is dark', as
the Chinese chronicles of the north-east province of Henan
recorded in a terse but eloquent evocation of total atmospheric
breakdown: 'Haze occurred again and again. Sky became dark.
Cannot see anything.'[17]

'*Sky became dark. Cannot see anything*': what on earth was happening to the weather around the world? Whatever the answer, it
was having a serious impact on human health, because all over
Europe, as the skies continued to darken with what the Belgian
diarist Baron de Poederlé described as 'that penetrating, unhealthy,
stinking fog', people in their thousands began to fall sick with
headaches, nausea and a variety of respiratory illnesses.[18] Nothing
like this deadly fog had ever happened before, and panic soon
began to spread, particularly in France, where, 'to the great benefit
of the priesthood', as a correspondent to the *Journal de Paris*
observed, 'some people of abilities declare they never remember
the like, while the timid dream of earthquakes and vast revolutions,
insomuch that among the low and superstitious part of the people
they talk very seriously of the end of the world.'[19]

'Some are weatherwise; some are otherwise', as Franklin had written in 1735, and, half a lifetime later, in spite of the fact that he was

overworked, unwell and anxious to be home, he found himself irresistibly drawn to the problem presented by this strange summer weather, of which the haze, it transpired, was only the beginning. For as the months went by, much of Europe would be plagued by a catalogue of extreme natural events: fog, thunder, lightning, earthquakes, volcanoes, fireballs, auroras and eclipses, which in turn gave way to a winter season that was, in Franklin's estimation, 'more severe, than any that had happed for many years.'[20]

None of it made the slightest bit of sense, at least not at first; but in the months that followed, after a number of French natural-ists had tried without success to provide an acceptable explanation of these summer-long phenomena, it turned out to be the hard-pressed Franklin who, in the midst of the minutiae of international diplomacy, and racked with pain from gout and bladder-stones, would find the answer to this riddle of the skies – and in so doing he would direct the world's attention to a new and important area for scientific research; an area which, more than two centuries later, would come to be known as climate change, and be ranked among the most pressing topics of global scientific concern.

II

For the time being, however, most commentators took the weather conditions to be a portent of some terrible event – and in fact something terrible had already happened, in a remote area of southern Italy, where, on 5 February 1783, a severe tsunamigenic earthquake destroyed the Sicilian port of Messina, as well as many of its neighbouring villages, killing an estimated thirty thousand people. But reports of the disaster had taken some time to get through to the rest of Europe, and for several months confusion reigned in the European press concerning the fate of Messina and Calabria. In the Netherlands, for example, the *Gazette van Gent* ran an article on 6 March that began by reporting 'the sad news that on the 5th at 19 hours according to the Italian clock a heavy

earthquake occurred at Messina in Sicily', but which then linked it
to a series of rumours concerning a sequence of other disturbances
across the region:

> The earthquake is ascribed to the bursting out of the Etna
> mountain which is situated 25 miles away. However, others
> assure us that this accident is the consequence of a most terri-
> ble thunderstorm. It is said that more than 20,000 inhabitants
> lost their lives in the waves or by the collapsing of their houses.
> One has counted more than 30 different earthquakes which
> were preceded by a heavy storm at sea and on land and accom-
> panied by excessive rain with thunder, lightning and a terrible
> darkness. For the rest, it is mentioned from Naples that the
> mountain Vesuvius throws out such a thick and uncommon
> smoke that one fears for many catastrophes.[21]

Such stories only fuelled a rising sense of geophysical alarm, which
intensified as further reports from southern Italy filtered through to
the rest of the world. This was a slow process, for in contrast to the
aftermath of the Lisbon earthquake, in which maritime links with
the rest of Europe had been largely unaffected, rural Italy was far
more vulnerable to the loss of its lines of communication. Even Sir
William Hamilton, the British envoy extraordinary in Naples, who
compiled an eyewitness account of the earthquake damage on
behalf of the Royal Society, was unable to dispatch it to London
until the beginning of July. Hamilton had already made his name
with a series of published papers on the eruptions of Vesuvius, and
as soon as his account of the earthquake was received, his moving
descriptions of the scenes of devastation were widely reprinted in
the British press. 'I travelled four days on the plain, in the midst of
such misery as cannot be described', he began; 'the force of the
earthquake was so great, that all the inhabitants of the towns were
buried either alive or dead under the ruins of their houses in an
instant; all lie in one confused heap of ruins.' Although Hamilton
was clearly horrified by what he saw, he nevertheless made calm
observations of even the most upsetting details – in every town that

he visited, for instance, 'the male dead were generally found under the ruins in the attitude of struggling against the danger; but the female attitude was usually with hands clasped over their heads, as giving themselves up to despair, unless they had children near them; in which case they were always found clasping the children in their arms' – but, given the prevailing mood of the time, it was the unusual natural effects which Hamilton described that attracted most attention from the press:

> At the time of the earthquake, during the night, flames were seen to issue from the ground in the neighbourhood of this city towards the sea, where the explosion extended, so that many countrymen ran away for fear; the flames issued exactly from a place where some days before an extraordinary heat had been perceived.
>
> After the great concussion there appeared in the air, towards the east, a whitish flame, in a slanting direction; it had the appearance of electric fire, and was seen for the space of two hours.[22]

By this time, of course, the sulphurous haze had descended over Europe, which, combined with accounts of the severity and the strangeness of the Calabrian earthquake, only heightened the impression that something terrible and momentous was occurring across the continent, and possibly the world – 'I am convinced that the whole damage has been done by exhalations and vapours', as Hamilton himself concluded, a comment that did much to strengthen the widely held suspicion that all these earthly events were somehow causally connected.

Horace Walpole, for one, thought it perfectly apparent that 'the dreadful eruptions of fire on the coasts of Italy and Sicily have occasioned some alteration that has extended faintly hither, and contributed to the heats and mists that have been so extraordinary.'[23] Given that earthquakes were still generally considered to be the products of high-pressure internal combustion deep within the bowels of the earth, it all made perfect sense, for it could easily

be imagined that the Italian tremors had unleashed a sort of
internal miasma – an 'electrical effluvium', as some commentators
described it – that had gone on to contaminate the atmosphere.
The earth, in other words, was choking itself to death, with an
escaped contagion dispersed by the slowly meandering winds.

It wasn't long, however, before a cast of other suspects had
been assembled and named as likely causes of the worldwide haze:
comets, meteors, sun-spots and eclipses, as well as unfavourable
conjunctions of the stars and planets, were blamed in turn for the
sudden corruption of the earthly atmosphere, alongside the more
dependable claim that it was the result of divine displeasure. In
France, according to an article printed in the *Edinburgh Advertiser* on
15 July, 'the superstitious part of the people had been wrought
upon by their priests to believe that the end of the world was at
hand', while sermons on the subject of the mysterious dry fog
were preached in churches and chapels throughout Europe. One
such sermon, delivered in Upper-Hessen, Germany, on 29 June,
described how members of the congregation had spent the previous week 'star[ing] at the sky and at the earth, at the unusual
sunrise and sunset, and at the horizon veiled in dark exhalations',
all of which effects, according to the preacher, the Revd Johann
Gottlob Schwarz of Alsfeld, were evidently messages that God had
written in the sky: 'The Lord speaks daily to us, and through nature
he shows us his omniscience, his omnipotence, his greatness –
extraordinary appearances therefore speak also, and capture our
attention. I praise your attention to the works of the Lord.'[24] An
article appearing in the *Gentleman's Magazine*, meanwhile, suggested that, 'although we are sensible that it is not the fashion of
this age to introduce Scripture into any comparison', there were a
number of striking parallels between recent events and a series of
biblical disaster prophecies, to be found in 'Matth. xxiv.7; Mark xv.8;
but particularly Luke xxi.25, 26':

> And is not the destruction of the cities of the plain, perhaps by
> the first earthquake after the creation, recorded in Genesis,

1. A panoramic view of pre-quake Lisbon seen from across the River Tagus, in a coloured engraving *c.*1750. The Castelo de São Jorge perches on the summit of the stylised hill to the left of the image, while the broad expanse of the Terreiro do Paço dominates the right-hand side.

2. The largest and costliest building in Europe, João V's great monastery at Mafra took nearly thirty years to complete, and virtually bankrupted the Portuguese economy.

3. Subduction occurs when one tectonic plate slips ('subducts') below another, to melt back into the mantle like the disappearing end of a conveyor belt. Jolts and slippages often occur during the process, however, giving rise to major earthquakes.

4. The Terreiro do Paço was the largest open space in Lisbon, and the venue for numerous public ceremonies including the Inquisition's notorious *autos da fé*. The square became the principal refuge for survivors in the hours following the earthquake, despite the violent incursion of the tsunami.

5. A theatrically time-compressed view of the earthquake, tsunami and fire which destroyed most of Lisbon's city centre, at a cost of between twenty thousand and ninety thousand lives. The image dates from 1887.

6. An estimated twenty-five thousand survivors moved into tents and shelters erected in fields outside the city. Note the gallows in the centre of the image: Pombal's preferred means of dealing with suspected looters.

7. Lisbon's sparkling new Royal Opera House had only been open a few months before it fell victim to the earthquake and fire. This view is from a set of six produced in 1757 by the French engraver Jacques-Philippe Le Bas, from a series of drawings made on the spot. The buildings on the right have been shored up with tree trunks.

8. A before and after view of Lisbon from a German atlas published in the 1770s. Pombal and his military surveyors devised a rectilinear street plan for Lisbon's rebuilt city centre, with the streets spaced out wide enough to allow survivors to escape in the event of another earthquake.

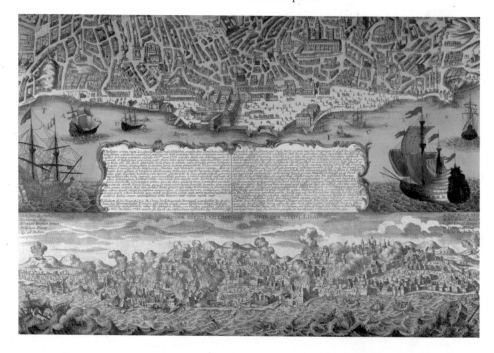

9. 'Think how this must appear among the Powder'd Heads of Paris', as Franklin wrote of his backwoodsman's hat in 1778. His cultivated air of rustic simplicity made him something of a fashion icon in pre-Revolutionary Paris, much to the irritation of his fellow American diplomats. Engraved versions of the original painting by Charles-Nicolas Cochin were circulated widely during Franklin's time in Paris.

BENJAMIN FRANKLIN, LLD. FRS.

10. The astronomer Edward Pigott, who was in York during the summer of 1783, made a number of journal entries in which he described the effect of the atmospheric haze on the appearance of the sun and moon. This entry, for 12 July, reads: 'Since the 24th of June the weather, excepting a few days, has been more or less in much the same state as on that day—the Sun and the Moon (last night) appear'd both of the same colour nearly thus*, but more vivid, exactly as the juice of cherries resembling this but more transparent.' *With kind permission of York City Archives.*

11. The artist Paul Sandby viewed the meteor of 18 August 1783 from the terrace of Windsor Castle in the company of a group of royal guests and employees, including Tiberius Cavallo of the Royal Society, who published a detailed account of the episode in the *Philosophical Transactions* for 1784.

12. Benjamin Franklin was in the crowd that gathered to watch the first manned ascent of a Montgolfier hot-air balloon from a field in the Bois de Boulogne on 21 November 1783. A few months later, Franklin took delivery of the world's first air-mail letter, carried by balloon from London to Paris.

13. This map from Saemund Magnussen Holm's published account shows the extent of the Laki fissures eruption of 1783, the largest single lava flow in recorded history. Marked on the map as *Ild-Havet* ('fire-ocean'), some fifteen cubic kilometres of molten basalt smothered nearly six hundred square kilometres of south-east Iceland. The letters marked on the map refer mostly to historic lava flows, as well as (D) to the *jökulhaup* ('glacier burst') that flooded the Súla river valley during the eight-month-long eruption.

14. This atmospheric image of the eleven-year-old seaman Sidney Tucker Baker was taken in a photographer's studio in Hong Kong during an early stage of the *W. H. Besse's* eventful journey to the East. A few months later, Baker would become a close-up eyewitness to the most famous volcanic eruption in history: Krakatau 1883.

15. The distinctive cone of Rakata in an engraving that appeared on the front page of the *Illustrated London News* on Saturday 8 September 1883, the caption of which read: 'Island of Krakatoa, in the Straits of Sunda, the centre of the late volcanic eruption, said to have disappeared.'

16. This iconic image of Krakatau in eruption was engraved from a photograph taken by a Mr Hamburg from the deck of the *Gouverneur-Generaal Loudon* on the evening of 27 May 1883; it turned out to be the last ever photograph of the island.

xix. 24–28, an exact counterpart of what happened in the plain of Calabria? A vapour, charged with electrical fire, or a kind of inflammable air; an overthrow, and the smoke of the country ascending like the smoke of a furnace: the same physical causes concurring under divine protection? – *Let us be wise, and consider these things.*[25]

But even in the middle of a fast-emerging weather panic, scriptural explanations failed to satisfy for long, and by the end of June, the editor of the *Journal de Paris*, the leading French newspaper of the day, had issued a direct appeal to the French Academy of Sciences for a more reasoned explanation of the weather. Surely someone among their number had, if not a fully worked-out theory, then something approaching an initial hypothesis to share among his readers?

The job of supplying it fell to a somewhat unlikely figure: Joseph-Jérôme Lefrançais de Lalande, one of France's leading astronomers, who responded with what amounted to a press release on behalf of the members of the Academy. Lalande made an unlikely choice of messenger because, exactly ten years earlier, in the summer of 1773, he had been responsible for an outbreak of national alarm when he had carelessly – and falsely – predicted that the earth was about to be annihilated by an approaching comet. As soon as the comet had passed on safely, millions of kilometres away from the earth, Lalande had been forced to issue a humiliating statement, in which he confessed that all his calculations had been hopelessly askew. There followed a brief but painful career as a national laughing stock – so ten years later, unsurprisingly, he was at pains to offer nothing but calm reassurance to the weather-panicked people of France:

To the Authors of the *Journal*: It is known to you, gentlemen, that for some days past people have been incessantly enquiring what is the occasion of the thick dry fog which almost continually covers the heavens? And as this question is particularly put to Astronomers, I think myself obliged to say a few words

on the subject, more especially since a kind of terror begins
to spread in society. It is said that a dangerous comet reigns
at present. In 1773 I experienced how fast these kind of
conjectures, which begin among the ignorant even in the
most enlightened ages, proceed from mouth to mouth, till
they reach the best society, and find their way even to the
publick prints. The multitude therefore may easily be supposed to draw strange conclusions, when they see the sun of
a blood colour, shed a melancholy light, and cause a most
sultry heat.

This however is nothing more than a very natural effect
from a hot sun after a long succession of heavy rain. The first
impression of heat has necessarily and suddenly rarefied a
superabundance of watery particles with which the earth was
deeply impregnated, and given them, as they rose, a dimness
and rarefaction not usual to common fogs.

This effect, which seems to me very natural, is not so very
new; it is at most not above nineteen years since there was a
like example, which period too brings the moon in the same
position on the same days, which appears to have some influence on the seasons. Among the meteorologic observations of
the academy for the month of July 1764, I find the following:
"The beginning of this month was wet, and the latter part dry;
the mornings were foggy, and the atmosphere in a smoke
during the day." – This you perceive bears a great resemblance
to the latter end of our June, so that it is not an unheard of or
forgotten thing. In 1764 they had afterwards storms and hail,
and nothing worse need be feared in 1783.

I have the honor to be, &c.

De la Lande, de l'Acad. des Sciences[26]

Lalande's article first appeared in the *Journal de Paris* on Tuesday
1 July 1783, the date chosen by some of France's more weather-
tormented divines for the imminent end of the world. While their
hopes were to remain disappointed, Lalande's article – the first officially sanctioned attempt to explain the cause of the still-persistent

worldwide haze – was widely translated and reprinted throughout the European press, since, apart from its brief diversion into astro-meteorology, it had managed to come up with what appeared to be a plausible explanation of the weather: the atmosphere had been severely fogged by an overabundance of evaporated rain. Moreover, by consulting the archives at the Paris Observatory, he had been able to compare the current conditions to those of an earlier summer, thereby coming to a reassuring conclusion, that 'nothing worse need be feared in 1783.' And perhaps this appeal to meteoro-logical history would have done the trick, had it not been for the fact that within days of the announcement, a series of severe electrical storms brought further devastation to much of northern Europe, while a sequence of renewed earthquakes of varying intensity rocked through southern Italy and France.

Poor old Lalande: he was already internationally renowned for making one false prediction, and now he had just issued another. It wasn't exactly his fault, but nevertheless, as the bad weather worsened and news of the earthquakes spread throughout Europe, what had started as a vague sense of geophysical unease began to escalate into a full-scale panic. Worse still, at least for Lalande, was that some of the same newspapers and magazines that had published and praised his scientific explanations were to follow them up, a week or so later, with attacks on his reputation instead. Reading them, Lalande must have experienced a certain dispirit-ing déjà vu – a return to the humiliations of 1773 – but, as he had become fond of declaring to the press, 'I am an oilskin for insults and a sponge for praise', which was just as well consider-ing the widespread pelting he received.[27] As the *Gloucester Journal* announced in its first-column leader for 28 July, 'the wretched inhabitants of Sicily and lower Calabria have again been visited with earthquakes, the most tremendous scourge that the divine vengeance employs in the punishment of a guilty world':

The news of these recent disasters immediately succeeding the publication of Mons. La Lande's letter, accounting for the

unusual appearance of the atmosphere, to remove the apprehensions of the vulgar, that great scientific genius has lost the
confidence which had been placed in his opinion. And these
dire calamities being observed to approach the western part
of Europe, many people cannot help expressing their fears
that we shall not be exempt from this visitation of the
Almighty.'

These fears, as the article went on to conclude, 'have contributed
very much to fill our churches', to the great satisfaction of those
among the European clergy who had felt their influence wane over
the years, as increasing numbers of natural philosophers came forward with new and compelling explanations for earthly processes
and events. John Wesley, for example, the 'dark and saturnine'
Methodist minister who had so welcomed the destruction of
Lisbon in 1755, was at it again during the summer of 1783, writing
happily of the 'good effects' of the recent spell of bad weather on
the people of Witney in Oxfordshire. 'Many thought the day of
judgement was come', as he noted in his diary on 16 July; 'the grace
of God came down in a manner never before known, and as the
impression was general, so was it lasting: It did not pass away with
the storm, but the spirit of seriousness, with that of grace and sup-
plication, continued.'[28]

The severe electrical storm that Wesley observed in Witney was
one of dozens that were caused by a series of unusually deep lows
that massed over northern and central Europe during June and July
1783. Few places were left unscathed by the lightning, hail and
floods, while a number of country towns and villages were virtually
destroyed. 'It would be too tedious to insert here the name of every
place, which I noted down in my journal, where I learned that the
thunder fell', as Robert Paul de Lamanon commented in the pages
of the *Journal de Physique*, which, in common with many other journals across Europe, carried detailed reports of the storms.[29] Witney
itself had fared particularly badly, the aftermath being described by
an agitated eyewitness (who was quoted in the *Ipswich Journal* for

12 July) as 'the most dismal scene he ever beheld; the whole town
was in the utmost fright and consternation [with] so many bodies
carried up the town apparently dead, he says, it seemed to make a
very awful impression.' The advent of these killer storms, added to
the ever-spreading haze, as well as to the rumours of yet more
earthquakes shaking large areas of southern Europe, was the cause
of enormous disquiet, and accounts of their violence filled every
newspaper from the Baltic to the Mediterranean.

One massive storm, for example, tore through central France
at the end of June, with the province of Bourbonnais suffering
the worst of the effects. According to a report in the *York Courant*
for 15 July, 'hail of an extraordinary size, driven by an impetuous
Wind, and followed by a heavy Rain that lasted almost three Hours,
laid all that Canton waste', with the estate of Condé, the country
seat of the Count de Viry, left in a terrible condition: 'the Castle
was unroofed, and all the Windows broke; many Trees were torn
up by the Roots, and the Harvest of ten Domains entirely ravaged;
so that neither Corn nor Hay can be expected this Year. It appears
that 10 or 12 neighbouring Parishes have shared the same Fate.'
In Lausanne, according to a report in the *General Evening Post* for
26–29 July, twelve people were killed and thirteen injured by a
single massive stroke of lightning, 'an effect without example in
this country', while in Scotland, according to the journals kept by
Janet Burnett of Disblair, Aberdeenshire, 'the thunder we had on
the 3rd July was very universal over all England and the South
of Scotland. Houses much hurt and a good many people killed.
This and such a continuance of thick fog is uncommon in this
country.'[30]

The storms that wracked Central Europe, however, were even
more severe. A Czech amateur meteorologist, parson Karel Hein of
south-western Moravia, kept a weather diary, in Latin, throughout
the summer of 1783, in which he complained of the constant fog,
as well as of the *'tonitrua horribilia'* ('horrible thunderstorms') that
persisted throughout June and July.[31] On 4 July, according to Hein,
lightning killed six bell-ringers in the Czech town of Doubrava, a

fate shared by many other bell-ringers throughout Central and
Eastern Europe.* An editorial in the *Gazette van Gent* for 17 July
claimed that 'many places in the German Holy Roman Empire
scarcely speak of anything other than the damage which has
been caused by the thunderstorms, the downpours and the inundations'; in Bohemia the town of Klatovy had been badly damaged
by lightning on 6 July, as had the neighbouring town of Zaclar,
where lightning struck eight times in one day, according to the
Gazeta Warszawska, and where 'it still thunders in a dense and
persisting fog.'[32] The Hungarian town of Cremnitz, too, was set on
fire by a lightning strike, and many of its wooden buildings burned
to the ground. All in all, the killer storms were more than living
up to their name.

The worst by far descended on Kłodzko (formerly Glatz), a
city on the Czech–Polish border. The storm was so extreme that it
was reported by newspapers all over Europe, with the following
account, from the *York Courant* for 22 July, being a typical example:

> The County of Glatz was visited with so dreadful a Storm,
> that there was no distinguishing it from an Earthquake. The
> whole Country was entirely overflowed by the Violence of
> the Rains, which, like a Deluge, carried away all the Bridges
> that have been built for 250 Years. The Claps of Thunder were
> so violent, that several Chimnies were thrown down and
> Walls shattered; whole Villages also were swept away by the
> Fury of the Torrents. Several Hundred Persons were drowned,
> and a great Number of Cattle lost. Our advices from Bohemia
> are as melancholy, and contain a Detail of several very
> unhappy Accidents.

The horror of these storms, particularly the one that destroyed
Glatz, lay partly in their blurring of the categories of disaster. There

---

* An edict banning the traditional (and suicidal) practice of ringing church bells as a
means of warding off storms would be issued later in the year by order of the Elector of
Bavaria.

was 'no distinguishing it from an Earthquake', as the *York Courant* put it, making an eerie connection to the current crop of earthquake scares then emanating from the south. The severe floods and land-slides, meanwhile, had taken on the quality of a biblical 'Deluge', as though they, too, had been sent from on high in punishment for earthly sins.

This confused sense that a mythic energy had been unleashed across the natural world inflected other reports of storm-related phenomena which were noted more for their strangeness than their severity. One widely circulated story in Britain, for example, was based on eyewitness accounts of the sky being set on fire. A letter from Leicester that was printed in the *Bath Chronicle* for 17 July, and then in many other papers over the following few days, described how on 'Thursday night last the inhabitants of this place were alarmed with a most awful appearance of lightning':

> It first began about nine in the evening at a distance, westerly, the sky clear, the atmosphere uncommonly hot and sultry; by degrees the clouds and lightning approached, exhibiting a wonderful spectacle of dreadful magnificence; before eleven o'clock the whole firmament seemed all on fire; the thunder, which till now had been heard at a distance, became loud and terrible, and the rain descended in torrents, mixed with smoke, sulphur and liquid fire; this scene of inconceivable horror continued for near an hour, when the lightning grew more faint, and the thunder less alarming; the clouds driving northwards; but in a short space returned with equal fury, and continued some time.

The letter's quasi-biblical language is almost as striking as the event it describes, and it gives some indication of just how terrified people must have been by what they evidently took to be appari-tions in the sky. With no modern terminology for things that had been seen but not yet understood, the natural recourse for eighteenth-century observers was to the language of the ancient texts, a language in which the sky is elevated to the 'firmament' and

lightning is transfigured into 'liquid fire', in tribute to the unknowa-
bility of the powers at work in the world.

The pyrotechnic storms continued over Europe for another
ten days, reinforcing the impression that the electrical outbursts
were causally connected to the still-persistent haze. 'It has been
conjectured that this extraordinary phænomenon is a natural consequence of the late uncommon state of the atmosphere, and
appearance of the sun, particularly at the hours of rising and setting', as the *Ipswich Journal* noted on 12 July, a sentiment which was
reiterated by papers all over Europe. 'We have experienced thunderstorms in many regions of the Kingdom', wrote a correspondent
to the *Gazette van Antwerpen* on 18 July, 'and these seem to be the
result of the general state of the atmosphere which has continued
for some time.' In Lincoln, as an in-depth article in the *Gentleman's
Magazine* observed, a severe storm on 10 July was preceded by 'a
thick hot vapour that had for several days before filled up the valley
between the hill on which the upper town stands and that which
descends from the heath, so that both sun and moon appeared
through it like heated brickbats, and as they sometimes do in a
morning fog near London'. As the author of the piece pointed out
in his conclusion, 'various conjectures had been formed on this
vapour by persons of different capacities; some conceived it the
electrical effluvia travelling hither from Calabria and Sicily; others
that the end of the world was approaching; others that it was
the effect of violent heats on the earth saturated before with cold
rain.'[33] But whatever the true explanation might have been, both
the haze and the storms persisted for the rest of July, with no sign
of improvement in the weather. A particularly severe storm in
London on 26 July was described in the *Gentleman's Magazine* as 'the
most awful and tremendous storm of thunder and lightning that
has been felt this summer in or near the metropolis.' It broke a large
number of windowpanes, destroyed a stand of trees in St James's
Park and shattered roof-tiles from Borough to Barn Elms, while
'in the Isle of Dogs the cattle were seemingly much affected. In
short, nothing like the violence of this storm is remembered in the

environs of London.'[34] Meanwhile, another report, published in the *Ipswich Journal* for 2 August, suggested that the violence of the thunder and lightning had actually served to rid the atmosphere of some of the lingering contagion. According to this account, the storm, as it passed over south London and parts of Kent, had 'a remarkable effect, deserving the particular notice of the public':

> the lightning was observed to set fire to the noxious vapour with which the atmosphere has been loaded for more than a month past. The whole expanse was successively in a blaze after every flash, without any thunder being heard, and even after the thunder and lightning had ceased, which did not continue violent for more than half an hour; the blaze of the vapour resembled what is called the white lightning, seen after summer's heat, but much more illuminated; as the light was momentarily so bright, that one might have seen to read by it. Since this phænomenon, the leaves of the summer shoots of the fruit-trees, that were before covered with vermin, appear to be cleared, and the clammy, glutinous substance with which they were covered, totally dried up.

Honeydew, the 'clammy, glutinous substance' mentioned by the correspondent, had been unusually prevalent throughout Europe that summer, adding a further cause of worry to farmers and gardeners, whose crops had already suffered in the stifling dry haze. A sugary substance excreted by aphids and adelgids, honeydew was a familiar sign of infestation, but it was thriving in the hot weather like never before, as Gilbert White of Selborne discovered to his distress:

> In the sultry season of 1783 honey-dews were so frequent as to deface and destroy the beauties of my garden. My honeysuckles, which were one week the most sweet and lovely objects the eye could behold, became the next the most loathsome; being enveloped in a viscous substance, and loaded with black aphides, or smother-flies.[35]

Similar blights were reported from locations all over the Continent, with the fruit trees of Hungary and Estonia, the cornfields of Slovakia and the vineyards and vegetable gardens of Croatia suffering from the lingering haze and its unwelcome swarms of aphids.

As the strange weather continued to stalk the European continent, so did the general mood of dread, a mood which turned out to be entirely justified, for church records throughout Europe show a sharp mortality peak occurring during the summer of 1783, a time when, as the *Bath Chronicle* declared on 3 July, 'from the unwholesomeness of the air, the scarcity of food, and the neglect of cleanliness, the lower class of people in the country were never known to be so unhealthy as at present. A fever of the putrid kind rages in many parts, which the people term the black fever, and carries off great numbers. In Wales, it has been so fatal, that at Carmarthen 20 and 30 people were daily carried off by this distemper.'

The situation, as we have already seen, was just as bad in France, where, according to the journal of the Abbot of Bazingham, 'putrid illnesses occurred due to the great heat of the summer, and one counted a larger number of deaths than births during the year.'[36] The same was true in the Netherlands, Germany, Switzerland and Spain, a sudden escalation of disease and death sweeping the length of Europe, the bringer of which was clear for all to see: 'One has probably to seek the causes of these illnesses in the state of the sky, the temperature of the air and the season of the year', wrote Mathias van Geuns, Professor of Medicine at the University of Harderwijk, while in Barcelona, the fifth Barón de Maldá had kept a diary throughout this period, in which he described how 'the great heat and the extreme droughts turned into a constellation of illnesses which were malignant fevers, from which no few persons died', a suspicion that has been borne out by examination of the burial records.[37] In Britain, for example, recent research at the University of Cambridge has identified some eleven and a half thousand anomalous deaths between August and September 1783

– usually the months of minimum mortality – which can be attributed to the effects of the pollutants in the haze, as well as to illnesses exacerbated by the unusually high summer temperatures: 'many whom I left in my parish well are dead, and many dying', as Charles Simeon wrote on 19 September, on his return to Cambridge after a six-week absence; 'this fever rages wherever I have been.'[38] The summer of 1783 was a summer not only of strange skies but of fevers, sweats and bronchial diseases for which basic medical attention remained beyond the reach of most, although it wasn't long before advertisements such as the following, which appeared in the *General Evening Post* for 19–22 July, became a familiar feature of everyday life in Europe:

> For most of the disorders that are now prevalent, such as putrid fevers, ulcerated sore throats, and all others which are occasioned by the intense heat of the present season, Freake's Tincture of Bark has been found particularly serviceable, and is recommended in preference to other preparations, as it contains every active property of the Bark, and may be given in smaller quantities than is usually prescribed, without overloading the stomach, as it frequently does when taken in substance. Sold by A. Freake, No. 3. Tottenham-Court Road, and by F. Newbery, No. 45. St. Paul's Church-Yard, in bottles, price 3s. 6d. each.

Tincture of bark, derived from the quinine-rich Peruvian cinchona tree, had been introduced to Europe in the seventeenth century by Spanish Jesuit missionaries, who had witnessed the benefits of its widespread use among the South American Indians. Once in Europe it was soon established as a familiar household remedy, and John Wesley, for one, became an enthusiastic advocate, recommending in his *Primitive Physick* (a Methodist home-doctoring manual compiled in 1747) that it should be soaked for an hour in a glass of port. Wesley was right to recommend its use, for malaria was one of eighteenth-century Europe's deadliest killers, and it spread to near-epidemic levels in the warm, mosquito-ridden summer of 1783, a grimly appropriate condition, given that its name derived from the Italian for 'bad air'.

Meanwhile, there was also the matter of the alarming series of earthquakes that were being experienced throughout Italy and France. A letter from Dijôn, published in the *General Evening Post* for 17–19 July, described 'a violent earthquake, which was followed by others at intervals', while in Beane, apparently, 'it was felt in a still more violent degree, considerable damage was done, and the sub-terranean noise is said to have been terrible beyond description. From many other parts of the kingdom we have the like dreadful accounts.' And soon the whole of Europe was being shaken from below – 'we just now learn from Geneva that the shocks of the earth have been so violent there, that they at one time thought the city was at an end', as the editor of the *General Evening Post* reported. And not even London would be spared: on the afternoon of 1 August, Horace Walpole sat writing a letter to his friend the Earl of Strafford:

> Have you had your earthquake, my Lord? Many have had theirs. I assure you I have had mine. Above a week ago, when broad awake, the doors of the cabinet by my bedside rattled, without a breath of wind. I imagined somebody was walking on the leads, or had broken into the room under me. It was between four and five in the morning. I rang my bell. Before my servant could come it happened again; and was exactly like the horizontal tremor I felt from the earthquake some years ago.[39]

Walpole was referring to the pair of earthquakes that had shaken London in 1750, causing widespread panic and alarm, even though only one person had been hurt (a maid-servant in Charterhouse Square, who had tumbled out of bed and broken her arm), and there had been little in the way of damage to buildings beyond the loss of a couple of chimneys. The scale of the alarm was due largely to the fact that the first tremor had been felt on Thursday 8 February, while the second, heavier shock came on Thursday 8 March. The coincidence of the dates led to hundreds of people fleeing London during the first week of April 1750, convinced that a third, massive earthquake would arrive to destroy the city on the 8th. 'Jupiter, I think, has jogged us three degrees nearer the sun', as Walpole joked at the time, but for others it was a serious affair.[40] Thomas Sherlock, the Bishop of London, published a sermon on the tremors in the form of an open letter to the people of the city, in which he castigated them for their multifarious sins and omissions, and urged them to ignore the words of the 'little philosophers, who see a little, and but very little, into natural causes.'[41] The escalating pair of earthquakes, he thought, had clearly been a merciful warning, while the third in the seismic trinity, due in exactly one month's time, would turn out to be the city's final judgement.

Needless to say, the April apocalypse never came, although the Lisbon earthquake of five years later was taken by some to be the predicted third strike, albeit mysteriously delayed and somewhat off-target. Perhaps, it was suggested, so many Londoners had been chastened by the warnings that their punishment was no longer deserved, or else the economic ties between the two corrupt cities were close enough to render them seismically the same.

Thirty-three years later, that same model of escalation remained at work on the popular mood. Oliver Goldsmith had commented on it in his early comedy *The Good-Natur'd Man*, which was first performed at Covent Garden in 1768. In it, Mr Croaker, an amateur natural philosopher with a penchant for earthquakes, tells his friends about a letter which he has just had published in a news-paper:

> what if I bring my last letter to the *Gazetteer* on the encrease and progress of earthquakes? It will amuse us, I promise you. I there prove how the late earthquake is coming round to pay us another visit, from London to Lisbon, from Lisbon to the Canary Islands, from the Canary Islands to Palmyra, from Palmyra to Constantinople, and so from Constantinople back to London again.[42]

As we have already seen, such images of seismic circulation were widely entertained in the public prints, and did much to keep the population in a state of nervous expectation. As an editorial in the *General Evening Post* expressed it, 'there seems lately to have been an almost universal perturbation in nature. All Europe has been shaken by some uncommon convulsions; and it appears from the different relations of the effects of the recent thunder storm, in different parts of the country, that this island has not escaped a participation in the general calamity.'[43] In other words, whatever had been responsible for causing all the summer's troubles appeared to be drifting slowly across the Continent, and nothing could be done to prevent it. Even domestic animals seemed to pick up on the disturbance, with the *Whitehall Evening Post* for 2 August declaring that, 'to the extreme heat of the weather we impute that canine madness which now very much prevails', while the *London Recorder* for 27 July reported that killer wolves of a new species, 'an unknown kind, differing from other wolves in having a larger head, larger feet, and sharper claws, have made their appearance in that part of Brittainy called Cornovalle; they glut upon human blood; dogs dare not face them; fifteen persons have fallen victim to their ferocity (including the Chévalier du Couedick); and proper steps are taken for their destruction.' As these and other rumours spread unchecked throughout the summer, everything in nature, from the animals to the atmosphere, became caught up in the universal convulsion.

But by the middle of August, things had begun to settle down. The brief spate of earthquakes had come to an end, the worst of the storms had blown themselves out and even the strange summer haze was appearing to ease, although no one had managed to come up with a credible explanation of its cause. Lalande's 'mist' hypothesis had not been taken up, while a number of competing explanations continued to do the rounds: earthquake exhalations, electrical effluvia, meteor fragments and comet-tail debris remained the most popular candidates for blame, along with other shorter-lived hypotheses that appeared over the course of the summer, including smoke drifting over from peat-burning in Ireland, solid evaporation rising up from the earth and solar emissions streaming in from an overheating sun. All were perfectly valid suggestions, yet all were clearly the result of speculation rather than research.

In fact only in France had there been any attempts to conduct first-hand investigations into the atmospheric haze. One experiment, held at the Paris Observatory in mid-July, saw a group from the French Academy of Sciences send a linen kite high into the air in order to collect atmospheric samples. When the kite was pulled back down to earth it was found to be blackened and discoloured by what was described in the report as 'moisture prejudicial to plants' (presumably a diluted form of sulphur dioxide, the substance that would later be known as 'acid rain'); meanwhile, at Grenoble in the south of France, according to an article in the *Journal de Physique*, a laboratory analysis of a sample of foggy air yielded inconclusive results:

> On the 4th of July, at five in the morning, M. Nicolas, physician at Grenoble, and M. Plana, apothecary, took four measures of fog and mixed them with two measures of nitrous air: the absorption was 1-4th, and nothing remained but a gas, in which a candle became extinguished several times. Atmospheric air generally contains nearly 1-3d of pure air (oxygen gas) and 2-3ds of mephitic air (azotic gas). Fontana's eudiometer gave the same result on the 7th of July: of three hundred parts of atmospheric air, thirty-two were absorbed. The air of the fog, mixed with inflammable (hydrogen) gas, did not prevent it from exploding when a lighted taper was presented to the neck of the bottle in which it was contained.[44]

Outdoor trials were also conducted by the energetic naturalist Robert Paul de Lamanon, who set out to discover just how high the fog extended. 'Having learned from the public papers that this phenomenon was not local, but almost general throughout Europe', as he noted in his article in the *Journal de Physique*, 'I made new observations, and traversed the highest Alps of Provence, Dauphiny and Piedmont'. An enthusiastic Alpine explorer, de Lamanon ended up on the summit of a 3,000-metre-high mountain in the Alpes du Dauphine in his search for the upper limits of the fog:

> When I was on the top of Mount Ventoux, nearly 1040 toises [2,027 metres] above the level of the sea, I saw it far above me . . . On the 22d of September I ascended the highest Alps of Dauphiny, to the height of 1660 toises [3,235 metres] above the sea. (No one has yet been higher in Europe.) The shepherds, who served me as guides, all assured me that this fog had however passed over these mountains. The lowest part of the fog was the thickest and driest. I assured myself of this by proceeding from the borders of the sea to the summits of the highest mountains. It is probable, according tò every account, that this fog overspread almost all Europe, the islands of the Mediterranean, and a part of Africa. It covered the whole Adriatic Sea, but extended only to the distance of 100 leagues [c. 500 kilometres] on the ocean. It was properly a continental fog.[45]

Having made considerable efforts to encounter and describe the limits of the phenomenon, Lamanon then went on to attempt an explanation of its cause. He began by casting doubt on the idea that the fog had been a consequence of the Italian earthquakes – 'the earthquakes in Calabria and Sicily took place chiefly in February, and the fog did not appear till the middle of June; that is to say, till more than four months after' – claiming instead that the various strange phenomena that had marked out the summer of 1783, including the Italian earthquakes, had a single common cause in the actions of the so-called 'subtle materials' of the earth. According to Lamanon, these subtle materials were noxious exhalations deriving from 'the remains of animals and vegetables still distinguishable, and which occupy so much room in our globe; the acids which attack them; the aëriform fluids disengaged from them; the metals and pyrites brought to perfection, or decomposed; the fires separated, or collected; the fermentations and effervescences; in a word, the innumerable decompositions and recompositions of all the parts of the earth.' According to him, these various exhalations circulated perpetually between the earth and the sky, but depending on a varied set of climatic and geographical factors, as well as the 'intestinal motions' occurring deep within the body of the earth, their movements could sometimes stall, as it were, thus forming a dense layer of atmospheric fog: and this, he claimed, was precisely what had happened during the summer of 1783.[46]

Sadly, Lamanon's research efforts didn't stop at the Alpine summits, and two years later, in 1785, he joined the ill-fated La Pérouse expedition to the south Pacific, during the course of which he conducted tireless magnetic and atmospheric observations. But on 11 December 1787 he and ten other expedition scientists were killed by a war party on the beach at Tutuila, an island in eastern Samoa, and so he never did learn the true explanation for the fog that had covered the Alps.

In contrast to their French counterparts, the majority of British naturalists who paid attention to the haze stopped short of conducting first-hand experiments, or even of putting forward their own explanations. One of the reasons for this difference in approach was that French scientific life was centrally organized and generously funded (as in many other northern European countries), while in Britain it was still pursued as an individual, and largely amateur, indulgence. Apart from the prestigious Royal Society of London, which was socially selective and expensive to join, Britain had little in the way of organized science, with most practitioners being self-funded members of debating clubs with limited access to equipment. They tended, as a consequence, to be more modest in their claims, though their enthusiasm for fieldwork was irrepressible, and there was hardly a cleric or physician in the country who did not own a barometer or a pair of celestial globes, or who hadn't sent a letter or two to the *Gentleman's Magazine* describing unusual natural phenomena in their local vicinities.

Gilbert White of Selborne, one of English literature's best-loved nature writers, was a classic example of the breed. An Oxford-educated country cleric, from a respectable family of modest financial means, he lived far from the centres of scientific life, pursuing an essentially private passion with a high degree of scholarly rigour. Though best known today for his botanizing and his bird-watching, he maintained a lifelong interest in meteorology, and enjoyed setting up instruments in his Hampshire garden in order to note the fluctuations of the outside air – although his enjoyment was badly dented on the unusually cold winter's night of 9 December 1784, when he decided to road-test two new thermometers: 'On the 10th, in the morning, the quicksilver of *Dollond's* glass was down to *half a degree below zero*; and that of *Martin's*, which was absurdly graduated only to four degrees *above zero*, sunk quite into the brass guard of the ball', as he complained in a letter to his friend Daines Barrington, 'so that when the weather became most interesting this was useless.'[47] But aside from the distractions caused by unreliable equipment, White had always found the weather to be a rewarding subject, and his account of the summer of 1783 went on to form the grand finale of his classic study, *The Natural History and Antiquities of Selborne*, a book that has never gone out of print since its first appearance in 1788. For White, as for everybody else at the time, the whole prolonged episode was both inexplicable and alarming. 'The summer of the year 1783', he began, 'was an amazing and portentous one, and full of horrible phenomena':

> the peculiar haze, or smokey fog, that prevailed for many weeks in this island, and in every part of Europe, and even beyond its limits, was a most extraordinary appearance, unlike anything known within the memory of man. By my journal I find that I had noticed this strange occurrence from June 23 to July 20 inclusive, during which period the wind varied to every quarter without making any alteration in the air. The sun, at noon, looked as blank as a clouded moon, and shed a rust-coloured ferruginous light upon the ground, and floors of rooms; but was particularly lurid and blood-coloured at

rising and setting. All the time the heat was so intense that butchers' meat could hardly be eaten on the day after it was killed; and the flies swarmed so in the lanes and the hedges that they rendered the horses half frantic, and riding irksome. The country people began to look with a superstitious awe at the red, louring aspect of the sun; and indeed there was reason for the most enlightened person to be apprehensive; for, all the while, Calabria and part of the isle of Sicily, were torn and convulsed with earthquakes; and about that juncture a volcano sprang out of the sea on the coast of Norway.[48]

White was clearly worried by the thought of a connection between the lingering haze and the ongoing sequence of Italian earthquakes, but he was at one with his rural neighbours in having no idea of what that connection could be. Neither, for that matter, did his close friend Thomas Barker, the famous vegetarian squire of Lyndon Hall in Rutland, who had acted as the Royal Society's weather correspondent for more than forty years, but who was also unable to venture beyond pure description in the end-of-year report he sent to London:

> During the showery time an uncommon haziness began, which was very remarkable all the rest of the summer: the air was all thick both below the clouds and above them, the hills looked blue, and at a distance could not be seen; the sun shone very red through the haze, and sometimes could not be seen when near setting. There was more or less of this haze almost constantly for a month, and very frequently to the end of the summer, and it did not cease till Michaelmas; and neither rain nor fair, wind nor calm, east nor west winds, took it away; and it was as extensive as common, for it was the same all over Europe, and even to the top of the Alps. This haze was very like Virgil's description of the summer after Julius Cæsar's death, which was probably the same case,
>
> *Cum caput obscura nitidum ferrugine texit,*
>
> for rusty iron is a very good description of the colour the sun shone.[49]

The sun, as Virgil recounted in Book I of the *Georgics*, had dimmed to a rusty colour as a mark of mourning for Caesar, but in spite of the illuminating choice of image – the product of an English landowner's classical education – this was hardly an adequate explanation for the veil that covered the skies (see picture 10). As keen weather-watchers and lifelong friends (the squire had married Gilbert's sister, Anne, in 1751), Barker and White arranged to meet in order to share their mutual disquiet over the season's strange events. Squire Barker made the journey to Selborne at the beginning of August 1783, covering 190 kilometres (118 miles) during three of the hottest days of the year, much to the concern of Gilbert White, who worried about the effects of the ride on the health of his sixty-two-year-old brother-in-law. But he needn't have worried, for Squire Barker – an early advocate of regular exercise and a strict vegetable diet – was possessed of an indefatigable constitution, and 'at every dining place, while the horses were baiting, he walked four or five miles in the heat in his boots with his wig in his hand', according to White (who was, in truth, a little taken aback by his old friend's physical fitness: 'He still has a streight belly, and is as agile as ever; and starts up as soon as he has dined, and marches all round Hartley-park. This morning [27 August] he ran round Baker's Hill in one minute and a quarter'[50]). But in spite of their spontaneous cross-country conference, and the hours spent gazing up at the discolorations of the sky, the pair remained unable to come up with any kind of credible explanation.

Back in France, meanwhile, the unabashed astronomer Joseph-Jérôme de Lalande had just submitted another of his announcements to the press, with a translation of his article (entitled 'Physics'), soon appearing in papers such as the *Morning Herald* for 26 July. It began with a summary of the situation so far: 'The hot fogs still continue at Paris; the heat has been excessive, and thunder storms frequent', before going on to tackle the most recent manifestations of the earth's inner turmoil:

> On the 6th of the present month, two small shocks of an earthquake were felt through all the towns of Bourgogne

and Franche-Comté, from Dijon to Besançon. The trembling continued about three or four seconds, accompanied by a rumbling noise, like the wheels of a chariot rolling with rapidity over the pavement. The terror was greater than the damage: there was no mischief done, except a few old chimnies thrown down, and cielings [sic] cracked.

Still seeking to reassure a nervous public, Lalande evidently couldn't resist another opportunity to promote one of his trademark explanations:

It is not probable these provinces can have any thing to fear, as there have never hitherto been any appearance of volcanos in them; and that this earthquake is only subterranean thunder, or an electric explosion, produced by the dry and elastic fogs, with which the whole face of France has been covered for such a considerable length of time. It is known that lightning sometimes issues from the earth, as well as from the clouds, which is mutually occasioned by the want of a due equilibrium between the earth and air: hence we may easily conceive, that if the accumulation of electric matter becomes immense, the shock it gives must be felt at a great distance.

Once again, poor old Lalande; it was almost as if his convoluted attempts to explain the earth's geophysical activities actually made conditions worse, for no sooner had he issued this latest pronouncement concerning volcanic eruptions and electrical matter than the story broke that a new and active volcanic island had just arisen in the sea off Iceland, and then, on the evening of 18 August, a huge flaming fireball passed low in the skies above Britain and northern France, casting fresh eddies of panic in its wake.

Firstly, the erupting island. As the front page of the *Morning Herald* announced on 31 July, 'a *new Island*, of about two leagues in circumference, has recently made its appearance in the seas of Iceland. It contains several volcanoes, and is supposed to have been an effect of the dreadful earthquakes, that have caused such havock in Sicily' – although the idea that an eruption in the North

Atlantic might have anything to do with an earthquake in Sicily was soon disputed in an article published in the *Gentleman's Magazine*, which suggested that 'those who consider its neighbourhood with Hecla, the second volcano in the world, will rather attribute it to some intestine commotions of that mountain.'[51] The island had apparently first been sighted by the crew of a Norwegian trading vessel during their return journey south to Trondheim, but at first their incoherent report of a flaming, smoke-spewing island rising from the waters was dismissed as a seafarers' tale. Soon after that, however, the captain of a Danish merchant ship made the same strange sighting, and reported the new island's location to the governor of Iceland, who dispatched a naval vessel to investigate. Once its existence was confirmed, the governor lost no time in claiming this new territory on behalf of the Danish crown, an act that generated some amusement in the pages of the next day's *Herald*:

> The *new Island* which the *King of Denmark* has taken posses-
> sion of in the sea of Iceland, does not most certainly produce
> either corn, wine or oil; but as there are several *volcanos*
> upon it, his Danish Majesty no doubt means to open a traffic
> with the inhabitants of Greenland, and other cold regions
> of the North, and barter *red-hot pumice stones* for a return of
> *snow-balls*!

The origins of the island, which, according to the newspaper, 'the curious here are much engaged in investigating', provided a great deal of speculation for the next few days, although further information from close at hand remained difficult to obtain. The haze, it seemed, remained particularly bad in Iceland, just as it had been all summer long, and the new island was only visible from the shore when the wind was blowing in a northerly direction; otherwise it was completely obscured by smoke.

But interest in the Arctic island was fated to be short-lived, eclipsed as it was by the sudden appearance of a flaming meteor, just before nine o'clock in the evening of 18 August 1783. It was

travelling, by all accounts, in a south-westerly direction, appearing
first over the Shetland Islands, and then hurtling along the coasts of
Scotland and England, before crossing the Channel and exploding
somewhere over France. There were, naturally, hundreds of eyewitnesses, many of whom wrote down their impressions and sent
them either to their local newspapers or to the editors of the leading London journals. Although few observers seemed to have
expressed alarm at the prospect – meteors were familiar celestial
phenomena in the days before light pollution banished them from
sight – all were impressed by its unusually low altitude, which
allowed for a spectacular close-up view of its brief career through
the sky (see picture 11). An eyewitness in Sheffield, for instance,
wrote to the *Gentleman's Magazine* describing 'a sudden light,
resembling the glare of pale lightning, which gradually increased to
a most brilliant refulgence, illuminating the whole atmosphere;
when, upon looking out of my chaise, I saw a ball of fire with a long
train, resembling a sky-rocket, moving with great rapidity from
NE to SW.'[52] 'It gave a light equal to that of half a dozen rockets',
wrote another, who claimed that as it passed overhead, it dropped
'particles of fire of bluish colour, of the size of a star', although a
later search failed to find anything on the ground connected to the
fiery apparition.[53] One of the best descriptions of all was written
by William Cooper, Archdeacon of York, who had happened to be
in his carriage on the way to Hartlepool, 'set out upon a journey to
the sea-side. The weather was sultry, the atmosphere hazy, and not
a breath of air stirring', as he wrote in a letter to Sir Joseph Banks,
President of the Royal Society. 'As we proceeded, I observed to
my attendants, that there was something singularly striking in the
appearance of the night, not merely from its stillness and darkness,
but from the sulphureous vapours which seemed to surround us
on every side.' Suddenly, the darkness of the Yorkshire night was lit
by 'a brilliant tremulous light' which appeared on the north-west
horizon:

> At the first it seemed stationary; but in a small space of time it
> burst from its position, and took its course to the S.E. by E. It

passed directly over our heads with a buzzing noise, seemingly
at the height of sixty yards. Its tail, as far as the eye could form
any judgement, was about eight or ten yards in length. At last,
this wonderful meteor divided into several glowing parts or
balls of fire, the chief part still remaining in its full splendor.
Soon after this I heard two great explosions, each equal to the
report of a large cannon carrying a nine-pound ball. During its
awful progress, the whole of the atmosphere, as far as I could
discern, was perfectly illuminated with the most beautifully
vivid light I ever remember to have seen. The horses on which
we rode shrunk with fear; and some people we met upon the
road declared their consternation in the most expressive
terms.[54]

Some observers took the opportunity to make detailed notes
and calculations of the meteor's progress. One eyewitness from
Canterbury, who signed himself 'J.R.' at the end of his letter to the
Gentleman's Magazine, managed to track the course of the meteor
until it appeared to explode or burst, some forty-five degrees above
the horizon. Exactly five minutes later the sound of 'a great explosion' reached his ear, and by correlating the angle with the time
elapsed, J.R. calculated that the meteor had been approaching
Boulogne, sixty-five miles away from him, and only forty-six miles
above the ground when it finally burned itself out; 'I therefore
imagine that it was generated in the atmosphere over the German
ocean, and as soon as it took fire directed its course to the S.W.,
mounting in its passage until it arrived at the utmost limits of the
atmosphere, which, by its rarefaction at that time, might have
exceeded its mean height, which is generally supposed to be 44½
miles.'[55] The meteor was thus extraordinarily close (although it
burned out long before it reached the stratosphere), and its unusual
proximity, as well as the direction from which it appeared to have
travelled, led to the inevitable observation that it had 'been occasioned by some of the vapours issuing from the volcanoes upon
the New Island lately sprung up in the ocean, about nine leagues
to the S.W. of Iceland, or perhaps from that profuse exhalation of

vapours occasioned by the excessive warm and dry weather we have experienced this summer.'[56]

Oh, yes: fogs, storms, lightning strikes, earthquakes, volcanoes, rabid dogs, killer wolves, and now this low-flying meteor exploding in the sky somewhere above the English Channel. Who wouldn't be worried by the summer's strange proceedings? Horace Walpole, of course, supplied a typically facetious account, writing that 'we have had pigmy earthquakes, much havoc by lightning, and some very respectable meteors', but others were not so sanguine, with the *General Evening Post* declaring, at the end of a long and worried editorial, that, 'in short, we have had the most melancholy tidings from all parts representing the recent disasters as to the general convulsions of Nature in disorder!'[57]

This widespread mood of bewilderment and despair was keenly felt by the poet William Cowper, who was still suffering from anxious depression at the general turn of events. In common with many other evangelicals, he subscribed to what (by the 1780s) was a rather antiquated reading of geophysics, in which phenomena such as earthquakes and meteors were seen as physical evidence of the planet's moral decay. Having been created by God in a state of smooth perfection, the Earth was falling into craggy ruin as the result of a series of extreme events that had begun with the biblical Flood, and which seemed to be proliferating faster than ever, their root causes being, of course, the multifarious sins of mankind. For Cowper and his friends, events such as the lingering haze and the low-flying meteor provided further evidence that 'th' old and crazy earth' was coming to the end of the road, a view that he espoused with characteristic fervour in Book II of *The Task*, the epic poem on which he had been hard at work during the summer of 1783. His outline argument for Book II, 'The Time-Piece', reads: 'Prodigies enumerated—Sicilian earthquakes—Man rendered obnoxious to these calamities by sin—God the agent in them—The philosophy that stops at secondary causes reproved', while the verses them-selves reveal the strength of Cowper's escalating fear of 'a world that seems to toll the death-bell of its own decease':

> When were the winds
> Let slip with such a warrant to destroy?
> When did the waves so haughtily o'erleap
> Their ancient barriers, deluging the dry?
> Fires from beneath, and meteors from above,
> Portentous, unexampled, unexplained,
> Have kindled beacons in the skies, and th' old
> And crazy earth has had her shaking fits
> More frequent, and foregone her usual rest.
> Is it a time to wrangle, when the props
> And pillars of our planet seem to fail,
> And nature with a dim and sickly eye
> To wait the close of all?[58]

For the sake of William Cowper's sanity, if for no other reason, a credible explanation of the strange summer weather was now needed more than ever.

III

By 1783 Benjamin Franklin had been famous for well over thirty years, and was at the height of his personal popularity both in France and North America. The esteem that he had once enjoyed in Britain, by contrast, had eroded as the American war went on, and as a leading representative of an enemy power, he had been denounced as a traitor by many of his former friends. 'I look upon him as a dangerous engine', as Viscount Stormont, the British Ambassador in Paris, declared, 'and am very sorry that some English frigate did not meet with him by the way.'[59]

Among the many fears that had grown to haunt the British administration during the final stages of the American campaign was the fear that Franklin had put his considerable scientific and technological knowledge at the military disposal of the French. Worried British spies, who had evidently convinced themselves that Franklin was somehow in possession of supernatural powers, circulated extraordinary rumours concerning his secret work on weapons of mass destruction:

> The Doctor with the assistance of French mechanics is prepar-
> ing a great number of reflecting mirrors which will reflect so
> much heat from the sun as will destroy anything by fire at
> a very considerable distance. This apparatus is to be fixed at
> Calais on the French coast so as to command the English
> shore whereby they mean to burn and destroy the whole navy
> of Great Britain in our harbours. During the conflagration the
> Doctor proposes to have a chain carried from Calais to Dover.
> He, standing at Calais, with a prodigious electrical machine of
> his own invention, will convey such a shock as will entirely
> overturn our whole island.[60]

Despite the colourful Archimedean allegations (an invading Roman fleet was burned off Syracuse in 212 BC, using a system of refract-ing mirrors designed by Archimedes), the Doctor was in fact spending tedious hours appealing for funds for the cash-strapped American forces, in between bouts of pleasurable philosophizing in the pre-Revolutionary salons of Passy. A wide array of subjects and ideas was discussed by Franklin and his aristocratic friends in the course of his regular attendance at their soirees, but the electrifica-tion of the English coast was unlikely to have been among them.

The spies' reports, though, were a curious conflation of aspects of Franklin's earlier fame as an electrical pioneer with elements of his current role as a revolutionary leader. 'He seized lightning from the heavens and the sceptre from tyrants', as Baron de Turgot famously remarked, and the British intelligence services had appar-ently taken this implied connection seriously.[61]

The idea of an electrical chain that could pass a current over a body of water dated back to the 1740s, and a series of large-scale experiments undertaken both in Europe and America. The most famous of these had been conducted in Paris by the French cleric and natural philosopher Jean-Antoine Nollet, who had taken an electrical charge (stored in a foil-lined container known as a Leyden jar) and passed it along the joined hands of a line of nervous volunteers. Once the last person in the chain had completed the circuit by placing one hand on a metal conductor, the charge passed rapidly along the line, causing each human relay to convulse or jump as it passed through his or her body. In the garden at Versailles in 1746 a chain of a hundred and eighty soldiers was electrified in front of the king, and later, it was claimed, a current was successfully passed through the hands of more than six hundred people arranged in an open field. It was soon discovered that metal wire could conduct electric charges over even greater distances, and ambitious demonstrations were held in the Tuileries Gardens in Paris, across Westminster Bridge in London, and between the banks of the Schuylkill River in Franklin's home town of Philadelphia. It was the success of these experiments that first inspired Franklin to take up the research into the nature of electricity that would later ensure his fame throughout the world.

Franklin's electrical research had begun as a hobby in the early 1740s, when he was still earning his living as a printer and pamphleteer, but it had soon taken over his life. 'I never was before engaged in any study that so totally engrossed my attention and my time as this has lately done,' as he wrote to a friend in London in 1747, 'for, what with making experiments where I can be alone, and repeating them to my Friends and Acquaintance who, from the novelty of the thing, come continually in crouds to see them, I have during some months past had little leisure for anything else.'[62] It may have been 'just' a hobby, but by the end of the 1740s Franklin had made a number of important discoveries in the field. By then, natural philosophers had already determined that most solid bodies contain an electrical charge, which was considered to be essentially fluid in nature, and that this 'fluid' came in one of two forms: vitreous electricity, which could be produced by rubbing glass with a piece of silk; and resinous electricity, which could be produced by rubbing resin with a piece of wool or fur. These charges, moreover, could be stored for later use in a Leyden jar (which Franklin later modified and renamed 'the electrical battery'); the stored charges could then be transferred between conducting objects, as the chain-of-hands experiments had shown. But it was pointed metal objects, as Franklin quickly noticed, that proved the best means of 'drawing off and throwing off the electrical fire', and he performed dozens of experiments to demonstrate his important observation that 'the electric fluid is attracted by points.'[63]

Franklin was particularly interested in the noisy electric sparks that he was able to produce with his home-made machines, and, in common with many other electrical researchers, he was convinced that the phenomena of thunder and lightning were merely vast natural versions of the same effects. 'Electrical fluid agrees with lightning in these particulars', as he wrote in a now-famous diary entry in 1749, listing the twelve key ways in which the two kinds of spark were alike:

1. Giving light. 2. Colour of the light. 3. Crooked direction. 4. Swift motion. 5. Being conducted by metals. 6. Crack or noise in exploding. 7. Subsisting in water or ice. 8. Rending bodies it passes through. 9. Destroying animals. 10. Melting metals. 11. Firing inflammable substances. 12. Sulphureous smell.[64]

All electric sparks, as he had long observed, were strongly attracted by metal points, but since 'we do not know whether this property is in lightning', he devised an ingenious experiment that would determine the answer. On the top of a high tower or church steeple, 'a kind of sentry box' would be installed, featuring a long metal rod pointing upwards to the sky. If lightning truly was an electric spark, this rod ought to be able to 'draw it off' from a suitably low-lying storm cloud. An observer positioned inside the darkened box would be able to see the sparks as they passed down the rod and into the ground via a wax-handled wire that the sentry would hold in his hand.[65] Franklin was apparently unaware of just how dangerous this experiment was, but nevertheless, when it was successfully performed in France in May 1752, the electrical nature of thunder and lightning was finally and irrefutably confirmed.

But it took some time for Franklin to receive the news that his proposed experiment had yielded results, and he remained at work on further attempts to prove the same hypothesis. And so, only a month after the French experiment, on a stormy day in June 1752, he and his twenty-one-year-old son William ventured into a field on the outskirts of Philadelphia to fly a kite into a cloud. The home-made kite, which he had fashioned from a silk handkerchief stretched onto a basic wooden cross, had a sharp metal point attached to its tip, and a metal key suspended near the bottom of the string. Franklin, who again seemed remarkably unaware of how perilous his experiment was, managed to fly the kite deep into a passing thundercloud; after a time, by holding his knuckle up close to the key, he was rewarded with a stream of electric sparks that he had drawn down to earth from the sky. These sparks, as he soon discovered, could be stored in a Leyden jar, transported home and used to perform the same experiments that he conducted with his electrical apparatus.

Once Franklin had independently established that lightning really was a form of static electricity, he began to develop an idea that had suggested itself during his research. If natural lightning, like his own home-made electric sparks, was so attracted to the point of a metal rod, why not put this discovery to practical use? Hundreds of buildings across America were destroyed every year by lightning strikes, but mightn't they be given some kind of protection by the use of a pointed metal conductor? 'The doctrine of points is very curious', as he wrote in a letter to the London researcher Peter Collinson, 'and the effects of them truly wonderful':

> and, from what I have observed on experiments, I am of opinion that houses, ships, and even towers and churches may be effectually secured from the strokes of lightning by their means; for if, instead of the round balls of wood or metal which are commonly placed on the tops of weathercocks, vanes, or spindles of churches, spires, or masts, there should be a rod of iron eight or ten feet in length, sharpened gradu-

ally to a point like a needle, and gilt to prevent rusting, or divided into a number of points, which would be better, the electrical fire would, I think, be drawn out of a cloud silently, before it could come near enough to strike.[66]

Franklin had just invented the lightning rod, and it wasn't long before the new invention was being fitted to public buildings throughout Pennsylvania. In Europe, however, there were loud objections put forward by a number of senior clerics, who – in an argument reminiscent of the clerical objections to the antiseismic rebuilding of Lisbon – claimed that the rod fulfilled a heretical purpose, which was the scientific subversion of divine providence in the form of lightning from above. In their view, the ringing of church bells was the only allowable form of benediction against an electrical strike: otherwise, what was the point of prayer if a piece of wire could be deployed instead? So in a world where the medieval motto 'Fulgura frango' – 'I break up the lightning' – was still being inscribed on newly cast bells, this American innovation faced stiff resistance. While Franklin and his supporters did their best to explain that churches were struck more often than other buildings simply because they tended to be the tallest objects in the landscape, and had attractive metal objects suspended in their bell-towers, the new invention went against centuries of established belief and custom, and continued to be opposed by Church authorities, who acted 'as though [they] thought it Presumption in Man, to propose guarding himself against the Thunders of Heaven!', as Franklin noted in 1753; 'Surely the Thunder of Heaven is no more supernatural than the Rain, Hail or Sunshine of Heaven, against the Inconveniencies of which we guard by Roofs and Shades without Scruple.'[67] But opposition didn't come only from the clerics, whose churches continued to be struck by lightning during severe electrical storms. Other objections included one made at the end of 1755, which claimed that a widespread use of lightning rods would lead to a dangerous build-up of electrical energy in the interior regions of the earth, causing an increase in major earthquakes such as the one that had just destroyed Lisbon.

Franklin did his best to refute such claims, but European prejudice against lightning rods continued for many years. Only in 1769, during Franklin's third sojourn in London, was the dome of St Paul's Cathedral fitted with an iron conductor, but three years later, in 1772, controversy broke out once again when Franklin was asked by the Board of Ordnance for his opinion on the best means of protecting the gunpowder stores at Purfleet, the chief naval depot on the Thames. Franklin naturally recommended the installation of a lightning rod: 'Its upper extremity should be carried ten feet above the summit of the roof, and taper off gradually till it ends in a sharp point', he advised, but a rival British electrical researcher named Benjamin Wilson, who was a prominent member of a Royal Society commission set up to investigate Franklin's advice, claimed that blunt rods rather than pointed ones should be used, since Franklin's own experiments had shown that points worked by actively attracting ambient electricity from the air.[68] Wilson insisted that the Purfleet rods be capped with rounded copper heads, but the Board of Ordnance preferred to stick with the tried and tested points. Following the outbreak of the American Revolution, however, Franklin (who was, after all, one of its leaders) was accused by Wilson of sabotaging Britain's naval supplies, an idea that so worried George III that pointed rods were removed from all London buildings by royal proclamation and replaced with patriotic blunt ones. Sir John Pringle, the President of the Royal Society and a long-term friend of Franklin, protested about the king's decision, saying that 'the laws of nature are not changeable at royal pleasure', as a consequence of which he was made to resign his presidency and was dismissed from the post of royal physician – victim of an overheated political dispute between the pointed rods of the American rebels and the blunt rods favoured by the loyalists.[69] An epigram that circulated in the wake of the king's decision summed up the episode well:

> While you, great George, for knowledge hunt
> And sharp conductors change for blunt
> The Empire's out of joint.

Franklin another course pursues
And all your thunder heedless views
By keeping to the point.[*70]

It was not the only time that Franklin's invention was caught up in wider affairs. At the end of May 1783, Maximilien Robespierre, then a twenty-five-year-old lawyer in the cathedral town of Arras, mailed Franklin a copy of a speech he had made against an ordinance prohibiting the use of lightning rods in the district of St-Omer. The case, which had been one of Robespierre's first, had attracted the attention of the national press, concerning as it did the controversial invention of France's most popular guest. The trouble had started a few months earlier, when a certain Monsieur de Vissery, a retired barrister from St-Ouen, decided to install a lightning rod on the roof of his family home. His neighbours, however, objected to the presence of what they regarded as a 'sacrilegious engine', and they engaged a bailiff who ordered de Vissery to remove it. De Vissery refused, pointing out that he hadn't broken any existing law, but when his neighbours threatened to remove the lightning rod themselves, he hired the ambitious young advocate Robespierre to contest the bailiff's order.

The case went to court in May, by which time Robespierre had engaged a number of leading French *philosophes*, including the Marquis de Condorcet and the Abbé Bertholon, both prominent members of the Académie des Sciences, to appear as expert witnesses. Their account of the scientific thinking behind the invention apparently impressed the jury, as did Robespierre's masterly presentation of the case, which began with the line: 'The arts and the sciences are the most noble gifts from heaven to humanity', and which ended with the demand that rational thinking be allowed to

---

[*] The controversy between blunt and pointed rods continues to divide meteorological opinion, although recent trials on a range of models at a lightning-prone test site in the mountains of New Mexico found that conductors with a 19mm diameter outperformed both the pointed and the mushroom-capped designs.

prevail over ignorance and superstition. Robespierre's speech was a great success, and the court found in favour of Monsieur de Vissery, whose lightning rod now pointed to the heavens under the full protection of the law.

Robespierre was a great admirer of Franklin, and sent him a copy of his court deposition with a note reading: 'I hope, Sir, that you will consent to receive this work with kindness, the object of which was to get my fellow citizens to accept one of your inventions.'[71] Franklin was touched by the young lawyer's praise, and gratified by the outcome of the case, but he could have had no way of knowing that Robespierre's efforts on behalf of civic reason had also caught the attention of several future members of the National Assembly, who appointed him as their Public Accuser in 1791. Two years later, as an elected leader of the Committee of Public Safety, he became the chief architect of the Revolutionary Terror, and was thus directly responsible for the deaths of more than thirty thousand people. 'Terror is nothing other than justice, prompt, severe, inflexible', he wrote, having turned his technological attentions from lightning rods to mass executions, helping pave the way for the introduction of Dr Guillotin's invention. But his appetite for rational vengeance was abruptly curtailed when he, too, fell victim to the general purge, and was guillotined, face up, on 28 July 1794, the last of the Revolution's leaders to die.

By the end of the summer of 1783, the possibilities of getting ever closer to the atmosphere had been enhanced by the development of another new technology: aerial ballooning. A pair of French brothers, Joseph-Michel and Jacques-Etienne Montgolfier, had spent the summer working on a prototype hot-air balloon, which made the first recorded ascent in history – from a field outside the village of Annonay – on the afternoon of Wednesday 4 June. Two months later, on 27 August (only a week before the peace treaty between Britain and France was finally signed) Franklin was among the crowd of more than fifty thousand spectators who had gathered to watch as Jacques-Alexandre-César Charles, one of the

Montgolfier brothers' principal rivals, sent an unmanned hydrogen balloon soaring into the hazy sky above the Champ-de-Mars in Paris. As the varnished silk balloon disappeared into the clouds a bystander is alleged to have said to Franklin: 'What is the use of this new-fangled thing?', to which the philosopher gave his celebrated reply: 'What is the use of a new-born baby?' (a remark that Michael Faraday was later to revive in response to a similar question concerning his invention of the electric generator).[72] Three months later, on 21 November, Franklin joined an even larger crowd, this time in Passy, to watch the world's first manned ascent in a hot-air balloon. Rising by means of a brazier full of burning straw, the gilded montgolfier reached a height of some 150 metres (500 feet) before sailing across the river Seine and bringing its two passengers safely down to earth in a garden in the middle of Paris (see picture 12). That evening, Joseph Montgolfier paid a visit to Franklin at the Hôtel Valentinois, where he heard him declare that this particular new-born baby had already grown into a giant.

With the rapid developments in ballooning technology, and the treaty between Britain and France now finally in place, it wasn't long before the first flight was made across the English Channel, piloted by Jean-Pierre Blanchard, the world's first celebrity aviator. His passenger on that historic flight from London to Paris was a young American army surgeon, Dr John Jeffries, who, in addition to conducting atmospheric experiments on behalf of Henry Cavendish, carried a letter in his pocket addressed to 'Benjamin Franklin, Passy', the soon-to-be recipient of the world's first air-mail delivery.

Franklin's ambassadorial duties were lightened by the signing of the peace treaty in September 1783, and in between his appearances at balloon flights and salons, he continued to ponder the problem of the year's unaccountable weather. None of Lalande's explanations had convinced him in the slightest, even though he and the astronomer had recently become friends, but it was not until the following February, when Franklin learned of an eight-month eruption of an Icelandic volcano that had only just come to an end, that he began to formulate a remarkable new hypothesis.

The winter of 1783–84 had been particularly severe all over Europe ('more severe, than any that had happed for many years', as Franklin had described it), with deep snow lying on the ground from mid-December until the end of February. Franklin wondered whether the global haze might have contributed to the cold snap's unusual duration, by acting as a screen against the warming effects of sunlight on the surface of the earth; and if that had been the case, might other fluctuations in global climate also be linked to atmospheric phenomena? This was a bold idea, and though Franklin had been thinking about the likelihood of long-term climatic change since the late 1760s, when he had written that 'the earth had anciently been in another position, and the climates differently placed from what they are at present', this was the first time that he – or anyone else – had identified an active agent in the process.[73]

By May he had given shape to these ideas in an extraordinary essay entitled 'Meteorological Imaginations and Conjectures', a copy of which he sent to Thomas Percival, his regular contact at the newly founded Manchester Literary and Philosophical Society, one of many such institutions that had appeared in Britain from the 1760s onwards. After being read and discussed at the Society's meeting on 22 December 1784, the paper was published the following year in their second volume of proceedings:

> During several of the summer months of the year 1783, when the effect of the sun's rays to heat the earth in these northern regions should have been greatest, there existed a constant fog over all Europe, and great part of North America. This fog was of a permanent nature; it was dry, and the rays of the sun seemed to have little effect towards dissipating it, as they easily do a moist fog, arising from water. They were indeed rendered so faint in passing through it, that when collected in the focus of a burning glass, they would scarce kindle brown paper. Of course, their summer effect in heating the earth was exceedingly diminished.

Hence the surface was early frozen.

Hence the first snows remained on it unmelted, and received continual additions.

Hence the air was more chilled and the winds more severely cold.

Hence perhaps the Winter of 1783–4, was more severe, than any that had happened for many years.

The cause of this universal fog is not yet ascertained. Whether it was adventitious to this earth, and merely a smoke, proceeding from the consumption by fire of some of those great burning balls or globes which we happen to meet with in our rapid course around the sun, and which are sometimes seen to kindle and be destroyed in passing our atmosphere, and whose smoke might be attracted and retained by our earth: or whether it was the vast quantity of smoke, long continuing to issue during the summer from *Hecla* in Iceland, and that other volcano which arose out of the sea near that island, which smoke might be spread by various winds, over the northern part of the world, is yet uncertain.

It seems however worth the enquiry, whether other hard winters, recorded in history, were preceded by similar permanent and widely extended summer fogs. Because, if found to be so, men might from such fogs conjecture the probability of a succeeding hard winter, and of the damage to be expected by the breaking up of frozen rivers in the spring; and take such measures as are possible and practicable, to secure themselves and effects from the mischiefs that attended the last.

PASSY, *May* 1784.[74]

Franklin, like Lalande before him, stressed the importance of consulting earlier records in the search for scientific clues, a method now in such common use it seems hard to imagine that it had to be invented. As far as the cause of the fog was concerned, it was Franklin's second suggestion that turned out to be correct, although it was Laki rather than Hekla that had erupted – in the biggest single lava flow in recorded history – and gone on to smother much of the northern hemisphere in a drifting plume of volcanic gas and smoke.

Mount Laki, in common with Iceland's many other volcanoes, is the product of a process known as sea-floor spreading: as the Eurasian plate and the North American plate slowly pull away from one another along the Mid-Atlantic Ridge, molten material rises up from the mantle to fill the ever-opening gap. At certain points along the 18,000-kilometre (11,000-mile) ridge, however, small volcanic islands have formed above active plumes of molten rock that are known to geologists as hotspots. Hundreds of such hotspots dot the length of the Mid-Atlantic Ridge, above which lies a series of islands, including Iceland, the Azores and Tristan da Cunha, the by-products of the endless slow separation of the plates (see map on pp. 14–15). Iceland, the largest of these plate-boundary islands, is still growing from the centre outwards at a rate of around a centimetre per year, the dividing ridge being clearly visible on the ground – in fact there are places in the centre of the island where you can stand with one foot in North America and one foot in Europe (geologically speaking) while the slabs on which the two continents sit pull slowly apart beneath you.

Mount Laki, which overlooks the Vatnajökull glacier in the south-east of Iceland, has been extinct for hundreds of years, but it has given its name to a twenty-seven-kilometre (seventeen-mile) chain of craters known as *Lakagígar* ('the Laki fissures') that extends north-east and south-west from the dead volcano's base. On 8 June 1783, in response to certain changes in underground pressure, caused presumably by movement along a section of the plate boundary, the fissure began a lengthy effusive eruption, which, over the course of the next eight months ejected a total of nearly fifteen cubic kilometres (three and a half cubic miles) of basalt, which spread to cover an area of nearly 600 square kilometres (230 square miles) to the south of the Laki fissures (picture 13). The eruption itself, by all accounts, was an awesome sight, flaring brightly through the clouds of ash that had descended over the entire country, with catastrophic effects. According to one observer, a

local clergyman named Saemund Magnussen Holm, columns of
fire could be seen from seventy or eighty kilometres away, while
'its thundering noise could be heard at the same distance, and
continued throughout the whole summer'. Holm's vivid close-up
account of the lava's whirlwind progress, which was published in
Copenhagen in 1784, remains an impressive piece of geophysical
reportage:

> It rushed with incredible violence and force, like the most ter-
> rible cataract, into the plain on the south, over which it rolled,
> amidst strong concussions of the earth and awful thunder and
> explosions in the atmosphere, carrying before it stones, rocks
> and small eminences. This flaming lake boiled and foamed in
> a dreadful manner with melted stones, iron and other sub-
> stances capable of being liquefied; some of the ignited rocks
> and stones, as big as whales and houses, were seen swimming
> on its surface, or driving up and down.[75]

Villages and settlements all over south-east Iceland were destroyed
or evacuated during the worst of the flows, with the exception of
the little town of Kirkjubæjarklaustur, where the interventions
of the local pastor, Jón Steingrímsson, were widely credited with
saving it from ruin. On 20 July, as a lava flow bore down on
Kirkjubæjarklaustur's outlying parts, Steingrímsson directed the
terrified townspeople into his church where he proceeded to
deliver a rousing sermon on the theme of deliverance from evil.
By the time his address had ended, the lava had stopped just short
of the church, at a promontory still known as *Eldmessutangi* ('Fire
sermon point'), but in spite of such powerful spiritual opposition, the *Lakagígar* eruption went on to cause six more months of
suffering for the Icelandic population, as fire fountains, explosive
noises and dense choking ashfalls continued intermittently until
February 1784. By then more than nine thousand people – nearly
a quarter of Iceland's population – had died, mainly from the
effects of crop-failure and fluorine poisoning caused by the eight-
month-long catastrophe that would be known to its survivors as

the *móðuharðindin*: 'the famine of the mist'. (Similarly, in north-east Scotland 1783 was named 'the year of the ashie').[76] The situation grew so severe in Iceland that the ruling Danish authorities considered evacuating the entire population and abandoning the island to the fire that had formed it, but once the worst of the eruption was over, life on the island began slowly to return to normal.

By then, of course, the rest of Europe had also suffered from the effects of the eruption, which had released an estimated 122 million tonnes of microscopic dust, sulphur dioxide and other volcanic gases into the atmosphere, which meandered across the northern hemisphere, carried by the persistent low-pressure systems that were also responsible for the severe summer storms. It was this vast aerosol of dust and sulphates that formed the semi-opaque and malodorous haze over much of Europe, and which, as Franklin correctly deduced, had been responsible first for the stifling summer fog, and then for the coldness of the subsequent winter (among the many casualties of which would be Gilbert White's thermometer). The cold was the result of the discoloured haze reflecting sunlight back from the earth, while slowly allowing trapped heat to escape back out to space, creating, in other words, the greenhouse effect in reverse.* Such global cooling has happened after numerous major eruptions, most recently in the early 1990s, following the eruption of Mount Pinatubo, in the Philippines, during June 1991. That eruption released eight cubic kilometres (nearly two cubic miles) of ash and twenty million tonnes of sulphur dioxide into the atmosphere, which spread around the earth as a vast acidic aerosol; the planet was shaded and cooled in exactly the same way as it was by the Laki fissures aerosol, the effect being enough to mask the overall global warming trend over the following two to three years.

There might seem, at first, to be a paradox in all this, since on

---

* This effect results from the fact that the aerosol particulates have a similar size to the short wavelengths of incoming sunlight, so they tend to reflect a proportion of it back to space, while the longer wavelengths of heat radiation are free to travel away from the earth, passing easily through the layers of aerosol haze.

the one hand, certain pollutants such as volcanic aerosols and ash, as well as visible smoke and particulates produced by the burning of fossil fuels, screen sunlight *from* the earth, thus exerting an overall dimming and cooling effect, while other kinds of invisible pollutants, notably greenhouse gases such as carbon dioxide and methane, serve to absorb reflected sunlight in the form of long-wave back radiation, thus exerting an overall warming effect. Taken together, one might ask, do the two competing effects not cancel each other out over long periods of time? The answer, unfortunately, appears to be no, and the warming effect is currently proving to be the dominant influence over our long-term climate, in spite of the enormous volume of visible pollutants that we, along with our volcanic neighbours, continue to pump into the air.

The idea that atmospheric pollution could have long-term effects upon climatic variation was to usher in new ways of thinking about the workings of the earth, and in the two and a quarter centuries since the publication of Franklin's essay, the study of climate change has developed into one of the most significant and collaborative branches of world scientific enquiry. The issue of global warming, as distinct from global cooling, might seem to be a historically recent preoccupation, but by the mid-nineteenth century atmospheric research had already established the role played by greenhouse gases in maintaining the global atmospheric equilibrium, and by 1896 the Swedish chemist Svante Arrhenius had hypothesized that human beings were altering the climatic balance through the widespread burning of fossil fuels. Arrhenius's calculations revealed that the hypothetical removal of all atmospheric carbon dioxide would cause the earth's temperature to drop by at least 20–30 degrees Celsius, and, conversely, that the doubling of atmospheric carbon dioxide (from its 1890s concentrations of *c.* 300 parts per million) would cause average global temperatures to rise by around 5 degrees C, with the greatest increase being seen at the pole, where 'the temperature of the Arctic regions would rise about 8 degrees or 9 degrees Celsius.'[77] Arrhenius thought that the human-enhanced doubling of atmospheric CO_2 would take around

three thousand years, but according to the fourth assessment
report, published by the Intergovernmental Panel on Climate
Change (IPCC) in 2007, pre-industrial levels of atmospheric carbon
dioxide are likely to have doubled by the middle of this century,
from a fairly constant and beneficial 275 parts per million – beneficial because its presence, along with that of the other greenhouse
gases such as methane and nitrous oxide, keeps the planet warm
and habitable by acting as a layer of global insulation, trapping
heat from the sun like the windows of a greenhouse.[78] So even
when the haze produced by major volcanic eruptions served to
cool the world by a couple of degrees, it was the presence of
these greenhouse gases that saved the planet from spiralling into a
permanent freeze.

Since the mid-eighteenth century, however, the atmospheric
ratio of carbon dioxide has risen steadily, to its current (2009) level
of some 390 parts per million, and is continuing to rise every year,
amplifying the naturally occurring greenhouse effect. Its influence
on temperature has been marked: since 1750, averaged global temperature has risen by around $0.8°C$, with most of that rise having
taken place since the 1950s. 'Warming of the climate system is
unequivocal', as the IPCC's fourth assessment report stated, con-
cluding that 'most of the observed increase in globally averaged
temperatures since the mid-20th century is *very likely* due to the
observed increase in anthropogenic greenhouse gas concentrations.'[79] Franklin's original insight – that climate was not merely
subject to change, but subject to rapid and large-scale change due
to relatively sudden alterations of atmospheric composition – is
thus being borne out, with projections by the IPCC suggesting that
a rise in average global temperatures of only 2 degrees C above
pre-industrial levels will be the point of no return for much of our
environment, with a carbon dioxide ratio of 550 parts per million
widely cited as the so-called 'tipping point' from which such a temperature rise would result. Since the current rate of increase in
atmospheric carbon dioxide stands at two parts per million per year,
it is clear that there is little time left in which to organize the serious

and lasting reductions of our global emissions needed if we are to avoid some of the predicted irreversible consequences of runaway global warming: these include the melting of the West Antarctic and Greenland ice sheets, the rising of global sea levels, worsening fresh-water shortages throughout the overheating southern hemisphere and, in the most dramatic (though least likely) outcome of all, the switching-off of the thermohaline ocean circulation, and with it the Gulf Stream, transforming much of the northern hemisphere into a permanent frozen desert.[80] This is what the environmental scientist James Lovelock has termed 'the revenge of Gaia', a doomsday scenario in which the Earth's own control mechanisms – the vast, cooperative assemblage of the chemical, physical and biological components that have so far helped to maintain life on earth – instead conspire to render the planet uninhabitable by man, as a drastic means of restoring its threatened equilibrium.[81] While Lovelock's is the most extreme of the array of competing climate-change projections, the mainstream scientific view, as represented by the findings of the IPCC, remains deeply concerned by the future implications of humanity's pursuit of business as usual, especially since remarkably little in the way of mitigating action has so far been initiated. Almost everyone agrees that drastic steps need to be taken, but all of us in the first world, from governments to consumers, have so far remained collectively inert, as though offering up an environmental version of the famously self-serving prayer: 'O Lord, make me chaste: but not yet.'

Franklin often used to say that he wished he hadn't been born so soon, as he would have loved to see how science and technology might evolve in the centuries after his death. 'It is impossible to imagine the Height to which may be carried, in a thousand years, the Power of Man over Matter', as he wrote in a letter to his friend Joseph Priestley; 'we may perhaps learn to deprive large Masses of their Gravity, and give them absolute Levity, for the sake of very easy transport. Agriculture may diminish its labour and double its produce; all Diseases may, by sure means, be prevented or cured, not even excepting that of Old Age, and our Lives lengthened at pleasure even beyond the antediluvian Standard.'[82] But although he was a confirmed optimist, Franklin was no technological utopian – 'Science without conscience is the ruin of the soul', as François Rabelais had written in 1533 – and Franklin, too, was equally aware that without a firm foundation of political and ethical good will, advances in science and technology would mean little: 'O that moral Science were in as fair a way of Improvement', as his letter to Priestley continued, 'that Men would cease to be Wolves to one another, and that human Beings would at length learn what they now improperly call Humanity!'

Franklin pressed on with his retirement campaign, and eventually Congress agreed to his request. In July 1785 he set sail for Philadelphia, along with a hundred and twenty-eight crates of luggage, on his eighth and final voyage across the Atlantic Ocean. Although by then he was seventy-nine years old, and far from well, he had lost none of his curiosity about the workings of the world, and he spent most of the six-week journey engaged in a variety of maritime observations, tracking the course of the Gulf Stream, just as he had done during his seven earlier crossings. It was a subject of long-standing fascination with him, this river of warm water snaking through the surrounding ocean, and he speculated, correctly, that it might have something to do with the natural regulation of the global temperature, serving as it does to transport tropical heat from the Gulf of Mexico up towards the temperate shores of north-west Europe. He also busied himself with a range of associated speculations on new methods of navigation, on diets for the crew members, on lifeboat drills, the design of kayaks, the cure for smoky chimneys . . . He had claimed, in a letter to his sister Jane, that he was finally coming home for a well-earned sleep, but in truth he was as wide awake as ever, and within a few weeks of his return to Philadelphia, where he was greeted at the dockside by an enthusiastic crowd, he was easily persuaded to serve on the Supreme Executive Council of Pennsylvania, which nominated him as its president the very next day. By now the pain of his bladder stones was so severe that he was unable to walk even the short distance between his home and the State House, so he was carried there and back on a specially built sedan chair by four stalwarts recruited from the nearby prison, while he fantasized about ordering an air balloon from France, which he would modify so it was 'sufficiently large to raise me from the ground. In my malady it would have been the most easy carriage for me, being led by a string held by a man walking on the ground . . .'[83]

Benjamin Franklin was back at work.

PART THREE

FIRE

THE ERUPTION OF KRAKATAU

1883

I

On an autumn afternoon in Boston in 1946 a seventy-four-year-old American sailor named Sidney Tucker Baker submitted, reluctantly, to a tape-recorded interview with his daughters Mary and Elizabeth. It was the first time in over sixty years that he had agreed to speak at any length about the defining event of his life, but once he got going he ended up talking until the batteries in the tape machine ran out. But then, like many sailors of his age and experience, he had an extraordinary tale to tell.

'I'll tell you about Krakatau', he began. 'It was when I was a small boy, as you well know, on my father's ship with my mother, comprising his family which sailed around the world with him.'[1] Sidney's father, Captain Benjamin C. Baker, was the commander of the *W. H. Besse*, a three-masted American barque that, towards the end of June 1883, had been on her way home to Boston, Massachusetts, with a cargo of sugar picked up in Manila, the capital port of the Philippines. On board the *Besse*, as usual, in addition to her crew, was Captain Baker's wife and their resourceful eleven-year-old son Sidney, who had sat, or rather stood, for this atmospheric photograph in a Hong Kong studio during an earlier stage of the trip (picture 14).

The *Besse* had made good time since leaving Manila, but just as she was approaching the north-west corner of the Indonesian island of Java she suddenly collided with a coral reef to the west of the Duizend Eilanden ('the Thousand Islands') which punctured a hole in her hull – fortunately, the hole remained small enough to allow her to limp into the nearby port of Batavia, the colonial capital of the Dutch East Indies (later renamed Jakarta). When the captain learned that it was going to take between two and three months for the ship to be repaired, Sidney and his mother were dispatched to the hill station of Buitenzorg (now Bogor), a haven of tranquillity and relatively cool air some fifty kilometres (thirty miles) south of the capital. It was customary for wealthy European and American visitors to flee the heat and bustle of Batavia for the placid gardens of Buitenzorg – its Dutch name translated as 'not a care' – and a couple of months in its well-tended parks may well have been something of an idyll for an eleven-year-old boy who had missed the company of children his own age during the years he had spent at sea.

But by Sunday 26 August 1883, he and his family were back on board the fully repaired *Besse*, which had begun the next leg of the six-month journey that would take her through the Indian Ocean and up the Red Sea to the Suez Canal, then across the Atlantic Ocean and home.

Their interrupted journey, however, had only just resumed when it was fated to take an even more eventful turn, as Sidney Baker explained in the interview with his daughters, sixty-three years later:

> We started on our way towards home, down the Straits of Sunda, and it was a clear day as I recall it, and perhaps toward the afternoon we noticed the cloudiness in the atmosphere seemed to be filled with a haze and with dust, or with sort of a mist. A little later, the atmosphere commenced to cloud up, and there was evidence of a disturbance in the atmosphere. We put the pilot ashore; he had his own boat with him and, incidentally, we discovered that he never reached the shore. We started on our way, and the cloudiness increased. The air seemed to be filled with dust, so much so that we feared suffocation. It became black, so black that you couldn't see your hand before your face. I'd never imagined that the atmosphere could be so dense.

For the rest of that Sunday afternoon everyone on board the *Besse* listened intently as a series of loud percussive noises rumbled in the smoky distance. These noises, which were accompanied by a strange agitation in the water, implied that either a volcanic eruption or a major submarine earthquake was occurring somewhere close by. Knowing the likely consequences for a vessel running close to the shore, the remaining crew took in all the sails, let go both anchors and waited in the ash-filled darkness, praying for the danger to pass.

At dawn the next morning the rising sun was still obscured by lingering clouds of low-lying smoke, but the worst of the rumblings appeared to be over. The *Besse* raised her anchors and started slowly on her way south-west through the waters of the Sunda Strait. Suddenly, just after 10 a.m., the sound of a vast and deafening explosion blasted through the air, and a smothering bank of blackness came hurtling across the Strait as Krakatau 'blew its head off and practically the whole island went up in the air', the sky filling with 'tremendous rumblings, and crashings, and flashes off in the distance, which were unlike and greater than anything you could imagine':

> It was a terrible experience. The air was filled with dust and ashes. The reverberations of the explosions were something that are unbelievable. Adjectives fail to describe the racket and turmoil. But after a while the current subsided, or the tidal wave, rather, subsided. The atmosphere cleared, if I remember correctly, way late in the afternoon. We finally got up anchor and started for Anjer, which was at the entrance of the Strait.

But Anjer was not at the entrance of the Strait, at least not any more, for the small Javanese coastal town, complete with lighthouse and signalling station, had been entirely destroyed by a series of giant waves thrown out by the force of the blast. Much of it was now smashed and floating in the sea, with fragments of what had recently been roads, buildings and dozens of moored vessels striking the hull of the *Besse* as she passed slowly through the waters of the Strait. In his interview Sidney recalled how the barque moved through 'all kinds of debris, refuse, villages that had been swept from their locations by the tidal wave, dead bodies galore – really, we had a job dodging them – animals and all kinds of evidences of the upheaval.' There was so much ash and dirt in the sea that the *Besse* had to sail a further 800 kilometres (around 500 miles) out into the Indian Ocean before the water turned blue once again.

When, eventually, they made it back to Boston, the news of the eruption was well known to all, with many who had known of the *Besse*'s planned itinerary assuming that the ship had been lost. The family was treated upon its return, or so Sidney Baker subsequently recalled, like a group of spectral beings who had emerged from the depths of the sea. One Boston newspaper, which interviewed some of the crew members shortly after they landed, even suggested that they had been driven mad by the intensity of their experience:

> A suffocating sulphur smell penetrated the whole atmosphere and hindered breathing. The whole day the noises and sights were far worse than the most vivid imagination could produce: the screaming winds, the foaming and seething water, the dark and impenetrable veil above their heads, the ash, pumice and pieces of earth threatening to sink the ship in the abyss, all worked together to make the entire crew lose their senses.[2]

As has already been noted, newspapers have long relied upon the power of hyperbole to generate an atmosphere of newsworthy wonder, but in the case of the eruption of Krakatau no exaggeration was needed to account for what the survivors had seen. As in the aftermath of the Indian Ocean tsunami of 26 December 2004, thousands of bodies had been strewn along the shorelines of Java and Sumatra, or found floating in the water amid tonnes of debris from the hundred and sixty-five villages that had been destroyed in the blast. Sharks by the hundred came to feast on the dead: 'it was sickening to see them', as one English seaman recalled, and when the true scale of the death-toll eventually became known – nearly forty thousand dead, with many thousands more rendered home-less and destitute – an air of helplessness descended on the region as the survivors contemplated what was left of their lives along the shores of the Sunda Strait.[3]

And the rest of the world soon shared their horror, for even though Krakatau had been a small volcanic island in the middle of a patch of faraway ocean, the world had come to know of the erup-tion almost as soon as it had happened, for by 1883 the means of transmitting rapid information around the globe was already well established, in the form of thousands of kilometres of submarine telegraph cable. The first length of cable had been laid across the English Channel in August 1850, and had soon given rise to a com-plex network of undersea and overhead lines that connected every continent on earth. Suddenly the world seemed a great deal smaller now that nation could speak unto nation.

The urgent brevity of the telegraphers' Morse-coded messages, meanwhile, had given rise to a new kind of truncated poetry that was peculiarly well suited to conveying the horror of an event such as a major volcanic eruption. The series of bulletins that were dis-patched from the Batavia telegraph office on the day of the disaster were the first words the world received concerning the event, and in some respects they remain the closest that we can get today to understanding the immediate impact it must have had – not just on the people who were closest to the scene, and whose lives were disrupted by the carnage that ensued, but on the news-hungry inhabitants of the world beyond:

> Batavia, August 27: During night terrific detonations from Krakatau (volcanic island, Straits Sunda) audible as far as Soerakarta,—ashes falling as far as Cheribon—flashes plainly visible from here.
>
> Noon.— Serang in total darkness all morning—stones falling. Village near Anjer washed away. Batavia now almost quite dark—gas lights extinguished during the night—unable com-municate with Anjer—fear calamity there—several bridges destroyed, river having overflowed through rush sea inland.

Batavia 11 a.m. Today. Anjer, Tjeringin and Telok Betong destroyed.

11:30 a.m. – Lighthouses, Straits Sunda disappeared.

12 noon. – Where once Mount Krakatau stood the sea now plays.[4]

II

Mount Krakatau was a familiar landmark in the Sunda Strait, which in 1883 was one of the busiest stretches of water in the world. A star-shaped patch of ocean spanning some hundred and twenty kilometres (seventy-five miles) across each of its axes, tapering to a width of around thirty kilometres (eighteen miles) at its narrowest point to the north, the Strait divides the two main Indonesian islands, Java and Sumatra, while connecting the waters of the South China Sea with the blue expanse of the Indian Ocean (see map on p. 145). A number of islands dotted the Strait, including the aptly named Dwars-in-den-weg ('Thwart-the-Way'), a jagged lump of rock located, inconveniently for shipping, in the middle of the narrowest section of the Strait.* Immediately to the west lay the jungle-covered volcanic twins Sebuku and Sebesi, the home of a large and noisy troop of orang-utans, while just a few kilometres further to the south, was the group containing the familiar high-peaked volcanic island of Krakatau itself (see picture 15).

Flanked by Lang ('Long') and Verlaten ('Desert') islands, as well as by a small rocky islet known as Poolsche Hoed ('Polish Hat'), Krakatau was a compact, distinctively shaped island, some eight kilometres (five miles) long and five kilometres (three miles) across at its widest point. Known to local seafarers for thousands of years, the island had also served as a useful navigational aid to foreign

---

* The island is known to Indonesians today as Pulo Soengan, and it remains just as inconvenient to shipping as it was in the nineteenth century.

sailors since the late 1500s, although its name had been spelled by cartographers and ships' captains in at least sixteen different ways, including Carcata, Cacatoua, Krakatan, Cracatou, Kraka-towa, Cracketovv and Krakatão. By the early 1880s, however, the ocean-going world had settled on 'Krakatau' as the generally accepted spelling, although the British and the Americans continued to prefer the slightly more euphonious variant 'Krakatoa', a choice of spelling that, due to the international circulation of English-language reports on the eruption, did much to determine the destiny of the name: 'Krakatoa', as Simon Winchester mused in his valuable in-depth study of the 1883 eruption, 'a name now firmly annealed into the language, welded into the world's public consciousness, a name that has become a byword for nature's most fearsome potential for destruction.'[5] Like the little town of Pompeii, which was also destroyed by volcanic action, in AD 79, the little island of Krakatau was fated to be erased, so that its name might for ever be remembered.

As the principal shipping lane connecting the islands of South-East Asia with the rest of the world, the Sunda Strait was filled, day and night, with vessels from the world's great trading nations, especially since November 1869 and the opening of the Suez Canal, a man-made shortcut through the sands of Egypt that served to halve the journey time to Europe. Every year thousands of craft would pass within a few kilometres of Krakatau, an uninhabited and densely forested lump of rock made up of three connected volcanic vents. The main peak was named Rakata, and stood at 822 metres (2,700 feet); Danan, the middle peak, stood at 445 metres (1,460 feet); while Perboewatan, the lowest peak, was only 122 metres (400 feet) high. Several generations of European surveyors had worked on the assumption that the triple volcanoes of Krakatau had all been long extinct, but as Sidney Tucker Baker, for one, would find out at first hand on the morning of 27 August 1883, that assumption was entirely unfounded.

The thirteen thousand islands of the Indonesian archipelago are the products of an extremely active region of the earth's crust.

As described in chapter one, the crust is made up of a series of migrating sections known as tectonic plates, the varying movements and alignments of which give rise to the majority of earthquakes and volcanoes. In the case of the sixty-five volcanoes of Java and Sumatra, including the peaks of Krakatau that once lay in between, they are the visible results of a 4,800-kilometre (3,000-mile) subduction zone, the seam created by the edge of the northward-travelling Indo-Australian plate as it slips below the lighter crusts of the adjoining Eurasian and Burmese plates at around six centimetres (two and a half inches) per year. Millions of tonnes of oceanic plate material, as well as a large volume of associated seawater, plunge slowly ('subduct') into the hot mantle below, melting and bubbling, the weaknesses at the resulting Java Trench giving rise, over millions of years, to an extensive arc of volcanic islands formed from some of the melted material that has forced its way back to the surface (see picture 3).

For tens of thousands of years this long chain of islands (known to geologists as the Sunda Arc) has played host to some of the most explosive eruptions that the earth has ever known: Mount Toba on Sumatra, for example, at the far northern end of the Sunda chain, erupted more than seventy-four thousand years ago, leaving a fifty-by-ninety-five-kilometre (thirty-by-sixty-mile) depression known as a caldera (the word is from the Spanish for 'cauldron'), the sheer cliffs of which can still be seen rising several hundred metres above the lake that fills the crater. Or Mount Tambora, some 3,200 kilometres (2,000) miles to the east, which erupted in April 1815, burying more than ninety per cent of the Sumbawanese islanders under dense layers of ash and pumice. Nearly one hundred cubic kilometres (twenty-four cubic miles) of ejecta was blasted thirty kilometres (eighteen miles) into the earth's upper atmosphere, leading to one of the northern hemisphere's coldest years on record – 1816, dubbed 'the year without a summer', in which a number of the weather features of 1783–84 staged a disconcerting return.[6] The recent Indian Ocean tsunami was also a product of movements along the Java Trench, having been triggered by the sudden release of a long-stuck section of subducting plate, causing a 1,200-kilometre (750-mile) section of sea floor off the north-west coast of Sumatra to 'jump' by several metres, sending powerful waves of displaced seawater racing across the Indian Ocean.

All these Sunda Arc events, including the eruption of Krakatau, were caused by the same relentless physical processes that still play out, year after year, within the volatile regions below the earth's crust, although the complex chemistry involved in the eruptions is just as important as the physics. Just below the waters of the Sunda Strait, the edge of the northward-trending Indo-Australian plate, which, like other largely oceanic plates, is composed of heavy, dense and relatively unacidic basaltic rock, slips below the southern boundary of the continental Eurasian plate, dragging some of the latter's warmer, lighter and more acidic rocks and soils along with it into the depths. Some atmospheric air and a good deal of water-logged sea-bed gets dragged down, too, and it is the resulting mix of solid, liquid and gaseous material – plus the varying temperatures and pressures that this subducted material encounters during its journey into the mantle – that determines what kind of volcanoes will rise nearby, and what kind of eruptions they will generate. In the case of Krakatau – 'a gigantic and classical subduction-zone volcano', in the words of Simon Winchester – it seems that rising pressure within the ancient magma chamber that lies directly beneath the island had, for a period of some two hundred years since its previous eruption, been seeking an exit through the three volcanic vents of Rakata, Danan and Perboewatan.[7] It was as if a viscous plug of congealed rock and magma had become stuck in Krakatau's throat, and was about to be suddenly cleared. But then, at a particular moment during the eruption of 1883, and for reasons that remain obscure, the roof of the magma chamber collapsed, and then, either because cold seawater poured into the cauldron, or a sudden intrusion of superheated basalt ascended from a deeper source, the fate of the island was sealed by the ensuing explosive chemical reaction, which served to blow most of its constituent material fifty kilometres into the sky.

Although this final explosion was entirely unexpected, Krakatau had in fact erupted several times before, most recently in May 1680, when the captain of the Dutch yacht *de Zijp*, which was then only fifteen kilometres (nine miles) from the island, reported feeling an earthquake rock his vessel, 'followed by a tremendous thundering crash', which made him wonder if there had been some kind of landslide nearby. It was only when he drew closer to the island that he saw that 'Cracketovv had split', as he was later to describe it, while he and his crew 'smelled a strong and very fresh sulphur odour.'[8] No one on board seemed worried, however, since it was apparently only a minor eruption, and the crew of the *Zijp* were happy to collect bucketfuls of floating pumice 'as a rarity', samples of which the captain kept on his yacht for many years, showing them to his passengers during subsequent journeys through the Strait.

There are no reliable eyewitness descriptions of any of the unknown number of eruptions that occurred before 1680, although there is plenty of geological evidence to support early Javanese and Chinese accounts of what appears to have been a massive explosion in the Sunda Strait some time in the sixth century AD. The Javanese *Book of Kings*, a long and rhapsodic history of the islands that was compiled by a mid-nineteenth-century court poet named Ranggawarsita, describes an ancient eruption of 'the mountain Kapi', during which 'the whole world was greatly shaken, and violent thundering, accompanied by heavy rain and storms, took place':

> The water of the sea rose and inundated the land, the country to the east of the mountain Batuwara, to the mountain Raja Basa, was inundated by the sea; the inhabitants of the northern part of the Sunda country to the mountain Raja Basa were drowned and swept away with all their property. After the water subsided the mountain Kapi and the surrounding land became sea and the Island of Java divided into two parts.[9]

Ranggawarsita, writing in the 1850s, was unable to put a reliable date on what was evidently a massive tsunamigenic eruption – a familiar occurrence along the Indonesian coast – but it's possible, given the story's setting as well as the evidence on the ground, that his account of 'the mountain Kapi' refers to Krakatau in eruption some fifteen hundred years ago. Certainly tree-ring evidence from around the world, as well as ice-core samples extracted from both poles, suggest (whether or not Krakatau was the culprit) that a past eruption in the Sunda Strait was powerful enough to have blasted dust and aerosols high into the atmosphere, and that these were then distributed over much of the surface of the earth. It is likely, too, that Lang and Verlaten islands were the remains of this vanished precursor to Krakatau, the new, three-peaked island having slowly risen from the sunken caldera during the centuries following the blast.

Understandably, the life-threatening nature of these Sunda Arc volcanoes, as well as the frequency of local earthquakes and tsunamis, has done much to shape the islanders' traditional beliefs and practices. On Java, for example, with its thirty-six volcanoes, twenty-one of which remain active today, much of the folklore remains preoccupied with stories involving eruptions. One Javanese legend tells of a romantic rivalry between two adjacent mountain deities, Merbabu and Merapi, both of whom had fallen in love with the daughter of a local king. When the princess returned Merbabu's affections, the jealous Gunung Merapi ('the fire-giving mountain') staged a massive tantrum-eruption, hurling ash-clouds and *lahars* (the Javanese word for mud-flows) in an effort to block the young girl's path to his rival. This story may well have arisen in response to the devastating eruption of Gunung Merapi that took place in the early eleventh century, prompting the Hindu court of Yogjakarta to relocate to Bali. Merapi, which looms over the landscape of central Java, remains the sixth most active volcano on the planet, and is sacred to the Sultan of Yogjakarta, one of only two sultans left in the Indonesian islands, whose title at court – Susunan – means 'life-giving mountain' or 'volcano'.[10] His priests still guard a symbolic key to the gates of Gunung Merapi, and once a year they climb to the edge of the crater to leave offerings to the mountain's resident spirit, a sulphur-breathing dragon lurking deep inside.* The topography of eastern Java, meanwhile, is dominated by the smoking outline of Gunung Bromo, one of the world's most sacred and story-laden mountains. One legend tells how the local inhabitants, suffering after years of poor harvests, promised lavish offerings to the mountain spirits in return for providing them with a good crop of rice. Their prayers were duly answered, but in the midst of sudden plenty they forgot their obligations, and were punished later the following year by a massive volcanic eruption. Today, the volcano-dwellers take care to fulfil their ancestors' promise, and the annual festival of Kesodo sees hundreds of Tenggen villagers and priests trek at dawn to the edge of the vast caldera to offer prayers and offerings (including live chickens and goats) in return for Bromo's continuing mercy.

Such mercy is needed in densely populated Indonesia, where the majority of its two hundred million inhabitants live within sight of an active volcano. Nearly twelve hundred recorded eruptions – one sixth of the planet's total number – have occurred within the Indonesian archipelago, where the death toll over the centuries has been immense. A third of the people who have ever been killed by volcanic eruptions have been killed in Indonesia – and this estimate does not include the countless victims of tsunamigenic earthquakes such as the one that struck northern Sumatra in December 2004. Despite the impression given by much of the world's media, the only thing unusual about that earthquake was its magnitude: Indonesia experiences, on average, three or four earthquakes *per day* measuring 5.0 or more on the Richter scale, and at least four or five per year measuring 7.0 or above.† Created and defined by the relentless activity of the Java Trench, the Indonesian islands, as their long-suffering inhabitants are only too aware, are some of the least stable landforms on the planet.

---

* In June 2006, after nearly twenty years of rumbling and threats, Merapi erupted once again, forcing fifteen thousand villagers to flee their homes.

† For a discussion of the Richter and other magnitude scales see pp. 220–26.

So when European adventurers began to settle in the area towards the end of the fifteenth century, they soon gained first-hand experience of the islands' active volcanoes. Portuguese spice-traders in search of pepper, cloves and nutmeg were the first Western merchants to make their way to the Java Sea, and it wasn't long before they bore witness to some major volcanic events. In 1512, both Sangeang Api on the Lesser Sunda Islands, and Gunungapi Wetar in the Banda Sea staged significant eruptions, both of which were documented by Portuguese observers, while in 1586, Gunung Kelut, a 1,730-metre (5,680-foot) peak in eastern Java, erupted catastrophically, precipitating powerful *lahars* that destroyed a nearby Portuguese settlement, killing an estimated ten thousand people.[11]

But it was capitalism rather than volcanism that ended the Portuguese empire in the East, and by the time Gunung Ringgit erupted in 1686, claiming a further ten thousand lives in eastern Java, the last of the Lisbon spice ships had gone, forcibly removed by agents of the Dutch East India Company. This powerful monopoly of merchant-adventurers effectively governed the islands from 1602 until they declared themselves bankrupt in 1799 – at which point the Dutch government took colonial possession of what became known as the Dutch East Indies until Indonesia, after a long and bitter armed struggle, declared itself an independent republic in 1949.

There was more than a touch of colonial arrogance on the part of the hordes of Dutch administrators who were dispatched to the islands during the nineteenth century, and they seem to have paid little attention to indigenous accounts of seismic activity, preferring to rely on geological reports prepared by their own surveyors. But perhaps they should have listened more carefully to the local fishermen, rather than dismissing their stories of the fiery ghosts that haunt the islands of the Sunda Strait; the surveyors may have declared the volcanic islands extinct, but many fishermen remained extremely wary of the jungle-covered rocks that dotted the strait between Java and Sumatra, and were often kept awake at night by the rumbling echoes of the sulphur-breathing mountain spirit Orang Alijeh, or by the sighs of the sea-ghost Antoe Laoet, responsible, it was said, for summoning violent waves whenever he was roused to anger.[12] Did any of the Dutch administrators stop to wonder why Krakatau's earlier inhabitants had long abandoned their ghost-ridden island, while its neighbour Sebesi still supported a sizeable population?

And so, towards the end of May 1883, when Krakatau decided to stir once again, taking the European residents of the surrounding coastlines entirely by surprise, perhaps it really was the work of Orang Alijeh, or Antoe Laoet, or some other indigenous spectre of the scene, who had decided to remind the modern world that such spirits were still at large.

On the morning of Sunday 20 May a series of loud booming noises was heard in many of the villages along the north-west coast of Java, while a number of passing vessels reported plumes of smoke seen above one of the islands in the Sunda Strait. The captain of the German warship *Elisabeth*, which was then thirty-one kilometres (eighteen miles) north of Krakatau, recorded the presence of 'a white cumulus cloud rising fast' above the island; half an hour later, it had reached a height that he estimated to be around eleven kilometres (nearly seven miles). It started to spread 'like an umbrella' and after a while a fine ash began to fall, settling on the decks of the ship.[13]

A later report by the *Elisabeth*'s chaplain offered a more detailed account than the captain's, explaining that the ship had left Anjer at nine o'clock that morning, heading south-west towards the Indian Ocean. By the time the eruption of Krakatau began, at around ten thirty, all the crew were up on deck 'in clean Sunday clothes', and ready for morning prayers. They were soon distracted by the sight of what the chaplain described as 'an enormous shining wide vapour column' rising from the nearby island. 'It was convoluted like a giant wide coral stock', he wrote, 'resembling a club or, for that matter, a giant cauliflower head, except that here everything was in imposing gigantic internal motion, driven by the enormous pressure from beneath.' The chaplain, impressed by the island's display, was moved to conclude that, in spite of the ash-stains on their Sunday best, and the unwelcome job of scrubbing down the decks for the second time that morning, the crew of the *Elisabeth*, which was heading home to Germany after two years away, had been given a splendid send-off by the volcano.[14]

At the port of Ketimbang, meanwhile, on the south Sumatran shore, some forty kilometres (twenty-five miles) north-east of Krakatau, Anna Beyerinck, the wife of a Dutch colonial official, was being 'much bothered by the sounds and tremors' that continued all that morning.[15] The surface of the water barrels in her bathroom shimmered as the noises from the Strait rocked the air, while in Batavia, a hundred and fifty kilometres to the east, another Dutch resident, Mrs van der Stok, wife of the director of the Magnetic and Meteorological Observatory, was even more distressed, since a valuable Delft dinner plate had just been shaken from her dining-room dresser and had broken on the flagstone floor. Her husband, who had already noticed a faint trembling of the windowpanes, made a careful note of the time at which the dinner plate was lost: 10:55 a.m. Although Dr van der Stok didn't know it at the time, Krakatau had just claimed its first casualty.

Examining his recording instruments in the observatory next door, van der Stok soon realized that the plate was not the victim of one of the regular local earthquakes, as he had initially supposed, but what appeared to be a volcanic disturbance coming from the direction of Sumatra. It was probably Gunung Merapi or Gunung Kaba, two of the island's more active volcanoes, or possibly even Rajah Bassa, the high volcanic peak overlooking Lampong Bay, although at this stage it was impossible to tell. It wasn't until the early hours of Monday morning that the Lloyd's agent in Anjer, a certain Mr Schuit, dispatched a hasty telegram to his head office in Batavia, which, by the time it had been transcribed at the receiving end, read: 'Krakatan casting forth fire, smoke and ash accompanied by explosions and distant rumblings.'[16] The story of the eruption of

Krakatau had begun, complete with the first of many misspellings of the island's problematic name, presumably committed by the night-shift operator on duty at the Batavia office.

A visit to the island the following day by Anna Beyerinck's husband William, a government official whose responsibilities included the Sumatran side of the Sunda Strait, confirmed that Perboewatan, the northernmost and the lowest of Krakatau's peaks, was in full eruption. In fact some fishermen from Sebesi had paid him a visit the previous day to tell him that they had seen the beach on Krakatau in flames, but typically he had discounted their story until a telegram message arrived from Batavia, asking him to take a closer look. By then the umbrella-cloud had spread for several kilometres, and the decks of dozens of passing ships had been covered with thick layers of glutinous ash, which left them looking 'like a mill ship, or more precisely, like a floating cement factory', according to the chaplain of the home-bound *Elisabeth*.[17] Rafts of floating pumice stones had also appeared, and the master of the *Conrad*, a Dutch mail steamer on its way to Batavia, reported that his passage north through the Sunda Strait had been delayed for several hours by a two-and-a-half-kilometre (one-and-a-half-mile) carpet of pumice that had been ejected from the mouth of the vent.

But the eruption didn't seem to be getting any worse, and, once they had recovered from their initial disquiet, the European residents of Bantam and Batavia were delighted to have a newly active volcano within easy reach of the capital. The majority of Java's liveliest volcanoes, such as the celebrated holy mountains Merapi and Bromo, lay a couple of hundred kilometres to the east, too far overland for most Batavians to venture, but Krakatau could easily be visited in a day. So, early the following Sunday morning, 27 May, the *Gouverneur-Generaal Loudon*, a mail steamer belonging to the Netherlands-Indies Steamship Company, took a party of eighty-six day-trippers from Batavia to see the new sight for themselves. The passengers had paid twenty-five guilders each for the excursion, and were apparently in a state of some excitement. Among them was a mining engineer named J. A. Schuurman, who took copious notes during the trip to the smoke-belching island, recording its appearance, as the *Loudon* drew near, as 'a picture of total destruction rising from the sea.'[18] What only a week before had been a densely forested mountainside was now burnt and bare, and covered with drifts of pale volcanic ash. A vast column of smoke rose from within 'with incredible beauty and thundering power', he wrote, and engineer Schuurman's awed description remains the most vivid account of the beginning phase of what would turn out to be Krakatau's three-month death throes:

> Overpowering was the impression of this proud natural scene, which reminded me in all seriousness of the angry, driven play of the elements, to which the rising, black, changing to a silver-white column of smoke, was attesting. It took a long time to get over the amazement of this immense spectacle and for the attention, tired of its attempt to comprehend everything, to focus on a single point of observation. But then the column of smoke made the most fantastic impression, with its constantly changing, never returning, phases. Although rising continuously, it increased significantly in size from its foot, through extremely powerful exhalations of smoke clouds every 5 to 10 minutes, which announced themselves with a frightful rumbling, and it was during these periodic eruptions that the dark-colored smoke which was belched out rose with much higher speed than normal and caused a hail of stones to fall from a height of approximately 200 metres, which on board looked like black dots flying through the air.

At one point a bolt of lightning shot through the smoke cloud, illuminating both the ash-blackened sky and the transfigured island below. So much dust and ash had fallen over Krakatau that the northern half of the Sunda Strait looked more like a winter landscape than a tropical sea, and Schuurman was keen to take a walk in what looked like European snow. He persuaded Captain Lindemann of the *Gouverneur-Generaal Loudon* to lend him a lifeboat, and he used it to ferry a small landing party to the island's northern beach, immediately below the erupting cone of Perboewatan. The members of the party stepped onto the shore, which was ankle deep in ash and pumice, and then, following a brief discussion about the wisdom of the venture, headed towards the scene of the eruption. Above them the vast plume of smoke billowed noisily upwards, drifting eastwards as it rose, breaking up at around 3,000 metres (9,800 feet) to fall as a kind of backdrop to the scene.

The visitors climbed through drifts of pumice and burnt-off tree-stumps, until, some 200 metres (650 feet) up, they came to the edge of the crater wall, from which, in engineer Schuurman's words, 'the powerful column of smoke escaped with a frightening noise, from a circular area of approximately 50 metres in diameter on the west edge away from us.' There was no sign of active lava in the crater itself, but around the edge were a number of vents of sulphurous steam that hissed furiously amid the roaring of the smoke. The whole thing looked and sounded like a blast furnace operating at full production. It didn't feel like a particularly safe place, and so, after collecting a number of samples of rocks, pumice stones, ash and cinders, the party made their way back to the boat. 'And this ends my story', as engineer Schuurman concluded. 'We started our return trip to Batavia at 8 o'clock in the evening, thankful for the beauty and for a spectacle which made a deep impression on all.' And it was then, as the *Loudon* was leaving the island, just before eight o'clock in the evening of 27 May 1883, that one of the passengers, an otherwise unknown Mr Hamburg, took the now iconic photograph of Krakatau in the early stages of its eruption. An engraved version of the picture appeared in the *Graphic* on 11 August 1883, an eerie foretaste of what would occur in just over a fortnight's time, when the island stepped up its eruptive activity, transforming itself from a local curiosity to a full-blown global phenomenon (see picture 16).[19] It was the last photograph ever taken of the island of Krakatau.

After that, the volcano went quiet for a while, although the black cloud continued to billow out from the island's active crater. Public interest in the eruption gradually abated, and there were no more day trips, until another explosion was heard on 16 June, and a second column of smoke was seen alongside the first. Danan, the middle peak of Krakatau, had just begun its own display, doubling the island's volcanic activity overnight.

The waters of the Sunda Strait were again filled with floating rafts of pumice stones, 'as far as the eye could reach', according to a passenger on board the *Quetta*, a British mail steamer that passed nervously through the Strait on 9 July, and a large area of Krakatau was now on fire.[20] This time the only person to risk a visit to its burning shores was Captain H. J. G. Ferzenaar, Chief of the Surveying Brigade in Bantam, who was sent to assess the feasibility of conducting a detailed survey. He made the trip on 11 August, paddling alone in a native boat, since no one would accompany him to what was, in fact, at that particular moment, the most dangerous spot on earth. He ventured as far as he was able onto the rubble-strewn slopes of the erupting island from which, as he described in his report, 'colossal dirty grayish white- and pink-coloured columns of smoke' rose continuously.[21] There were, he estimated, at least a dozen active vents distributed over the lower parts of the island. He carried out some digging on the beach below Perboewatan, where he identified a top layer consisting of 'gray ash, ash mixed with sulphur underneath, and at last pumice; these stones thus seemed to have been ejected first.' He also prepared a rapid sketch map, the last image ever made of the old Krakatau, which showed the position of the newly opened vents. Sensibly, given the extent of the eruptive activity, he rejected as 'inadvisable' the proposal mooted by the Chief of the Topographic Service, of making further surveying trips to the volcano. Thus, Captain Ferzenaar – as far as we can tell – was the last person ever to set foot on Krakatau.

Shipping, meanwhile, continued to ply the Sunda Strait, and captains' logbooks filled with references to the growing cloud of volcanic smoke that towered over an increasingly wide area, discolouring the sky and filling the air with an irritating sulphurous smell. Thunder and lightning flashed and growled in the upper regions of the column, which had once again climbed to a height of

3,500 metres (just over two miles), and from which fell a fine rain of dust and ash. But the first sign that things were about to get really intense came on the afternoon of 25 August, when a series of unusually loud booms – the unwelcome voice of Orang Alijeh – were heard to reverberate throughout much of the Sunda Strait. That evening, when the captain of the Batavian mail steamer *Princess Wilhelmina* added a brief note to his ship's daily weather report, it seems that he little suspected what the noises actually meant:

> Saturday August 25th. In the afternoon about 7 shakes and heavy blows in the distance were heard (as from thunder) in the W and WSW. Wind variable. Bar: 762. Therm: 29°C.[22]

After this, the volume of the smoke-column increased, and heavy ash-falls were reported from settlements all along the south Sumatran coast, including the little town of Ketimbang, where Mr and Mrs Beyerinck lived, and Telok Betong, a busy port located further up the shore, at the head of Lampong Bay. The rain of ash continued late into the night, but at least there were no more disquieting bangs like those heard earlier in the day.

The following morning, 26 August, turned out to be surprisingly breezy and pleasant, even though the familiar pall of smoke still hung over the islands of the Strait. But in spite of the proximity of the newly active volcano, with the accompanying layers of drifting ash that seemed to get into every corner, life continued as normal in the surrounding towns and villages, as well as on board the numerous vessels which were passing through the Strait. The *Gouverneur-Generaal Loudon*, for example (the steamship that had taken the party of trippers to Krakatau) was working just as hard that morning, having left Batavia for Anjer at 8 a.m. with instructions to pick up a work-party of a hundred and eleven labourers and take them over the Strait to Telok Betong. By midday she had overtaken the *W. H. Besse*, which, fully repaired and with everyone back on board, had left Batavia harbour at 6 a.m. to resume her journey home to Massachusetts. Sidney Tucker Baker, who was up on deck as usual, and glad to be on his way once again, watched the *Loudon* steam past as the two ships approached St Nicholas Point, the north-eastern entrance to the Sunda Strait. A number of other vessels were also heading towards the channel (divided so annoyingly by Thwart-the-Way Island), including two British ships, the *Sir Robert Sale* and the *Norham Castle*, whose crews, in common with those of their neighbouring craft, were soon to bear witness to the coming eruption from pumice-laden decks (see map below).

At the opposite end of the Strait, meanwhile, and heading north-east towards the Java Sea, were two more vessels whose courses would take them past the ill-fated island of Krakatau. In front was the British cargo barque *Charles Bal*, nearing the end of a voyage to Hong Kong, while thirty-two kilometres (twenty miles) behind her was the German paraffin-ship *Berbice*, commanded by a Scotsman, William Logan of Greenock, who was heading to

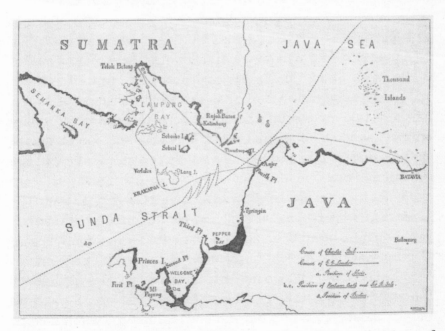

Figure iii. Map of the Sunda Strait, showing the positions and courses of the ships caught up in the eruption.

Batavia with a cargo of petroleum picked up in New York City.
So far, according to the captains' logbooks, that breezy Sunday
morning had passed without incident, but a few minutes after
one o'clock in the afternoon, just as the *Loudon* was beginning
her turn in to the port of Anjer, and the *Charles Bal* was passing
a mere sixteen kilometres (ten miles) south-west of Krakatau, a
sudden loud explosion echoed over the Strait, and another vast
cloud billowed into the sky.

It was immediately obvious to all who saw and heard this new
display that it dwarfed the eruptions that had occurred over the
previous three months. The sound was deafening, and rattled
windows as far away as Batavia and Buitenzorg, some hundred
and sixty kilometres (hundred miles) to the east, while the billow-
ing smoke-column, according to the captain of the *Norham Castle*,
had soon reached a height of twenty-eight kilometres (seventeen
miles), shrouding the sky in darkness. An elderly Dutch pilot, who
was to survive the destruction of Anjer less than twenty-four
hours later, claimed it grew so dark that Sunday afternoon that
he could 'not see my hand before my eyes.'[23] There were further
loud explosions throughout the day, although the strange acoustics
of the Sunda Strait (due to the complex arrangement of its inlets
and bays), meant that the inhabitants of some villages were shaken
by the blasts while others hardly heard a thing. But everybody
within a hundred-kilometre (sixty-mile) radius was soon aware of
the towering column of smoke and ash that completely blotted out
the summer sky.

It was the crew of the *Charles Bal*, under Captain W. J. Watson
of Belfast, who became the closest eyewitnesses to Krakatau's
final eruption, being only sixteen kilometres away when it began.
Captain Watson's account of the experience, which by the end of
1883 had been reprinted in newspapers and magazines throughout
the world, paints an unforgettable picture of the danger from flying
pumice stones, clouds of hot ash and storm-force winds created
by the turbulence of the eruption. His chronometer, however, had
apparently not been reset from Indian Ocean Time to Batavia Time

(the one-hour adjustment made by ships as they entered the Sunda Strait from the south), so his timings are all exactly an hour ahead of everyone else's on the day:

> At 2:30 p.m. we noticed some agitation about the point of Krakatoa, clouds or something being propelled from the north-east point with great velocity. At 3:30 we heard above us and about the island a strange sound as of a mighty crackling fire, or the discharge of heavy artillery at one or two seconds' interval. At 4:15 p.m., Krakatoa bore north-east, ten miles distant. We observed a repetition of the noise noted at 3:30, only much more furious and alarming; the matter, whatever it was, being propelled with amazing velocity to the north-east. To us it looked like blinding rain, and had the appearance of a furious squall, of ashen hue.[24]

The ship was soon being buffeted by Watson's 'furious squall', which turned out to be a storm of ash and pumice stones, 'of which many pieces were of considerable size and quite warm', and the crew had to work fast to cover the skylights in order to protect the glass. The afternoon sky was now completely dark, and the captain's attempts to move his ship forward were halted by the ash-fall, 'which covered the decks to 3 or 4 inches'; soon, Watson was forced to anchor his craft in the middle of the Sunda Strait, almost in the shadow of the erupting volcano.

'The night was a fearful one', he wrote; 'the blinding fall of sand and stones, the intense blackness above and around us, broken only by the incessant glare of varied kinds of lightning and the continued explosive roars of Krakatoa, made our situation a truly awful one':

> At 11 p.m., having stood off from the Java shore, wind strong from the south-west, the island, west-north-west, eleven miles distant, became more visible, chains of fire appeared to ascend and descend between it and the sky, while on the south-west end there seemed to be a continued roll of balls of white fire. The wind, though strong, was hot and choking, sulphurous,

with a smell as of burning cinders, some of the pieces falling
on us being like iron cinders.

In spite of the pummelling suffered by the ship, it was still too dark
and dangerous either to proceed or retreat, 'as we could not see any
distance, and knew not what might be in the Strait'; so there was
nothing for the crew to do but maintain their position, sixteen kilometres from an erupting volcano, and wait for the night to pass.

On board the *Berbice*, meanwhile, thirty-two kilometres behind
the *Charles Bal*, Captain Logan was growing increasingly anxious at
the prospect of carrying a flammable cargo towards what he at first
imagined was a tropical storm, but what was in fact – as he later
realized – a violently erupting volcano lying dead ahead. With several thousand gallons of petroleum sloshing about in the hold, he
quickly had the *Berbice* hoved to in the lee of Princess Island, near
the western entrance of the Sunda Strait, though it offered little
protection from the ash and sparks that rained down from above.
As the afternoon wore on, the eruptions continued, blasting thousands of tonnes of stones and ash high into the reverberating air,
and it is clear from Captain Logan's log that he was well aware of
just how perilous the situation had become:

> the lightning flashes shot past around the ship; fire-balls con-
> tinually fell on the deck, and burst into sparks. We saw flashes
> of lightning falling quite close to us on the ship; heard fearful
> rumblings and explosions, sometimes upon the deck and
> sometimes among the rigging. The man at the wheel felt
> strong electric shocks on one arm. The copper sheathing of
> the rudder became glowing from the electric discharges. Fiery
> phænomena on board the ship manifested themselves at every
> moment. Now and then, when any sailor complained that he
> had been struck, I did my best to set his mind at ease, and
> endeavoured to talk the idea out of his head, until I myself,
> holding fast at the time to some part of the rigging with one
> hand, and bending my head out of reach of the blinding ash
> shower which swept past my face, had to let go my hold,
> owing to a severe electric shock in the arm.[25]

Showers of sparks were falling thick and fast, and Logan, who was still unable to move his arm, ordered that the sails be taken down and nailed over the hatches, the rudder secured, and all hands sent below to shelter as best they could. By two o'clock in the morning the ash-fall lay one metre (three feet) thick on the deck of the ship, but some of these ashes, as the sleepless commander suddenly discovered, were hot enough to burn holes through the sailcloth covering the hatches, and so all hands were summoned back on deck to clear away the drifts, and to watch for any cinders as they fell. And that was how the rest of the night was passed, anchored in the howling Sunda Strait, with everyone on board the *Berbice* knowing that one loose spark falling into the hold would blow the ship clean out of the water.

On land, meanwhile, the sequence of eruptions was also causing panic and alarm. 'The ground shook and trembled as if "the Day of Judgement" had come', wrote Mr Schruit, the newly appointed telegraph master at Anjer, who at 6 p.m. was in the process of sending a message to Batavia ('Krakatau vomiting fire and smoke') when contact with the capital was abruptly lost. He hurried down to the harbour to see whether the undersea cable had broken, but all he saw, as he was later to tell a reporter from the local Dutch newspaper, the *Bataviaasch Handelsblad*, was 'a schooner and twenty-five or thirty praws being carried up and down between the draw-bridge and the ordinary bridge as the water rose and fell, and nothing remained unbroken.'[26] It was a worrying sight, this movement of the water, but since it gave no sign of overflowing the harbour, and the noise of the eruption seemed to be decreasing a little, the telegraph-master put it out of his mind and returned to his hotel for dinner. 'In the course of the evening', as he explained to the reporter, 'I had frequent occasion to exert my powers of persuasion to reassure several ladies who were greatly alarmed and excited by the surrounding phenomena, and indeed not without reason.' Schruit's wife and children were still in Batavia, from where he had intended to recall them just as soon as he found somewhere suitable for them to live. They, too, would have heard the distant booms from Krakatau, although many in the capital believed at first that this was merely the thunder of the monsoon arriving a little early. By Sunday evening, however, the telegrams received from Anjer and the other coastal towns confirmed it was the reawakened volcano in the Sunda Strait.

On the other side of the Strait from Anjer, at the Sumatran port of Telok Betong, the harbour master had spent most of the afternoon waiting for the *Gouverneur-Generaal Loudon* to arrive. For, in spite of Krakatau's renewed eruption, Captain Lindemann had set off from Anjer at 2:45 p.m., determined to deliver the boat-load of passengers he had been paid to ferry to Sumatra. Among those passengers, after all, were the hundred and eleven labourers who had been hired for the construction of a much-needed lighthouse in Lampong Bay, and Lindemann had no other option but to deliver them over to their foreman. He thought, at first, that he might be able to hug the coast off Ketimbang, keeping as far away from the erupting island as possible, but the *Loudon* was soon being buffeted by flying volcanic debris, as well as by heavy swells that had started to crash against the shore. By late afternoon the mail-ship was struggling badly, and Captain Lindemann began an unsuccessful attempt to dock at Ketimbang, some forty kilometres (twenty-five miles) south-east of Telok Betong.

The Dutch administrator William Beyerinck observed his efforts from the shore, where rising waves were now causing structural damage along the Ketimbang waterfront. Ketimbang was the settlement nearest the volcano, and as well as the sizeable waves crashing over the promenade, ash and pumice stones were raining onto the roofs while Krakatau continued to bellow like a gigantic cornered beast. By late evening (by which time the *Loudon* had abandoned all hope of docking and was steaming along the coast of Lampong Bay in a desperate attempt to escape the eruption), Beyerinck had decided to remove his wife and three young children into the hills for safety. Along with many hundreds of others, the family made for a series of huts and settlements on the

slopes of Rajah Bassa, from where, over the course of the following twelve hours, they would listen to the sounds of Ketimbang
being destroyed.

The port of Telok Betong, meanwhile, was faring little better
than its neighbour down the bay. By dusk the harbour master had
given up waiting for the *Loudon*, and, following a series of powerful
waves that had threatened to overwhelm the town, he decided to
retreat to the range of hills lying immediately to the west of the
port. From there he watched the rising waters wreak havoc on
his home, as vessels were dragged from their moorings, the houses
nearest the seafront were repeatedly pounded and many of the
people who had remained on the foreshore were hauled far out to
sea.

As night began to fall over the Sunda Strait, the situation in
Lampong Bay looked particularly bad, and by the time the flailing
Loudon finally made it to the anchorage at Telok Betong, the sea
was too rough for her landing boats to get anywhere near the
pier-head, most of which was already under water. Several other
ships were drifting dangerously in the bay, including the armed
government paddle-steamer *Berouw*, which had been moored near
the pier-head when the eruption began, but which had just been
wrenched from her cables by the increasingly violent sea. Fearing
a collision with an unmoored vessel, Captain Lindemann had the
Loudon steam back into deeper water, where, anchored as best
they could amid the bucking waves, he and his shipload of terrified
passengers waited for the morning to come.

In all the towns and villages around the Sunda Strait, as well as on
board the various ships that rode at anchor in its waters, that noisy
Sunday night was spent in darkness and terror, but as the sun rose,
just after 5 a.m., there was widespread hope that the worst of the
danger had passed. The volcano had quietened considerably during
the early hours of the morning, and though visibility remained
poor throughout the region, it looked as if the sky might be
beginning to clear. The rumble had ceased and a death-like calm

prevailed', as a British resident of a Javanese village some thirty-five kilometres (twenty-two miles) south of Anjer reported.[27] But the calm was not to last for long, for shortly after dawn the sounds of Krakatau resumed, noisier than ever, as the volcano began the final phase of its three-month act of self-destruction.

In Anjer, Mr Schruit the telegraph master, who had gone to bed late on Sunday night, 'suspecting no danger', as he later told the reporter from the *Bataviaasch Handelsblad*, 'rested till early in the morning of Monday, the 27th August, that unhappy day which will be written in history with such sanguinary letters.' At half-past five he was back at the harbour, overseeing the efforts to repair the broken cable, when there was a particularly loud explosion that unsettled everyone who heard it, for it sounded almost like an opening salvo, as if the volcano had woken up reinvigorated after slumbering quietly through the night. But nobody knew just how serious the effects of the latest sequence of explosions would be, until Schruit, who had just been offered a cup of tea by a neighbouring shopkeeper, and was waiting for it to arrive, 'happened to look up and perceived an enormous wave in the distance looking like a mountain rushing onwards, followed by two others that seemed even greater':

> I stood for an instant on the bridge horrified at the sight, but had sufficient presence of mind to warn the telegraphist and line-watcher of the danger, and then ran as fast as my legs could carry me. The roaring wave followed as fast, knocking to atoms everything that came in its way. Never have I run so fast in my life, for, in the most literal sense of the word, death was at my heels; and it was the thought of my wife and our children, who would be left destitute by my losing my life, that gave me superhuman strength. The flood-wave was hardly thirty paces from me. It had destroyed the draw-bridge, the hotel, the house of the Assistant Resident, in short, everything that it struck.

But suddenly the telegraph master stumbled and fell, exhausted by his burst of running, and he fully expected to be dragged to his death by the incoming water behind him. But, to his amazement, the wave crested and turned barely a metre from where he lay, plunging back down the hill towards the flooded and ruined town. 'I gasped for breath', he remembered, 'but a hearty offering of thanks to Heaven rose through my choking throat, for my deliverance and for the Providential care by which my family had been left in Batavia.' Had they been in Anjer with him, he said, 'there would have been no chance of safety, for I should at the first sight of the danger have hastened to their assistance, in which case we must all have been drowned.'[28]

But many of Anjer's other survivors were less fortunate than Schruit, having suffered the horror of seeing their families drowned in the raging tsunami. The wife of the assistant resident, Thomas Buijs, for example, was flung against her bathroom door when the wall of water burst into her home, and she was unable to save her husband or her young child, both of whom were borne away by the violent flood. Everything was chaos, and worse still, above the roaring of the waves, the renewed roaring of the nearby volcano could also be heard, as showers of hot mud and pumice began to fall from the blackened sky. By now there were hundreds of Anjer's townspeople flailing in the filthy water, 'carried along like a straw', as one survivor, an elderly Straits pilot named de Vries, described it in his account of the ordeal; he had been able to grab hold of a palm tree to which he 'clung closely, though it bowed and quivered from the fearful impulse of the water.'[29] De Vries had no idea how long he remained holding on to the swaying tree, but it was at least an hour after the morning's first eruption that the rushing waters began to recede from the town, though by then a second explosion had already been heard, which had sent another vast surge of water racing out in all directions. By 7:30 a.m., Anjer, in common with the rest of the neighbouring coastline, was once more under siege. The impact of that second wave was even more extreme, and according to one survivor, who had evaded the first wave by moving up to higher ground, 'the place where Anjer had been before was covered by a turbulent sea, upon which some trees and roofs of houses were still peeping out.'[30] The morning's explosion, with its accompanying tsunami, had all but destroyed the town.

At the village of Merak, meanwhile, twelve kilometres (seven miles) north of Anjer, the waves were coming in further and higher, due to the narrow configuration of the shoreline. One of the few survivors from the village, where some 2,700 people lost their lives, was a Javanese labourer who had been working in a rice-field at the time of the eruption. 'We had gone to work as usual, in spite of the volcano', as he later told the Revd Philip Neale, an English clergyman who undertook a tour of the affected area in order to gather information on the condition of the survivors: 'We did not think it would hurt us':

> And all of a sudden there came a great noise. We looked round at once and saw a great black thing, a long way off, coming towards us. It was very high and strong, and we soon saw that it was water. Trees and houses were washed away as it came along. The people near began to cry out and run for their lives. Not far off was some steep sloping ground. We all ran towards it and tried to climb out of the way of the water. It was too quick for most of them, and many were drowned almost at my side. I managed to get a long way up, and then the water came very near to me. When I thought I was safe I looked back and saw the wave wash the people down one after the other as they tried to scramble out of its way.

There was a sudden panicked rush to climb up through a narrow pass towards higher ground, causing a kind of human log jam, formed by dozens of people wedged together and unable to proceed. The horror of the ensuing scene, as described by the Javanese survivor, remains almost beyond comprehension:

> Then they struggled and fought, screaming and crying out all the time. Those below tried to make those above them move on again by biting their heels. A great struggle took place for a few moments, but all was soon over. One after

another they were washed down and carried far away by the rushing waters. You can see the marks on the side of the hill where this fight for life took place. Some of those who were washed off dragged others down with them. They would not let go their hold, nor could those above them release themselves from this death-grip. Many were high enough up to have altogether escaped if they had not been dragged down by their unfortunate companions.[31]

On the Sumatran side of the Sunda Strait, meanwhile, the relentless waves thrown out by the eruptions were also causing havoc and destruction. The little town of Ketimbang, the nearest settlement to the volcano itself, had started suffering the incursions of the sea during the sequence of eruptions on Sunday night, during which many of its inhabitants, including the Beyerincks, had decided to make for the slopes of Rajah Bassa. By 6 a.m., according to the report of a group of locals who had ventured back down the mountain to assess the extent of the damage, the town had completely disappeared. It wasn't clear when, exactly, the worst of the devastation had happened, but it seems likely that the town had been finally finished off by the first of the massive tsunamigenic explosions at 5:30 a.m., thirty minutes after which a twelve-metre (forty-foot) wave had smashed into the coastline, sweeping away everything before it. Not even a tree had been left standing on the deserted lake of muddy water where, only a few hours before, more than eight thousand people had lived and worked.

Further up the bay, at Telok Betong, where the crew and passengers of the *Gouverneur-Generaal Loudon* had spent an uneasy night, the series of fierce waves kept coming, but as dawn broke and the eruptions intensified, the situation became even worse. Several of the ships lying closer in to shore were wrenched from their moorings by the first big wave and hurled onto the rubbish-strewn beach; among them was the doomed government paddle-steamer *Berouw*, whose twenty-eight-man crew was almost certainly killed on impact when the ship first slammed into the shore. Not far from the *Berouw*, the salt barque *Marie* was also cast violently onto the beach: 'it was a terrible moment, I thought we were all going to die', as her commander later recalled, but most of his men were able to flee the stranded vessel before the arrival of the next tsunami, caused by a second explosion, which was heard on the beach at 6:44 a.m.[32] That second massive wave crashed into Telok Betong at around 7:45, lifting the battered *Berouw* from where she lay and flinging her into what remained of the town as its low-lying wooden buildings were reduced to floating splinters by the force of the sea.

All this was witnessed from the heaving deck of the 1,239-ton *Loudon*, which was now in serious danger from the waves, even though she was moored further out in the bay, where the swells were less destructive. 'About 7 a.m. we saw some very high seas, presumably an upheaval of the sea, approaching us up the road-stead', as Captain Lindemann noted, but his calmness on paper belied the seriousness of the situation as the second series of waves came in, and it was only through an extraordinary feat of seamanship and courage that Lindemann was able to steady his nerve and turn the vessel round by ninety degrees, just in time to face the wave head-on; thus, to the sound of Krakatau's roars, he rode the *Loudon* straight into the tsunami.[33] One of his passengers, a Dutch civil engineer named R. A. van Sandick, witnessed the entire operation from the *Loudon*'s ash-strewn deck:

> Suddenly, at about 7 a.m., a tremendous wave came moving in from the sea, which literally blocked the view and moved with tremendous speed. Immediately the crew set to under great pressure and managed after a fashion to set sail in the face of the imminent danger. The *Loudon* steamed forward in such a way that she headed right into the wave. After a moment, full of anguish, we were lifted up with a dizzy rapidity. The ship made a formidable leap, and immediately afterwards we felt as though we had plunged into the abyss; but the ship's blade went higher and we were safe. Like a high mountain, the monstrous wave precipitated its journey towards the land.[34]

Lindemann, who had watched as the wave went on to hurl the
Berouw like a toy, 'high upon the shore among the cocoanut trees',
decided to try to steer the *Loudon* back over the water to the shelter
of the harbour at Anjer, having no idea that the situation there
was just as bad – in fact the broken remains of Anjer had been
swept away by the force of the second wave only a few minutes
before. So, out in the darkening bay, the *Loudon* began slowly to
turn, but visibility had once more been reduced to almost nothing,
as Krakatau stepped up the deluge of ash and pumice stones. 'The
air grew steadily darker and darker', as Lindemann recorded in
his log, 'the wind was from the westward, and began to increase
until it reached the force of a hurricane', and it wasn't long before
he had given up the attempt to re-cross the Sunda Strait, having
now ridden out a third wave that flailed towards Telok Betong
shortly after 9 a.m., following yet another blast from the volcano.
The captain had no choice but to drop anchor once again, keeping
'the screw turning slowly at half speed in order to ride over the
terribly high seas which kept suddenly striking us, presumably in
consequence of a "sea quake", and made us dread being buried
under them.'[35] By now it was approaching 10 a.m., and Krakatau
was fast gearing up for its final act of destruction.

So far, most of the other vessels that had moored further out in
the Sunda Strait had been little affected by the sequence of waves,
for it is only as they approach the shorelines that tsunamis grow vast
and dangerous, slowing down and piling high due to friction caused
by contact with the rising sea floor; but with the nearby volcano
having just resumed its eruptive sequence, their crews still had
plenty to worry about. Everyone on board the *Charles Bal*, which
had sheltered all night within sight of Krakatau, had been roused
by the renewed activity, and they set off at first light in an effort to
put as much distance as they could between their vessel and the
erupting volcano. By 10 a.m. they had tacked nearly as far as the
Sunda Strait's north-east entrance, some fifty kilometres (thirty
miles) away from Krakatau, and not far from where the *W. H. Besse*
was also under way, heading slowly in the opposite direction,

towards the erupting volcano. Just ahead of the *Besse* were the two British ships, the *Sir Robert Sale* and the *Norham Castle*, both of which were still sitting quietly at the entrance to the Strait. The paraffin-ship *Berbice*, meanwhile, remained at anchor near Princess Island, a hundred kilometres to the south, with all her crew still occupied in keeping sparks from the flammable cargo (see map on p. 145). By now the sky above the Sunda Strait was completely black, 'just the same as on a very dark night', according to Captain Lindemann's log, when, at exactly two minutes past ten, the agitated island of Krakatau, after three months of low-level build-up, nineteen hours of escalating threats, and one long morning of increasing detona-tions, finally and definitively blew itself apart with an almighty, deafening explosion.

The end had come at last. This terminal eruption, compared to all those that had already happened, was in a separate order of magnitude altogether, a moment of sustained, elemental destruc-tion in which a portion of the earth tore itself apart with incredible upheaval and display. At two minutes past ten the vast magma chamber beneath Krakatau detonated upwards, accompanied by an unimaginable roaring and crashing – 'the reverberations of the explosions were something that are unbelievable; adjectives fail to describe the racket and turmoil', as Sidney Baker recalled – hurling twenty-five cubic kilometres (six cubic miles) of rock high into the air, creating a mighty mushroom cloud of fast-moving material atomized by the force of the blast.[36] Any ship within a twenty-kilometre radius would never have survived, but the *Charles Bal*, which by now was over fifty kilometres north-east of Krakatau, was still too close for comfort, as the entry in Captain Watson's log (still one hour ahead) makes clear:

> At 11:15 there was a fearful explosion in the direction of Krakatoa, then over 30 miles distant. We saw a wave rush right on to the Button Island, apparently sweeping entirely over the southern part, and rising half-way up the north and east sides, 50 or 60 feet, and then continuing on to the Java shore . . . At the same time the sky rapidly covered in; the wind came

strong from south-west to south; and by 11:30 a.m. we were
enclosed in a darkness that might almost be felt, and then
commenced a downpour of mud, sand, and I know not what,
the ship going north-east by north, 7 knots per hour under
three lower topsails. We set the side-lights, placed two men
on the look-out forward, the mate and second mate on either
quarter, and one man washing the mud from the binnacle
glass. We had seen two vessels to the north and north-west of
us before the sky closed in, adding not a little to the anxiety of
our position.[37]

One of the two nearby vessels was the *W. H. Besse*, which had
nervously resumed her journey at the break of day, when Captain
Baker judged, entirely mistakenly, that the worst of the danger had
passed. She was just over eighty kilometres (fifty miles) north-east
of the erupting island, and, like all the vessels in the Sunda Strait,
she was now exposed to the rain of volcanic ejecta that continued
to fall for the rest of the morning, 'the air being so thick it was
difficult to breathe . . . all hands expecting to be suffocated', as the
first officer recorded in his log.[38] Many on board the ships were
certain they would not survive the day, and in the cabin of the
Norham Castle, a couple of kilometres due west of the *Besse*, Captain
Sampson sat down to write what he believed would be the last
words of his life: 'I am writing this blind in pitch darkness; we
are under a continual rain of pumice-stone and dust. So violent are
the explosions that the ear-drums of over half my crew have been
shattered. My last thoughts are with my dear wife. I am convinced
that the Day of Judgement has come.'[39]

But the situation on board the *Gouverneur-Generaal Loudon* was
even worse, for though she was positioned slightly further from
the volcano, she was in much shallower water, having anchored
off the western shoreline of tsunami-shattered Lampong Bay. She
had already ridden out three vast waves, but now, along with a
heavy payload of flying rock and pumice, the final detonation of
the erupting island had sent the fourth and biggest tsunami so far
surging out across the surrounding waters, threatening everything

that still lay close to the shore, and the *Loudon* lay directly in its
path. The mail-ship's second engineer, whose name has come
down to us only as 'Mr S—', described the scene on board the
wallowing vessel as all hands struggled to save her – his timing,
however, appears somewhat confused, since Krakatau's final blast
occurred, as we have seen, at 10:02 a.m.:

> It was while we were thus enveloped in darkness that the
> stones and cinders discharged by the mountain began to fall
> upon the ship. In a short time the canvas awning and the
> deck were covered with ashes and stones, to the depth of two
> feet, and all our available men were employed in removing
> the falling mass, which would otherwise have sunk the ship.
> We had a large number of natives on board, and 160 European
> soldiers. The latter worked with the energy of despair at their
> task of clearing the deck, in spite of the twofold danger of
> being burnt and stunned by the hot falling stones. While we
> were engaged in this struggle, and enveloped in the sheer
> blackness of a veritable hell, a new and terrible danger came
> upon us. This was the approach of the tidal wave caused by the
> final eruption, which occurred at about 12.30–1 p.m. The wave
> reached us at 2 p.m. or thereabouts, and made the ship tumble
> like a see-saw. Sometimes she was almost straight on end, at
> other times she heaved over almost on her beam-ends . . .[40]

Lindemann kept the *Loudon* steaming up to the anchors, just as he
had done before, using the engines' full forward power to ride out
the giant waves, first as they swept in towards the coast, and then
as they crashed back out to sea. 'All the passengers and crew gave
themselves up for lost, but there was no panic, and the Captain
handled the ship splendidly throughout', according to the testimony of engineer S—, who gave a glowing account of Lindemann's
'indomitable courage in saving the ship and passengers; well, you
can fancy what it was like when I tell you that the Captain was
lashed with three ropes along the engine-room companionway,
while I was lashed down below to work the engines.' Everyone else

on board was hurled around the heaving ship as the waves and the
flying debris tried their utmost to destroy her.

Back at Telok Betong, however, the fate of the town, and of the
stranded *Berouw*, was about to be sealed for good. The battered
paddle-steamer currently lay on her side in the middle of the town's
Chinese quarter, near the mouth of the Koeripan River, surrounded
by the ruins of dozens of wooden houses and uprooted coconut
palms. The first of the morning's giant waves had killed her entire
crew, while the second and third had hurled her further into
town, but when the fourth wave came in just after 11 a.m., 'as high
as a seven-story building and traveling at the speed of a train', in
Ian Thornton's words, it proceeded to carry the ship on a violent
journey inland along the course of the Koeripan River valley, where
it eventually deposited her, at a drunken angle, nearly three kilometres (two miles) from the shore and eighteen metres (sixty feet)
above sea level (see picture 17).[41] But the town that the ship left
behind had been erased, leaving what one eyewitness would later
describe as 'a plain bare and laid waste. Nothing is left of Telok
Betong or any of the surrounding villages.'[42]

Further along the bay, meanwhile, the party of refugees from
Ketimbang had still been sheltering in their bamboo huts a hundred and twenty metres (four hundred feet) up the south-west slope
of Rajah Bassa when Krakatau finally exploded. Anna Beyerinck
remembered being thrown to the ground by the force of the blast,
'then it seemed as if all the air was being sucked away and I could
not breathe. Large lumps clattered down on my head, my back
and my arms. Each lump was larger than the others. I could not
stand.'[43] Like many others she had been badly seared by the heat of
the eruption, and her skin was hanging off her back and arms in
large folds, sticky with a gruesome paste of ash and blood. Deafened
by the explosion and in terrible pain, she crawled out of the hut into
the dark volcanic storm, as 'the hot bite of the pumice pricked like
needles', where she lay beneath the shelter of some nearby trees
and silently waited to die. All around her were the burnt bodies of
other Ketimbang refugees, the only people who were actually killed

directly by the heat of the eruption, rather than by the impact of the four gigantic tsunami waves which, even as the people on the mountain lay dying, continued their reign of destruction below.

In certain places around the shoreline the fourth wave had reached over thirty-six metres (a hundred and twenty feet) in height, and few who witnessed its arrival would survive to tell the tale; one who did described 'the ocean advancing like an enormous rampart of water', before hearing 'an awful roaring noise as the sea struck the land.'[44] Telegraph master Schruit, who had run inland from Anjer after escaping the first wave at 6 a.m., had heard the last of Krakatau's explosions some four hours later, 'a frightful sound . . . followed by a heavy fall of ashes and flashes of lightning'; not long after he met a group of Javanese villagers who were running uphill, shouting, '*Ayer datang, ayer datang!*' ('The water is coming, the water is coming!'); their nearby fishing village, Waluran, less than two kilometres from Anjer port, had already been badly damaged by the preceding waves, but this last tsunami swept everything away, including the village's stone-built mosque, which having survived the earlier waves, was crowded with people seeking refuge.[45] The handful of villagers Schruit met on the hillside were the settlement's only survivors.

Meanwhile, on the sheltering *Berbice*, nearly a hundred kilometres to the south of Anjer, a high wind had just started up, which caused the ship to start listing badly from the weight of ash on her masts and rigging. But worse was still to come, according to Captain Logan's account, for an hour or so after Krakatau's final explosion, 'a heavy sea came rushing on about 3 [sic] in the afternoon. It rose to a height of 20 feet, swept over the ship, making her quiver from stem to stern with the shock.'[46] As the *Berbice* righted itself, the wave continued at a hundred kilometres per hour towards the south-east entrance of the Sunda Strait, from where it radiated out across the Indian Ocean, gaining speed as it reached deeper waters. Some five and a half hours later the tsunami reached the east coasts of India and Sri Lanka: 'the wave reached halfway up to Calcutta on the Hooghly', as the Tidal Survey of India recorded, while the *Ceylon Observer* carried a report that in the southern port of Galle the sea had receded to the end of the jetty before rushing back in with surprising force, while a few kilometres further along the coast, a woman working in a paddy field was swept away and drowned. Five hours after that 'a great tidal disturbance' was reported at Aden on the Arabian Peninsula, while metre-high waves were also seen to strike the harbours at Cape Town and Port Elizabeth on the South African coast, more than 7,500 kilometres (4,600 miles) away from the now dematerialized volcano.[47]

As the day wore on, the waters of the Sunda Strait slowly calmed, and survivors started taking stock of the impact of the morning's events. Every ship within a hundred-kilometre radius had been left in a sorry state, with decks, masts and rigging scorched by flying cinders and covered in drifts of ash. 'The *Loudon* looked terrible!', wrote engineer van Sandick, 'everything was covered with foul, stinking mud. Zola could have described it well. If the ship would have been sunk for about 10 years and then raised, this is what she probably would have looked like.' It took the crew all day and late into the night to remove the mud – a sticky amalgam of waterlogged ash and other debris. The *Charles Bal* had fared little better: 'the ship, from truck to water-line, was as if cemented', wrote Captain Watson, 'spars, sails, blocks, and ropes were in a terrible mess; but thank God nobody hurt nor was the ship damaged. But think of Anjer, Merak, and the other little villages on the Java coast!'[48]

Yes, think of all the villages along the inundated coasts, wiped out of existence by the force of the incoming sea. A total of a hundred and sixty-five towns and villages were completely destroyed by the giant waves, with a further hundred and thirty-two settlements damaged almost beyond repair. It was hard to know how to describe the carnage, for as we have already seen, Telok Betong, Ketimbang, Anjer and Waluran had been swept away, and there were scores of other settlements whose names would be the only things to survive: Beneawany, Beteong, Chikandie Udik, Penimbang, Tandjoeangan, Tampang, Tanot Bringin, Tjaringen . . . all had gone, many without a trace, except, here and there, for the bodies of the dead, crushed together in heaps, or strewn over wide areas, according to the particular manner in which the water had come in and receded; two thousand five hundred dead in the village of Beneawany, where everyone had been assembled in the open air for an emergency meeting with the colonial Resident; seven hundred dead in the village of Tanara; three hundred dead at Karang Antoe, where the bodies were found eerily stacked in the corner of what had been the crowded Monday market. Death was everywhere, as a crewman on the ship *Samoa* later recalled, in a letter published in the London *Times* on 12 December 1883. His craft sailed south-west through the Sunda Strait, through what appeared to be an ocean of dead: 'masses of dead bodies', he wrote, 'hundreds and hundreds striking the ship on both sides – groups of 50 to 100 all packed together, most of them naked' (picture 18). Over the course of a single morning the quartet of waves had swept the entire coastal area clear of almost every sign of life. 'All gone', as the Lloyd's sub-agent in Serang described the south-west coast of Java in a five-word wire to head office in Batavia: 'All gone. Plenty lives lost.'[49]

III

News of the eruption spread quickly around the world via the submarine telegraph system, with newspapers such as the Boston *Globe* and the London *Times* reporting within a matter of hours that 'a terrific volcanic eruption took place last night on the island of Krakatoa.' Having no reporters of their own on the scene, many papers simply printed the incoming wires verbatim, which, from today's perspective, serves to impart a powerful air of immediacy to their coverage. The *Times* for 30 August, for example, ran a series of telegrams from Batavia under the headline, 'THE VOLCANIC ERUPTION IN JAVA', with the first, dated 28 August, beginning: 'All quiet. Sky clear. Communication Serang restored', and ending: 'Knows nothing further of fate of Anjer, but believed all lost.' The next, dated 29 August, 10 a.m., was a masterpiece of abbreviated reportage:

> Sky continues clear. Temperature fell ten degrees on 27th, now normal; native huts all along beach washed away. Birds roosted during ash rain; and cocks crowed as it cleared away; fish dizzy; town covered with thin layer ashes, giving roads quaint bright look. Sad news just coming from West Coast. Shall wire again.

The sad news coming in from the coast was passed on an hour later, at 11 a.m., the wire reading simply: 'Anjer, Tjeringen, Telok-betong, destroyed', with further bulletins dispatched over the course of the afternoon confirming that Anjer and the other ports had been 'completely destroyed by the tidal wave which followed the eruption of Krakatoa . . . There has been enormous loss of life, both among Europeans and natives in North Bantam. Property has also been damaged to an immense extent.'[50]

Of course none of this was news in Batavia itself, which had also suffered some of the effects of the blast, having been covered in ash since Sunday night; then at 12:30 the following day – some two hours after the final explosion – a sizeable body of water inundated the city's main canal, overflowing its brick-built banks and causing some structural damage to the downtown area, a kilo-metre or so inland. The colonial capital had been struck by the fourth tsunami, and although loss of life was reported to be small, the violence of the wave impressed upon the city's inhabitants the seriousness of the situation further down the coast. As worsening reports from Serang and Banten continued to arrive in the capital, it became increasingly apparent that something needed to be done to alleviate the suffering of the survivors. So, only a few days later, a fund-raising committee was put together by a group of leading Dutch residents, who gave it the rather grand-sounding title: 'The Central Committee for the Relief of Sufferers from the Outburst of Krakatau'. By the end of September 1883 the committee had raised nearly 658,000 guilders, a sum equivalent to around $3.5 million in today's money, most of which had come from individual donors in the Netherlands. The Straits government, according to a report in the *Liverpool Daily Post* for 4 September, had given $25,000 in aid, while the Dutch government had sent a paltry 5,000 guilders 'towards the relief of the distress caused by the earthquake' [sic].[51] Just as in the aftermath of the Indian Ocean tsunami in 2004, government remittances were put to shame by the generosity of individuals living far from the scene, and resentment was later expressed by some of the Indonesian survivors who felt that the Dutch colonial government, wealthy as it was, had done little to materially assist its principal overseas possession. This sentiment is easily understood if one considers that between 1830 and 1900 the Netherlands earned over two billion guilders from Javanese revenues alone, in which context it is hardly surprising that the few thousand given in emergency aid would be viewed as a grudging return.

But plenty of blankets and tents were dispatched from Batavia, as were several hundred cases of petroleum for burning some of the thousands of bodies that were strewn along the shorelines of Java and Sumatra. At first, this work had fallen to the surviving villagers, though it soon became apparent that in certain areas so few people had been left alive it was only by appealing to inland villages, and then by recruiting gangs of prisoners (in return for shortened sentences), that enough labour could be mustered to finish the task. The workers were paid at the rate of five guilders per body, and as the weeks went by, several hundred a day were burned or buried, while the shorelines were drenched in carbolic acid in an attempt to prevent the spread of infection. Soon, there were thousands of freshly dug graves lining every beach along the Sunda Strait. 'We could scarcely take a step anywhere in one part of the district without walking on a grave', the clergyman Philip Neale observed, the whole place having become, as he described it, 'nothing more or less than a huge cemetery.'[52]

But in spite of the aid that was dispatched from Batavia, the situation worsened as the weeks went by, due mainly to the shortage of food and fresh water caused by widespread volcanic contamination. 'The misery is great', as one Sumatran survivor complained; 'our buffaloes, cattle, and horses have nothing to eat; deer and wild pigs even come into the villages in search of food. Rice is short, and there is a lack of drinking water. All the available water tastes of sulphur and is muddy', and these problems grew increasingly acute, with the loss of coastal roads and moorings rendering many of the outlying regions impossible to reach.[53] As Philip Neale discovered during his journey to Java's west coast, 'the well-made road from Batavia to Merak – on which we had thus far travelled – now came to an abrupt ending. Its metalled track had suddenly disappeared, partly washed away at first, and a little farther on completely swept away. A ruined bridge was all there was to show where once the road had been.'[54] And it wasn't just the roads: rafts of floating pumice blocked the entrances to many of the smaller bays, preventing aid ships from accessing some of the worst-affected areas.

Those who had fled to the hills during the height of the eruption were greeted with scenes of desolation when they returned over the following few days. The Beyerincks, for example, who had sheltered on the slopes of Rajah Bassa, staggered onto the beach near the ruined village of Kali Antoe on Friday 31 August, after three days spent crawling down the mountainside through perilous drifts of ash. Their youngest child, a baby boy, had not survived the journey, and they had been forced to leave his body behind, along with the thousand or so others who had also died on the mountain. Anna Beyerinck was now in a terrible state, her skin burnt and badly swollen, her hair matted and heavy with ash, and her two remaining children drifting in and out of consciousness due to hunger, pain and exhaustion. 'No human tongue could tell what happened', she later recalled, 'I think hell is the only word applicable to what we saw and went through.'[55] But now they had finally made it back down the mountain, they were still surrounded by a scene of destruction, with hardly a tree or a house left standing on the scoured plain of mud and rubbish that had once been a village teeming with life. Scores of bloated bodies marked the new treeline, now more than a hundred metres further inland. The family spent that night on the beach, and by the following morning they had just about given themselves up for dead, when suddenly the dark shape of the *Kedirie*, a rescue barge sent out from Batavia, was seen pushing through the pumice-filled water along the northern shore of Lampong Bay, her crew on the lookout for survivors. Their attention was soon attracted by the group of figures on the beach, and, with some difficulty, a boat was rowed ashore, in which the starving Beyerincks were ferried to the waiting vessel. The *Kedirie* turned around amid the floating pumice and headed back to Batavia with the Beyerincks on board, where all of them, eventually, would recover from their injuries.

Out in the Sunda Strait, meanwhile, the stricken ships began to make their way towards land, their crews unsure of what they might encounter there. At half-past six on Tuesday morning, 28 August, Captain Lindemann piloted the *Loudon* slowly south-east through drifts of pumice and uprooted trees that were so densely packed together that it seemed as if they were moving overland. He had intended to return to Anjer on the opposite shore, but the route was so transformed by the islands of debris that he ended up closing in on what was left of Krakatau. 'The middle of the island had disappeared', he observed, while the outlying fringes appeared, to his disquiet, to be producing a regular column of smoke. But as the *Loudon* approached the coast of Java, his disquiet grew stronger when he saw that the Fourth Point lighthouse – a familiar landmark to the south of Anjer – had been 'entirely washed away', while all along the shoreline, as far as the eye could see, was nothing but a wide expanse of ash-grey wasteland, devoid of trees and buildings. Anjer had simply disappeared, 'wiped away, no trace, no stone can be seen any more', as engineer van Sandick described the view from the deck of the *Loudon*; 'a more complete destruction is unthinkable.'[56]

As the *Loudon*'s passengers stood gazing from the rail at the scene of total devastation, the *W. H. Besse* headed south-west towards the open expanse of the Indian Ocean, her weary crew having already borne witness to the fate of Anjer town. 'The city had gone under water completely', as Sidney Baker remembered, recalling an observation made by his father (who had lodged in the town the previous year) that they could have sailed right over the Anjer Hotel and dropped anchor down its chimney.[57] As the *Besse* sailed south towards Princess Island, she passed the paraffin-ship *Berbice* heading slowly in the opposite direction, towards Anjer. Like all the vessels that had been close to the eruption, the *Berbice* had been smothered with volcanic mud and ash, which the crew had spent the previous few hours removing as best they could. According to Captain Logan, more than forty tons of debris had to be thrown overboard before the *Berbice* could get under way, but she was to make slow progress through what Logan described as 'large banks of pumice between 18 English thumbs [inches] and 2 feet thick', in amongst which the bodies of people and animals, including tigers, were clearly visible. They didn't draw near to Krakatau until the following afternoon – 'as far as I could see, the island was separated into three parts by two gaping openings', wrote Logan – but apart from his sighting of the *Besse* the previous day, he encountered no other vessels anywhere in the Sunda Strait.[58] All surviving craft had evidently fled the scene at first light on Tuesday morning; by the following afternoon, one of the busiest stretches of water in the world was empty of traffic, temporarily abandoned to the smoking stump of rock that glowered like a beacon at its centre.

As has already been seen, the series of vast tsunamis generated by the force of the erupting volcano had made their way across the Indian Ocean at speeds approaching 650 kilometres (400 miles) per hour, reaching the eastern shores of Africa some ten hours after the explosions. The sounds of the detonations, meanwhile, had travelled nearly twice as fast, radiating through the humid air for thousands of kilometres. Within the space of an hour or so, the noise of Monday morning's final blast had reached Thailand, Sri Lanka, the Philippines, Australia and, at its furthest extent, the island of Rodriguez, more than halfway across the Indian Ocean, 4,775 kilometres (2,968 miles) to the west, where according to the local chief of police, it sounded like the roar of distant cannon. Covering nearly 8 per cent of the planet's surface, it remains the furthest that any sound has been known to travel, making the eruption of Krakatau the loudest noise ever recorded on Earth.

But even those who didn't hear the explosions were brushed by the shock waves that they set in train, as vast invisible ripples of disturbance – *an earthquake in the air*', as Simon Winchester aptly described it – hurtled round the globe no fewer than seven times, their journeyings clearly inscribed on the drum rolls of barographs in observatories all over the world.[59]* Barograph papers were usually changed once a week, and tended to show the rise and fall of atmospheric pressure in the form of long, sinuous curves; but when the rolls came to be removed at the end of the week of 27 August, it was immediately obvious to anyone who handled them that something unusual had happened, for in graphic contrast to the usual pattern, a series of sharp peaks had been recorded at regular intervals over a five-day period, beginning on the Monday afternoon. For the rest of the week, massive pressure-waves had rippled and refracted around the planet, causing 'temporary derangements of atmospheric pressure', in the words of a paper read three months later at a meeting of the Royal Society of London. That paper, entitled 'Notes on a Series of Barometrical Disturbances which Passed over Europe between the 27th and 31st of August 1883', was destined to have a greater long-term impact than its modest-sounding title might suggest, for as its author, Robert H. Scott (the secretary of the Royal Society's meteorological division), had apparently realized, these barograph readings from around the world were the first indication that the eruption of Krakatau should be viewed as a global phenomenon.[60] The fact that everyone on the planet had been physically touched by the volcano's silent

---

*   The barograph was a recording barometer, designed in the early nineteenth century to trace the fluctuations of atmospheric pressure on slowly revolving clockwork drums.

pressure-waves as they hurtled through the atmosphere at close to
the speed of sound was a powerful image, and served as a reminder
of the scale and connectedness of the earth's natural forces, as well
as our ever-present human vulnerability. Everyone on the planet,
whether they knew it or not, had experienced the eruption at first-
hand, and it seems to have been this idea that motivated the Royal
Society to establish a 'Krakatoa Committee', a thirteen-strong scientific body tasked with investigating the global repercussions of
the event. So, with appeals for eyewitness accounts of the disaster
beginning to appear in newspapers around the world, and with a
generation of scientists devoting unprecedented levels of attention
to such a faraway event, Krakatau 1883 soon turned into the most
studied eruption in history.

In a coincidence widely noted at the time, 1883 was also the
centenary year of the Laki fissures eruptions, and though the two
events were very different in kind – Krakatau had been violently
explosive while *Lakagígar* had been poisonously effusive – both
eruptions jettisoned enormous quantities of volcanic particulates
deep into the atmosphere, which drifted over much of the world
with impressive and disturbing results. Just as in 1783, following the
vast emissions of dust and sulphates from the Icelandic fissures,
Krakatau's forty-six cubic kilometres (eleven cubic miles) of ejected
dust and gases also formed themselves into a semi-opaque band
that threaded slowly westwards around the equator, forming memorable sunsets and afterglows across the earth's lower latitudes –
and were also responsible for a worldwide temperature drop of
almost 0.5°C over the following months, just as had happened
during the winter of 1783–84. A few weeks later, the aerosol veil
began to spread outwards from the tropics to the poles, and by
November 1883 most of the world was being subjected to the same
displays of lurid discoloration that had so transfixed northern
Europe a century before, caused by the slowly falling high-altitude
material as it scattered the incoming light. Blue moons and green
suns appeared amid skies suffused with an array of mercurial hues,
'burnished gold, copper, brass, silver, such as Turner in his wildest

dreams never saw',[61] as one observer in the South Pacific described the effects (see picture 19).* 'The glow is intense, this is what strikes everyone', observed Gerard Manley Hopkins in the course of a long and lyrical essay on 'The Remarkable Sunsets' that he published in the journal *Nature* in January 1884; 'it has prolonged the daylight, and optically changed the season; it bathes the whole sky, it is mistaken for the reflection of a great fire':

> But it is also lustreless. A bright sunset lines the clouds so that their brims look like gold, brass, bronze, or steel. It fetches out those dazzling flecks and spangles which people call fish-scales. It gives to a mackerel or dappled cloudrack the appearance of quilted crimson silk, or a ploughed field glazed with crimson ice, the lilac disappears; the green deepens, spreads, and encroaches on the orange; and the red deepens, spreads and encroaches on the green, till at last one red, varying downwards from crimson to scarlet or orange fills the west and south. While these changes were going on in the sky, the landscape of Ribblesdale glowed with a frowning brown.[62]

Like William Cowper a century before, here was a leading religious poet responding to a sequence of atmospheric anomalies that had been created by the eruption of a distant volcano, but unlike Cowper in 1783, Hopkins wasn't writing from a position of scientific ignorance. The century since the *Lakagígar* weather panics had seen large numbers of professional and semi-professional scientific observers established in locations all over the world (including at Stoneyhurst College, Lancashire, where Hopkins was on the staff between 1882 and 1884), the vast majority of whom – thanks to the advent of rapid communications – knew exactly what they were witnessing. They still wanted to prove it to their own satisfaction, however, and a great deal of amateur and professional research was

---

* The choice of Turner was an interesting one, as he had painted a sequence of earlier volcanic London sunsets, following the eruption of Tambora on the island of Sumbawa in April 1815.

17. The armed paddle-steamer *Berouw* (from the Dutch for 'remorse') was carried several kilometres inland from the town of Telok Betong by the waves thrown out by the force of the eruption.

18. Ships that sailed through the Sunda Strait in the weeks following the eruption encountered floating islands of dead bodies, 'hundreds and hundreds striking the ship on both sides', as one crewman described the scene in a letter printed in the London *Times* in December 1883.

19. The English painter William Ascroft was captivated by the Krakatau sunsets, and spent many evenings between 1883 and 1886 making pastel sky-sketches on the banks of the Thames. He was well aware of similarities to the 1783 effects, and in his *Catalogue of Sky Sketches* (1888), he cited Gilbert White's description of the sun at noon shedding 'a rust-coloured, ferruginious light on the ground.' He went on to exhibit five hundred and thirty of these lurid pastels in the South Kensington Museum, the forerunner of London's Science Museum, in the repository of which they remain today, little known and rarely seen.

20. The geologist Rogier Verbeek was commissioned by the Dutch colonial government to survey what remained of Krakatau in the months after the eruption. He and his team made five field-trips to the pumice-covered stump of Rakata, the west side of which is shown here, in a chromolithograph from Verbeek's 1885 report.

21. Anak Krakatau ('Child of Krakatau') broke the surface of the Sunda Strait in 1928, since when it has been growing at an alarming rate: it currently stands at around three hundred metres, almost half the height of its parent volcano. This image, showing lava flows in progress, was taken from the Ikonos satellite in June 1998.

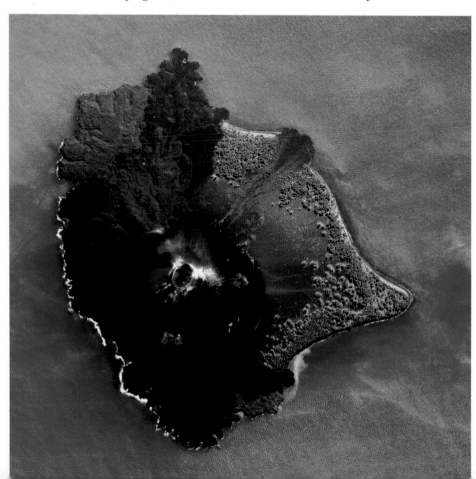

22. Laupahoehoe Point as it looked before the tsunami swept ashore on 1 April 1946. The school buildings can be seen on the right-hand side of the image, with the teachers' cottages down by the water, just beyond the playing field.

23. Art Deco buildings began to appear in downtown Hilo in the late 1930s. By then the population of the city was approaching fifty thousand. This view is of Kamehameha Avenue.

24. The wave races shorewards over Coconut Island, Hilo Bay, 1 April 1946.

25. Running from the wave: a barber named Cecilio Licos turned and took this vivid snapshot of the third wave as it crashed in to downtown Hilo on the morning of 1 April, 1946.

26. Hilo's celebrated Café 100 was
badly damaged in the 1946 tsunami.
It reopened a few months later, and in
early 1960 it moved to new premises
a few metres inland, where it was
destroyed once again on 22 May
by the tsunami from Chile.

27. A railroad car shoved under a
bakery building by the force of the
tsunami, Hilo, April 1946.

28. The cleanup begins:
volunteers help sort out the mess
at the Hilo Dry Goods store,
Kamehameha Avenue. The buildings
on the other, ocean side of the road
bore the brunt of the wave damage,
leaving those on the *mauka* (mountain)
side damaged but not destroyed.

29. The names of the twenty-four children and adults lost at Laupahoehoe Point were inscribed on the memorial that looks out to sea from the site of the former school playing field.

30. A familiar sight along the Hawaiian coastline, tsunami warning sirens play a central role in the state's Civil Defense programme.

31. Just before midnight on 22 May 1960, sightseers ignore the warning sirens and gather near the Hilo fish market to wait for the long-range tsunami from Chile; sixty-one people were killed in Hilo, as were a further hundred and forty in Japan.

32. A row of steel parking meters bent to the ground by the force of the retreating wave, downtown Hilo, May 1960.

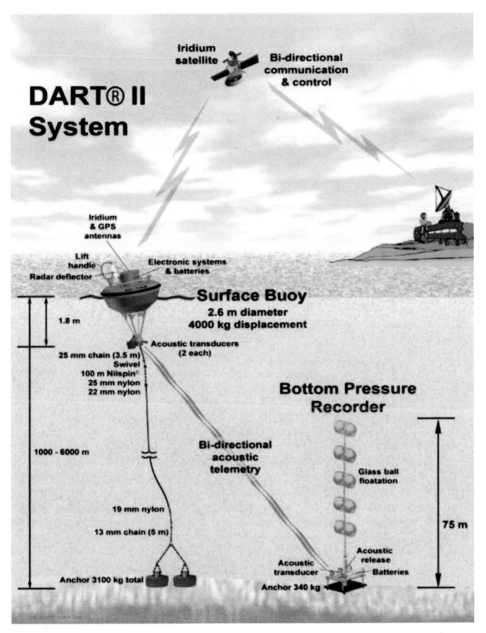

33. The Deep-ocean Assessment and Reporting of Tsunamis (DART II) system consists of anchored sea-floor pressure recorders which send real-time information on wave activity to surface buoys, which then transmit the information to the Pacific Tsunami Warning Center via satellite. The technology is expensive to maintain, however, and out of the price range of most Indian Ocean governments. (NOAA/National Weather Service).

34. The melancholy site of the former Japanese-Hawaiian township of Shinmachi, rebuilt after the 1946 tsunami, but left bare after its subsequent destruction in May 1960.

35. The Waiakea Town Clock, stopped at 1:04 a.m. on 23 May 1960 by the Chilean tsunami, stands as a memorial to the lost Hilo neighbourhood, as well as a reminder of the ever-present dangers of the sea.

devoted to confirming the assumed connection between the Krakatau eruption and the sequence of strange winter skies.

In suburban Philadelphia, for instance, a metallurgist named Joseph Wharton had been entranced by 'the splendid roseate glows' that descended every evening through the hazy sky, and devised his own experiment for testing whether they really had been caused by the 'stratum of fine solid particles suspended at a great height in the atmosphere', which had floated around the world from Krakatau. After extracting samples of the dust that had fallen to earth in a snowdrift near his house, he set about comparing them with ground-up pumice that had been gathered in the Sunda Strait by the crew of the *J. E. Ridgeway*, a Philadelphia cargo steamer that had returned to port in February 1884. Looking through his home microscope, Wharton saw that the two sets of particles were identical in composition, consisting, as he described them, 'of irregular, flattish, blobby fragments, mostly transparent and showing no trace of crystalline structure.' As a control measure, he compared his snow-caught sample with dust collected from other sources, such as nearby steel works and blast furnaces, in order to rule out the possibility of industrial contamination. None of these other samples was a match for Wharton's 'snow-dust', which – as he had just demonstrated to his own satisfaction – must have landed in Pennsylvania after a 'long voyage of more than ten thousand miles of space and more than four months of time.'[63]

The Krakatau dust and its atmospheric impact became a subject of particular fascination for scientists all over the world, and the Royal Society's 'Krakatoa Committee' ended up devoting nearly two-thirds of its final report to a global catalogue of what it termed 'the Unusual Optical Phenomena of the Atmosphere'.[64] Their exhaustive tracking of the 'twilight phenomena' grew into a valuable resource for understanding the behaviour of the earth's upper atmosphere, and it was soon acknowledged that the eruption had been just as significant in the development of meteorology as it had been in that of volcanology – the study of its global after-effects revealing much about the workings of stratospheric circulation, as well as the optical and climatic effects of floating high-altitude particulates. Ever since Franklin's brilliant intervention, a century before, the atmosphere had increasingly been seen as a vast, gaseous mechanism that was susceptible to large-scale planetary processes;* now, in the wake of the Krakatau eruption, it was as if a kind of dye had been added to the upper layers of the atmosphere, rendering their hitherto invisible movements suddenly and thrillingly visible as they made their way from the equatorial regions out towards the higher latitudes. Thus, in contrast to the earlier episode, the longer-term fluctuations of trade winds, jet streams and large-scale convection cells could be tracked by scientists through the medium of the drifting dust-veil. And unlike the relatively short-lived aftermath of the Laki fissures event, which had lasted only a few months, the Krakatau dust remained aloft for the next three years, allowing intensive study of its immediate visual effects, as well as of its slow, drifting circulations via the newly visible wind streams. All in all, as the Prussian physicist Johann Kiessling was moved to declare in 1887, the eruption of Krakatau had been nothing less than 'a turning point for the science of meteorology.'[65]

For geologists, meanwhile, the eruption supplied an equally valuable opportunity for studying the mechanics of a large-scale subduction-zone volcano. First on the scene was Dr Rogier Verbeek, a mining engineer from Utrecht, who had worked on a geological survey of the Sunda Strait only three years before the great eruption. Within weeks of the event he had been instructed by the Dutch colonial authorities to return to the remnants of

---

* This idea has found modern expression in James Lovelock's celebrated Gaia hypothesis, in which the earth and its inhabitants are held to constitute a single, self-regulating system, comprised of physical, biological and human components. According to the Gaia idea, early plants and other organisms rendered the earth habitable by altering the chemistry of its atmosphere, although human activity has speeded up the process to an unsustainable rate, through the rapid release of long-buried fossil carbon.

the island volcano in order to prepare a scientific assessment. In October 1883 he and his team set off on the *Kedirie* (the vessel that had ferried the Beyerinck family to safety), but when he set eyes on Krakatau again, he was amazed, for most of the island that he remembered had gone, leaving only a crescent-shaped stump of cliff that had once been part of Rakata, the highest of Krakatau's three peaks. The rock was covered in thick black streaks that, on closer inspection, turned out to be sizeable mud flows, which must have streamed over the earlier deposits some time after the main explosion. Lang and Verlaten islands, meanwhile, appeared to have grown, having been smothered by thirty-metre drifts of pumice-stone and ash, but the volcano itself, as Verbeek soon concluded, was no longer an active threat, and he and his team were happy to camp out on its ruins in order to conduct their research (see picture 20).

Over the course of the next eighteen months, Verbeek conducted another four field trips to the ruined volcano, which culminated in an impressive 546-page report, *Krakatau*, which was published in Batavia, at government expense, in May 1885. Unlike the Royal Society's later report, which considered the eruption in its global dimension, Verbeek's assessment was principally concerned with the immediate local impact, although, as he made clear in his foreword, this was 'an exceptionally important eruption, whose consequences were observed over all of the earth', and the book did go on to discuss the more distant repercussions of the sea waves, the pressure-waves and the meandering optical effects.[66] But the real value of Verbeek's book lay in his detailed first-hand observations, the results of which included his now celebrated conclusion that the island had not simply blown itself apart, as most commentators had initially assumed, but that much of it had in fact collapsed back into the sea to form a large sunken caldera more than 350 metres (1,150 feet) deep. This insight, when applied to other volcanic sites around the world, greatly advanced the understanding of island eruptions and the formation of calderas, especially when linked to Verbeek's prophecy that 'in any renewed activity of the volcano, it is to be expected that islands will arise in the middle of the seabasin that is surrounded by Rakata Peak, Verlaten and Lang.'[67] And that is exactly what has been happening since January 1928, when Anak Krakatau – 'The Child of Krakatau' – first broke the surface of the Sunda Strait, just above the spot where Krakatau's middle peak had last stood, forty-five years before. According to Verbeek, the island that erupted in 1883 had itself grown up within the ancient crater walls of an earlier caldera, one presumably created by the massive eruption that occurred some time in the sixth century AD, and the same process was certain to continue, 'just as formerly the craters Danan and Perboewatan themselves formed in the sea within the old crater wall.'

Rogier Verbeek died, aged eighty-one, in April 1926, just missing the spectacle of his predicted new volcano rising noisily from the Sunda Strait amid billows of smoke and flames. Plenty of other geologists had assembled in his place, however, and over an exhilarating two-year period they watched from a nearby observatory as the peak of Anak Krakatau rose and dipped beneath the waters, while the opposing forces of volcanism and wave erosion slowly battled it out. Finally, on 11 August 1930, the submarine vents were able to establish a permanent landform, succeeding in their 'concerted attempt to sculpt a lasting memorial on the surface', in Simon Winchester's elegant phrase, and ever since then, the adolescent island has been growing upwards and outwards at an average rate of thirteen centimetres (five inches) a week.[68] By 1960, the island was nearly two kilometres in diameter and stood 166 metres (545 feet) tall, with a rapidly growing cinder cone emerging from a crater on its south flank, which was soon producing regular eruptions (see picture 21). Ever since then, its activity has been monitored by the Volcanological Survey of Indonesia (a body established in 1920), which issues warning bulletins whenever an increase in seismic activity is registered on the island. The most recent warnings were given out on 16 May 2005, when the Alert Level at the volcano was raised from 1 (dormant) to 2 (restless), and

again on 26 October 2007, when the Alert Level was briefly raised
to 3 (local eruption threat), following a sudden increase in seis-
micity, accompanied by a plume of dense grey ash that billowed
a kilometre above the island.*

But it isn't only earth scientists who take an active interest in
the new volcano. For life scientists, such as the Belgian biologist
Edmond Cotteau, who visited Rakata in the summer of 1884 in
search of living remnants of the island's ruined ecology, the discovery of a microscopic spider busily spinning a web across a
fire-blackened rock precipitated a question that remains a focus
of biogeographical research today: was all life entirely destroyed
by the blast, or were there certain creatures, including Cotteau's
spider, that somehow survived the conflagration? This question,
which is still known as the Krakatau Problem, goes right to the
heart of understanding the dynamics of ecological recovery: how,
exactly, do ecosystems restore themselves after major calamities
such as volcanic eruptions? Does life only ever return from outside – borne on the wind, or on the waves (perhaps clinging to the
husk of some migrant coconut) or on the feet of visiting seabirds –
or are there particularly hardy species of seeds and rhizomes that
can withstand the stresses of a paroxysmal blast? After all, there
are numerous specifically adapted life-forms that thrive in the hot,
sulphur-laden waters around undersea volcanic vents, so it seems
highly likely that something living – if only a few billion bacteria
– would have survived the final eruption. The jury is still out on
the question, though most life scientists tend to the view that even
if one or two lower organisms did manage to survive the blast, the
major system of repopulation would still have been colonization
from outside. Ian Thornton, for example, the Australian biologist
and author of the seminal study *Krakatau: The Destruction and*

---

* There are two main volcano alert grades in current international use, one colour-
coded: Green (dormant), Yellow (restless), Orange (local eruption or eruption threat)
and Red (significant or explosive eruption); the other numerical: 0–5, with 0 signifying a
dormant state and 5 a major eruption currently in progress.

Reassembly of an Island Ecosystem (1996), describes the relic of the Krakatau eruption as 'a *tabula rasa*, or clean slate', which was subsequently repopulated by an array of plants and animals that made their way to the island stump by a variety of means.[69] The process, though complex, was remarkably rapid: within a year of the eruption, significant patches of green vegetation had already been observed on Rakata's surviving flank, and two years after that, in 1886, a botanical expedition discovered fifteen species of flowering beach plants, two mosses and eleven ferns, while the following years saw more and more arrivals establishing themselves on the ruined island. Grasses, ferns, orchids, sugar cane, fig trees and palm all came and thrived, and within twenty years the vegetation had grown so thick that explorers had to hack their way through with machetes, while trying to avoid being bitten by the swarms of insects that had made the new jungle their home.

But that was only the old island: after 1930, once Anak Krakatau had become a permanent new landform neighbouring the stump of Rakata, the question of ecological colonization versus ecological recovery took on a whole new dimension. It was as if a large-scale pristine laboratory had suddenly been dropped into the middle of the Sunda Strait, right next door to the earlier lab, affording 'a very rare and unquestionable example of a primary xerosere', as Ian Thornton has characterized this virgin ecology, 'a biotic succession starting on a "clean slate", a substrate initially devoid of life.'[70] So the question was: how would the colonization of this new and initially lifeless lump of rock compare with that of its rapidly regenerating neighbour?

The first biologist to make landfall on the new island was the British arachnologist William Bristowe, who visited the six-month-old site in February 1931. No plant life had yet established itself, although Bristowe did discover a beetle (*Anthicus oceanicus*), a mosquito (*Aedes vigilax*), a leaf-mining moth and several ants, as well as a number of wind-borne spiders, all of which were apparently thriving on the naked surface of the island. A year later, and the first plants had begun to take root along the flotsam-strewn beach, where migratory sand-plovers were seen foraging for the insects and small crustacea that continued to make their way over the Strait. Colonization was thus just as rapid as it had been on Rakata, and today, seventy years on, even though the vegetation suffers regular erosion from the island's ongoing volcanic eruptions, a settled community of wind- and sea-dispersed flora and fauna has established itself as a more or less permanent island ecosystem. Anak Krakatau's regular lava flows have so disrupted the patterns of vegetation, however, that a much smaller range of species has established itself compared to the neighbouring island. As Ian Thornton has commented, 'the mixed forest clothing of the three older islands testifies to the relentlessness of the gradual process of natural recuperation and recovery. The visitor has a glimpse of two sides of the same coin, both the destructive and the healing powers of nature, each seeming to exceed by far anything that human power, with all its technological aids, can yet achieve.'[71]

The 1883 eruption of what is still the most famous volcano in the world was a crucial event in the history of science, for it was the first natural catastrophe to occur at a time when there were enough observers stationed around the world to make sense of its progress and aftermath; and as Mike Rampino (Professor of Earth and Environmental Sciences at New York University) has pointed out, the result of their endeavours was 'the first real study of a volcano that showed us how volcanoes work', and many of these lessons are still being debated by volcanologists in universities all over the world.[72] But the eruption was also the first catastrophe to be experienced on a global scale, with the instantaneity of the telegraph reports serving to create an entirely new category of disaster: the universal news event, a story followed, in the case of Krakatau, by more than half of the world's population.[73] This novel perception of the earth as a single realm of shared experience meant that, for the first time, discrete local observations, such as Joseph Wharton's Philadelphian snow-dust, or Gerard Manley Hopkins's lyrical descriptions of the Krakatau sunsets over the Ribble valley, assumed a contemporary global significance, while encouraging the evolution of a new view of earth as a connected series of natural systems, seismic, volcanic, oceanic, atmospheric, each a potentially fearsome expression of our home planet's relentless energies, perpetually engaged in the pursuit of equilibrium.

Anak Krakatau, meanwhile, is fast turning into an extremely dangerous volcano: an eruption in 1993 claimed the life of one unlucky visitor, and injured another five, while shipping is currently advised to give the island a wide berth, not least because magnetic anomalies cause compasses to behave erratically when passing within a few hundred metres. More alarming still, the island continues to grow at something like six metres (twenty feet) a year, and currently stands at nearly 300 metres (980 feet) high – nearly half as high as its ancestor stood in August 1883, just before it blew itself apart. By the middle of this century, perhaps, the young island will have grown into the image of its eruptive parent; and then it won't be long, at least not in geological terms – perhaps less than a thousand years – before the fiery adolescent has reached eruptive maturity, and will be ready to take over the family business, by detonating all over again.

PART FOUR

WATER

THE HILO TSUNAMI, HAWAII

1946

I

Shortly before seven in the morning on 1 April 1946, the yellow-painted school bus turned off the Hamakua coastal highway, some fifty kilometres (thirty miles) north of the Big Island port of Hilo, and began to descend the steep cliff road leading down to Laupahoehoe Point (see map on p. 185). It was an overcast Monday morning, but the children on board were in a state of some excitement, having spent the journey teasing one another with an escalating series of Fool's Day frauds, so the shouts that came from the row of children sitting at the front – 'Hey, there's no water in the ocean, no water in the ocean!' – were greeted with laughter from the back. One of the older boys, fifteen-year-old ninth-grader Bunji Fujimoto, who was sitting with his brothers, Takeyoshi and Toshiaki, responded: 'What, there's no water in the ocean? April Fool, April Fool!', but as the bus turned the bend at the top of Laupahoehoe cliff, he saw to his surprise that it was true. The sea, which usually came halfway up the boat-ramp at Laupahoehoe Point, really had gone right out, leaving the rock-studded seabed exposed to view for a distance of a hundred metres or more. 'So we looked, and okay, it's funny, but nobody knew what it was', as Fujimoto later recalled; 'it was unusual, something different.'[1]

His class-mate Masuo Kino, who was also on the bus that morning, described how the children couldn't wait to get down the hill for a closer view: 'everybody was really excited, "Hey, this looks real fun"'; but he also described how a group of Hawaiian construction workers, who were doing roadside repairs about a kilometre above the school, tried to stop the bus from descending any further, shouting to the driver 'that the sea was very dangerous, or something to that effect. But that just made us more interested', and since the driver still had another morning run to complete, he chose to ignore the men's advice and continue on his usual route to the waterside school. As soon as the bus pulled in to the entrance, just behind the baseball field that overlooked the ocean, most of the children ran from the bus to see what had happened to the water. By this time there were dozens of children gathered along the shoreline, some of whom had started to venture out across the exposed sea floor, stopping to investigate the contents of the rock pools that had been left behind in the reefs. Bunji Fujimoto, who had just stepped off the bus, joined some of his friends on the playing field near the school entrance, but most of the other children, including his younger brother Toshiaki, and his classmate Masuo Kino, made straight for the beckoning rock pools. 'I walked around for a minute or two looking for anything of interest', recalled Masuo, 'but I didn't find any, so I came back up on the knoll and joined the other boys still standing there.'

It was then that the sea began to return, sweeping in fast and low, 'not the great big wave that people kinda think of', as Fujimoto remembered, 'but like filling a cup with water; when it reaches the brim, it doesn't stop. That's what happened here.'[2] The water came in as far as the road below the school, which 'was, under normal circumstances, quite high. It never came up there before.' But no one was unduly worried, and as the water started to recede once again, Fujimoto remembered thinking, ' "Oh, I guess that's it" . . . to me, wasn't anything to panic about because it wasn't a rolling kind of huge wave that you see or imagine later on.'

Everyone else on the Laupahoehoe shoreline appears to have felt the same way. Even the school teachers, a number of whom lived in a row of wooden cottages overlooking the ocean at the edge of the playing field, seemed unperturbed by the sea's unusual behaviour. In cottage number one, for instance – situated nearest to the school itself – were four young women, all newly qualified *haole*

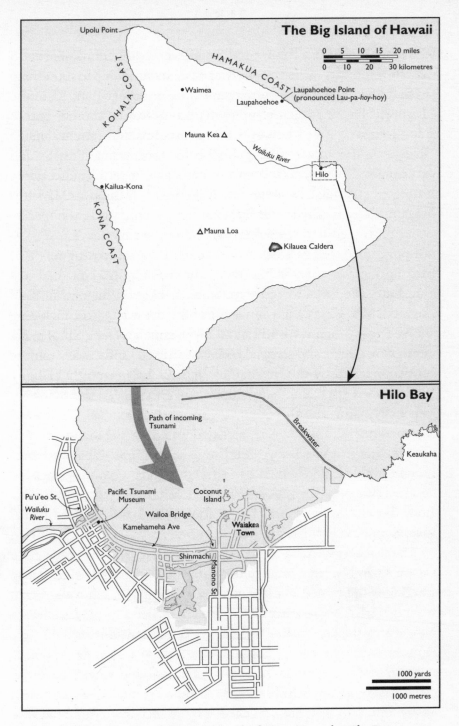

The Big Island of Hawaii

Upolu Point

KOHALA COAST

HAMAKUA COAST

0   5   10   15   20 miles
0   10   20   30 kilometres

• Waimea

Laupahoehoe Point
(pronounced Lau-pa-*hoy*-hoy)

Laupahoehoe •

Mauna Kea △

Wailuku River

Hilo

• Kailua-Kona

KONA COAST

△ Mauna Loa

Kilauea Caldera

Hilo Bay

Path of incoming
Tsunami

Breakwater

Keaukaha

Pu'u'eo St

Pacific Tsunami
Museum

Coconut
Island

*Wailuku
River*

Wailoa Bridge

Kamehameha Ave

Waiakea
Town

Shinmachi

Manono St

1000 yards

1000 metres

Figure iv. Map of the Big Island of Hawaii, with Hilo Bay.

(white) teachers from the United States who had come to Hawaii only a few months earlier, on the first civilian cruise ship to cross the Pacific following the Japanese surrender in September 1945. All four – Dorothy Drake (aged twenty-two), Fay Johnson (twenty-one), Helen Kingseed (twenty-two) and Marsue McGinnis (twenty-one) – had been appointed to Laupahoehoe School during a post-war recruitment drive organized on the mainland in response to staff shortages in schools across Hawaii. 'It was an idyllic spot', as Marsue McGinnis later recalled, 'our little cottage on the beach, the black lava sand, the lazy surf, the eternal spring' (see picture 22). That morning, however, they had been woken before seven by one of their ninth-graders, Daniel Akiona, who, passing by their cottage door, had called out to his form teacher, Helen Kingseed: 'Miss Kingseed, Miss Kingseed, you want to see tidal wave? Come, come quick.' The women were still in their pyjamas, so had quickly put on dressing-gowns and stepped out onto their veranda, where they were confronted by the mysterious sight of an apparently empty Pacific seabed stretching before them, 'as if the ocean had taken a deep, belly-filling mouthful of its own water', as Marsue McGinnis described it. Then, as the teachers stood watching, the first big wave came in, and just like Bunji Fujimoto and his friends, the teachers thought nothing of it. 'The ocean sucked out like a bathtub empty-ing', said Marsue, 'then it came back in and it came up a little bit above the high-water mark. So we looked at that, "That's a tidal wave? Something's wrong here, you know."'

The teachers went back indoors and began to get ready for eight o'clock assembly, but a few minutes later they heard Daniel Akiona shouting to them that another wave was coming in, 'and this one more better!' This second, larger wave had been spotted advanc-ing towards the shore from a point on the distant horizon, but in common with the earlier surge, its landfall proved a disappoint-ment, except to the bands of excited children who were clutching at the pao'o (blenny fish) that were stranded in the shallow pools. 'As the four of us watched', recalled Marsue McGinnis, 'Fred Kruse, a Hawaiian who taught history in the high school, splashed by with

five boys. I shall never forget his beaming smile. "Good fun", he
called to us.' Dorothy and Helen went back inside the cottage
again, but Marsue and Fay, both now dressed in sports shirts and
jeans, stayed out on the veranda, watching the sea retreat once
more, 'fast this time, with a vast, deep sigh. The deep pool just off
the rocks, where we had gone swimming, drained suddenly dry.
Then we both saw it at the same time':

> A tremendous wall of water was gathering out to the left of
> the lighthouse, and for the first time I felt fear, an almost
> paralysing fear . . . I noticed that Fred Kruse and his science
> students were out there on the rocks looking at the uncovered
> sea floor, the seaweed that was uncovered, and he was stand-
> ing out there. This wave just got bigger and bigger. That was
> the first time that anybody around us, anybody, thought to
> be afraid. Here we were, landlubbers, and it never occurred
> to anyone to be afraid.

As the giant wave headed shorewards, everyone who saw it sensed
that this was something different from the earlier incursions.
Masuo Kino, who had wandered back up to the playing field after a
couple of minutes spent exploring the rock pools, was looking out
to sea when he saw the third wave massing on the horizon 'as a
huge wall of water. And it wasn't a beautiful wave like you see in
surfing magazines. It was just a wall of gray, black water. And as we
just stood there and watched it got bigger and bigger and closer and
closer. When it was maybe about 150, 200 yards away, everyone
realized that we were in grave danger. We took off.'

The seaside atmosphere had suddenly vanished, and everywhere there were people running in fear. Fay Johnson and Marsue
McGinnis hurried into their cottage, where the four young women,
after a moment's hesitation, ran towards the back door, which
faced away from the ocean, all thinking the same thought, according to Marsue: 'should we risk the dash across 50 yards of lawn to
the hillside beyond?' But then the wave struck, and 'there was a roar
like all the winds in the world':

I looked back to see brown water fighting at the windows, heard the crash of shattering glass as the windows burst in, and the sharp cracking of parting timbers. The four of us clung to the sides of the doorway as the cottage began to tilt and move. "It's going to tear the cottage down," Helen said. She spoke calmly . . . No one screamed; we just braced our feet against what suddenly became nothing, and then the four of us were thrown into the water. Helen, struggling to keep her head above water, sank right in front of me. I reached down and caught her under the armpit, but the rushing water jerked her from my grasp and she was gone.

A hundred metres further in from the rapidly disintegrating teachers' cottages, the wave caught up with Masuo Kino and his friends, who had been running towards the higher ground just in front of the school. Masuo remembers tripping over a patch of long grass, before 'the wave flipped me over and carried me toward the lava rock wall that rimmed the school. I recall telling myself, "Gee, I'm going to die. I'm going to hit head first into that rock wall, and I'm going to die." ' All around him there were children running and screaming. Bunji Fujimoto, who had been standing near the school entrance when the third wave came, ran right through the school building and out the other side. 'I didn't stop until I got up to the highway, past the church on the hill', he said, while down below, on Laupahoehoe Point, the relentless ocean kept coming. Masuo Kino, who had been picked up by the wave and carried over the lava-block wall, was now 'rumbling along, rolling along with all the rocks. I wasn't high on the wave', he recalled:

I was on the bottom of the wave, and I don't know how high the wave was above me. My friend Seiki Oshiro claims it was over fifty feet, I wouldn't know. But all I know is I was under tons of water and I was getting hit by all these rolling rocks and debris, and I couldn't breathe. I was sixteen, but I guess I knew what mortality meant. I said to myself: "This is it, I'm going to die." And then, miraculously, by the wave action or something, I popped up to the surface of the water, took a breath, and looked around. I was about halfway across the park; and then I saw my good friend, Yoshinobu Sugino from Honohina. He surfed by on a piece of lumber. I don't know where he got a piece of lumber or how he got on it . . .

Masuo was carried far beyond the school buildings, where he was finally able to grab on to a high branch of a guava tree, to which he clung with all his strength as the water surged around him.

Meanwhile, back at the shoreline, the row of teachers' cottages had been completely destroyed by the incoming wave – 'the cottage went *whoomf*!', as McGinnis described it – pitching the women into the flood. Fay and Marsue managed to crawl onto what was left of the roof, which was soon being dragged towards the sea as the water began its retreat. 'Then we saw Dottie's head bobbing among the debris at the far corner of the roof. She was clutching the roof with both hands; her eyes were glazed with fear and panic. I started to inch down towards her, but her hands slipped off the edge and she sank . . . she was just wild-eyed', Marsue recalled; 'I never saw her again, never saw Helen again. Fay and I were holding hands . . . I never saw Fay again. And I thought: this is it, this is the end, and I went down. And it didn't matter how good a swimmer I was, I'm – I'm dead.'

Most of Laupahoehoe Point was now under several metres of water, as more and more waves kept sweeping in over the entire north-east stretch of the Big Island coast, wiping out roads and railway bridges all the way down to Hilo, where the situation was fast becoming even more perilous than at Laupahoehoe School. Kapua Heuer, who lived in a house overlooking Hilo Bay, remembers watching as the relentless wave train crashed into the city, 'hitting buildings, the lighthouse, and the railroad track and everything. And the roar. You could hear it all.

'And I said: "Oh, that's good-bye to Hilo."'

★

II

Even without the incursions of the sea, the people of Hilo (pronounced 'He-low') have always contended with more than their
fair share of water. The rainiest city in the United States, measur-
able precipitation falls on Hilo on an average two hundred and
seventy-eight days of the year, adding up to an annual tally of
some 330 centimetres (130 inches – that's nearly eleven feet), which
lends some credibility to the local saying that no one tans in Hilo,
they rust. It's little wonder that the Hawaiian language features a
hundred and thirty different words for rain.[3]

The reason for all this rain is the city's location on the windward
side of Hawaii, facing the north-easterly trade winds head on. These
winds, having travelled across thousands of kilometres of warm
Pacific ocean – picking up plenty of moisture on the way – hit the
volcanic mountains and lava-cliffs of Hawaii, and are swept upwards
into a colder layer of air. The winds' rapid cooling prompts their
cargo of vapour to condense into clouds, which then proceed to
pour their contents onto the sodden coastline below. The trade
winds, meanwhile, continue moving over the mountains, and by the
time they reach the island's western side, they've deposited almost
all their moisture, so the climate along the Kona coast is corre-
spondingly warm and dry. But it's the clouds and rain – along with
the rich volcanic soil from the island's two great active vents,
Kilauea and Mauna Loa – that make Hawaii such an agricultural
Eden, and the windward side is an extraordinary riot of orchids,
fruit trees and wild sugar cane, a natural bounty alluring enough for
a permanent settlement to have risen beneath the rainclouds.

The Big Island was probably the first of the Hawaiian chain to
be colonized by seafaring Polynesians, some time in the second
or third century AD. It was these early settlers who brought with
them the majority of the plants that would form the heart of the
Hawaiian economy: coconut palms, banana trees and the precious
sugar cane, all deliberate introductions imported by canoe from

Tahiti and the Marquesas by inter-island navigators in search of new land. But the history of the newly colonized islands, divided as they were into a number of separate chiefdoms, was not, as is often imagined, a paradise of uncorrupted living, but a series of long-term internecine wars of an astonishingly violent hue. This situation ended abruptly when a new wave of colonists, this time from Europe, arrived at the end of the eighteenth century. It was they who helped the Big Island king, Kamehameha I (pronounced 'Ka-*may*-ha-*may*-ha'), subdue all seven inhabited islands into the single unified kingdom of Hawaii. By the time he died in 1819, however, Kamehameha's ambitions had played directly into the hands of his foreign protectors, whose military presence, along with the tireless efforts of numerous North American missionaries, led to the United States' political and spiritual domination of the islands. The ancient Polynesian religion, with its complex system of laws and taboos, was replaced by Christianity within the space of a single generation, while the introduction of market capitalism by European and American traders saw many of the islanders abandon subsistence fishing and farming in favour of paid labour, beginning with the sandalwood trade in the 1790s, and then moving on to sugar in the 1830s. It soon became apparent that only large-scale plantations could exploit the economic potential of far-flung Hawaii, and by the 1840s most of the land along the Hamakua coast, a hilly stretch of rainforest running north-west from Hilo, had been converted into vast fields of cultivated cane.

It was the American Civil War that ensured the survival of Hawaii's newest industry, since the populous Northern states could no longer source their sugar from the South. The boom in Hawaiian production during the following decades led to an enormous influx of overseas labour, since there weren't enough native Hawaiians to work the sprawling plantations. Chinese field-workers were the first to arrive, during the early 1850s, followed by countless boat-loads of Japanese, Koreans, Filipinos, Scandinavians, Austrians, Puerto Ricans, Spaniards, Russians and Portuguese (mostly from the volcanic islands of Madeira and the Azores), all of whom arrived in Hilo port, destined for the plantation-camps of the Hamakua coast.* Plantation workers were usually indentured for a five-year term, by the end of which many had saved just enough money to go into business for themselves. While some chose to make the return journey home, most ended up staying in Hawaii, with those who had worked along the Hamakua coast tending to gravitate to Hilo. The city's ever-growing shops, bars, hotels, restaurants, cinemas, laundries, taxi firms and brothels were owned and run for the most part by ex-plantation workers, whose customers were drawn from the thousands of current plantation workers who descended on Hilo every weekend in order to spend their pay (see picture 23).

By the 1930s the Japanese formed Hilo's largest immigrant community, the majority of whom had settled on the banks of the Wailoa River, creating Waiakea Town on the east bank first, before developing the larger township known as Shinmachi (from the Japanese for 'new town') on the marshier flood plain to the west (see map on p. 185). By the time the Second World War broke out, working-class Shinmachi had become the heart of modern Hilo, with dozens of restaurants, shops and temples punctuating the narrow rows of dark wooden houses that had been built on stilts

---

* When Laupahoehoe School opened in 1883 to provide an education for the plantation workers' children, it must have been one of the most culturally diverse institutions in the world. Marsue McGinnis recalled the many Japanese and Filipino weddings to which she and her fellow teachers were invited, as well as the scores of Japanese, Chinese, Portuguese and Korean children who passed through the school every day. By then, these various outside cultures had integrated with Polynesian island culture to produce an alluring mix that the post-war world would embrace as uniquely Hawaiian. The Madeirans, for example, had introduced the four-stringed guitar known as the *braginha*, which, in response to the rhythms of Pacific island music, soon evolved into the better-known ukulele (a Hawaiian word meaning 'jumping flea'), and which is now, alongside the steel guitar (invented in Oahu in 1889), the most popular musical instrument in the Pacific. (The jumping flea itself, by contrast, along with the mosquito and the rat, was a far less welcome cultural introduction, having been deposited by American whaling ships on route from Alaska to the East.) The ubiquitous short-sleeved 'aloha shirt', meanwhile, had been improvised by Chinese tailors in Honolulu, and was mass-produced as a cruise-ship souvenir from the 1930s onwards, using pre-printed kimono silk imported from Japan.

along the flood plain. It was, by all accounts, an extraordinary place
– 'those were the days when people had little money, but lived', as
one former resident recalled – with its own weekly newspaper and
grand Theatre Royal, as well as, right in the centre, the Coca-Cola
bottling plant, one of the largest employers on that side of the
island, as well as the only concrete structure for many miles around.

When Japan launched its dawn raid on the American fleet at Pearl
Harbor on 7 December 1941, not only did the attack bring the
United States into the Second World War, it also had an immediate impact on the Japanese community in Hawaii. By that same
Sunday evening over a hundred Japanese civilians had been arrested
in Hilo alone, mostly on suspicion of having assisted the enemy in
preparing the attack. Over the next few months nearly two thousand Japanese Hawaiians were dispatched to internment camps
on the American mainland, including many of the tuna-fishermen
of Waiakea Town, whose fleet of radio-controlled sampans had
roused the suspicions of United States military intelligence. Soon,
every aspect of life in Hilo was conducted under military supervision, with an 8 p.m. curfew, barbed-wire fences around the city's
major buildings and military policemen on foot patrols, enforcing
martial law. The internments and blackout restrictions caused
widespread suffering across the Hawaiian islands, although they did
give rise to occasional moments of classic military absurdity. One
April afternoon in 1942, for instance, the giant volcano Mauna Loa
staged one of its periodic slow eruptions, but the US authorities
declared the event a military secret, on the grounds that their troops
might be disheartened to learn that a river of lava fifteen metres
(fifty feet) wide was creeping down the hill towards Hilo barracks.
But word got out when the Army Air Corps started bombing
the lava in a last-ditch attempt to divert its flow, their efforts only
giving rise to a new column of lava that ran parallel to the original,
before joining up with it further down the slope. Hilo was now
on evacuation standby, while 'Tokyo Rose' – the English-speaking
voice of Japanese propaganda – was radioing 'congratulations to

Hawaii on its fine volcanic eruption!' to thousands of American troops stationed throughout the Pacific.[4] By 7 May, the lava stood only eighteen kilometres (eleven miles) from downtown Hilo, at which point it stopped in its tracks, as abruptly as it had begun, and the Secret Eruption of Mauna Loa was over.

Following the destruction of Hiroshima and Nagasaki in early August 1945, and the Japanese surrender of 2 September, thousands of Japanese-American servicemen and internees returned home to resume their lives as best they could. Among the many Hawaiian veterans was Richard Miyashiro, born in Hilo to Japanese parents who had left Okinawa at the turn of the century to work in the Hamakua sugar fields. After the attack on Pearl Harbor, Miyashiro volunteered for the US Army, and was sent to Italy with the 100th Battalion of the 442nd Regimental Combat Team, a unit composed exclusively of Japanese-Americans, and the most decorated in US Army history – Miyashiro himself had received one of the unit's 9,500 Purple Hearts, the medal awarded to servicemen wounded or killed in action.

Soon after his return, Richard and his wife Evelyn bought the Sakura Café on the corner of Kamehameha Avenue and Manono Street, next to the Wailoa Bridge, and renamed it the Café 100 in honour of his old battalion. The café quickly established itself as the favourite meeting place of Hilo's many veterans, as well as the eating place for the famous 'loco moco', Richard Miyashiro's own invention, an extraordinary East–West culinary fusion involving a bowl of rice topped with a hamburger and a fried egg, drenched in a sticky brown sauce. Richard and Evelyn's Café 100 proved an immediate commercial and cultural success, and the couple, who lived above the premises, became well-known characters in the post-war Hawaiian scene.

But the Miyashiros' idyll was not to last for long. Just before 7 a.m., on Monday 1 April 1946, three months on from the café's grand opening, the couple were woken by a series of shouts coming from the street outside: 'Tidal wave, tidal wave, tidal wave!' They hurried downstairs and onto Kamehameha Avenue, but the only visible evidence of the wave that had passed was a few enormous puddles in the road, and a crush of people, some of whom had started to run inland, while others crowded onto the Wailoa Bridge, looking out to sea in some excitement. Richard and Evelyn (who was then six months pregnant with her first of three children) decided to join the crowd on the bridge in order to see what was happening in the bay.

A few minutes later their curiosity was rewarded by an unusually brisk wave that came powering up the Wailoa River, passing noisily under the bridge before turning the corner towards the Shinmachi flood plain, pursued by a large volume of discoloured water. Like the teachers in the cottage down at Laupahoehoe Point, who had also just watched this second wave arrive, Richard was, in truth, a little disappointed – as were some of the others on the crowded bridge, among whom were Alexander Riviera, the son of a Puerto Rican plantation worker, and his best friend Katsuyoshi Hayashida, known to his schoolmates as 'Kats'. The two fifteen-year-olds had been on their way to Hilo High School via Kats's house near the Wailoa Bridge, and had walked past Café 100 as they did every morning on their way downtown. But that morning was destined to be different, as Alexander later recalled. 'People was saying "Tidal wave! Tidal wave! No go school, tidal wave!", but what I going know about tidal wave? I don't even know what a tsunami is . . . I say, "Ah, those guys they pulling my leg again", so I went across the bridge', where he and Kats stood in the crowd, watching as the water in the Wailoa River began its rapid retreat. 'It was very, very unusual', he remembered. 'I look down and see the boats going out . . . I could see the bottom.' But he and Kats had no idea what any of this might mean, and no notion – at least not yet – that there was any reason to be afraid. 'It didn't dawn on me – maybe it's because I was so young – it didn't dawn on me that this was really going to be a catastrophe.'

★

On a bridge at the other side of town, meanwhile, a couple of kilometres west of Wailoa, a near-identical chain of events was unfolding. A young local policeman, Robert 'Steamy' Chow, was about to go on morning duty, and so shortly before 7 a.m. he had reversed his car out of his driveway onto Ohai Street, just over the Wailuku River from downtown Hilo. (The hills behind Hilo get so much rain that two separate rivers, the Wailuku and the Wailoa, flow through the city to the sea). As he turned right into Pu'u'eo Street, someone called out to him, '"Hey, Steamy, tidal wave", so I said, "Yeah, April Fool's," "No, real, real", so I say, "Yeah, April Fool's"', but as he drove over the Pu'u'eo Bridge and looked to his left towards the open ocean, he saw that a section of the railway bridge had collapsed into the water at the mouth of the river, and was being thrown about by the surf. The morning's first wave, which had caused very little in the way of damage else-where along the Big Island coast, had funnelled into the mouth of the Wailuku River and smashed into the bridge with some force. A large crowd of people who had gathered on the road were pointing at the ruined structure.

Alarmed by what he'd just seen, Chow headed downtown to the police headquarters, where, after changing into his con-stable's uniform, he was assigned to work the bay-front area along Kamehameha Avenue. He climbed into his patrol car, and was turning it around in the station car park, when what appeared to be another, larger wave, came roaring in from the sea. 'That's when people panic', he recalled. 'And I mean people didn't care if a car was coming or not, they just kept on running. So the only thing for me to do is just stop and let the people run.' But it wasn't only people who were suddenly on the move: 'all of a sudden I noticed the bridge that was in the water was floating upstream. It missed the Pu'u'eo Bridge by inches . . . and the same time, water came underneath my car and I was surrounded with water. And I had that eerie feeling, you don't know if you're going to be washed away or not. But I just held on and nothing happened.'

After a few tense minutes, during which his car was rocked on its wheels by the force of the retreating water, Constable Chow got out and headed back across the bridge on foot. He noticed that the Wailuku River, which only a few minutes earlier had been the scene of an incoming flood, was now virtually empty, with 'maybe six to ten inches of water at the bottom.' But all this was about to change once more as the third wave came racing in from the open ocean, 'just like a big block of ice moving towards land, and when it hit the bridge, just like everything exploded' – though by the time that happened, 'Steamy' Chow, along with everyone else from the Pu'u'eo Bridge, was running inland fast (see pictures 24 and 25).

That third wave smashed through an entire row of buildings along the bay-front section of Kamehameha Avenue, before surging up the slope into town for a hundred metres or more. Those who survived a close encounter with it would never forget its awesome power. One of them was sixteen-year-old Jimmy Low, who was driving his father's car, a Model 'A' Ford, on his first day in his new job, buying provisions for the family restaurant, the Sun Sun Lau Chop Sui House on downtown Kamehameha Avenue. Jimmy was driving extremely carefully, as he'd had to work hard to convince his parents that he was safe behind the wheel of his father's precious car. But he hadn't got far that Monday morning when a policeman stopped him, 'yelling out of his car for me to get out of there. Well, he used different language from what I said, "You get out of there!"' Jimmy nervously stopped the car, wondering what he might have done wrong, until he looked across the street towards the moving ocean and realized what the policeman had been trying to say:

> I couldn't believe my eyes because here was this huge, huge wave, nothing that I've ever seen in my life. It was like a wall of water that was rising in the bay and it was just rolling in towards the buildings. But I was still thinking to myself at that time – you know it happened so fast you didn't have enough time to kind of think – I was trying to figure out why the policeman yelled at me. So by the time I saw that wave it was already against the building that was on that block. So I turned

into the service station to try and make a u-turn to get out of there.

But in the short time it took him to turn the car around, the wall of water was already on him, and suddenly he was trapped inside the vehicle: 'I was neck deep in water and half petrified because I didn't know what to do, you know, I was in shock. And so I sat there for a while.' But when Jimmy felt the submerged car begin to move, as the water lifted it from the forecourt and out towards the flooded road, 'it kind of woke me up':

> I immediately jumped out of the car through the window, climbed through the window. A Model 'A', it's easy to get out of. I don't know if I could have opened the door or not because we were just under water. Anyway, I jumped out through the window, and I struggled to a fence that was between Island Motors and Moto's Inn. There was this little fence in there, about a ten-foot high fence. I climbed over the fence and ended up on the back side of Island Motors . . .

Soaking wet, bewildered by shock and having lost his shoes as well as his father's most prized possession – and all on his very first day in the job – Jimmy limped along the street towards home, worried more about the scolding he was certain he'd receive than the tsunami that had just engulfed the town.

Back on the crowded Wailoa Bridge, Anthony Riviera and his best friend Kats had also just encountered the terrifying sight of the third wave coming straight for them: 'I seen that wave coming', as Anthony recalled: 'Was very, very big. It seemed as though – just like it was boiling . . . boy, I'm telling you, it was the biggest and ugliest thing because it was black. It was black, see, the water over there is black because you have black sand beach. And it's all you saw, was this big black thing coming in. So I told Kats, "Kats, we gotta run! I don't know if we going to make it." ' The boys ran for their lives up Manono Street, looking back when they heard the wave smash into the Wailoa Bridge with a 'Boom! A terrific sound. Like an explosion. We could see the bridge, you know. Brrm, brrm. The bridge was broken on both sides.' They watched as the tsunami flooded buildings on both sides of the bridge, including the three-month-old Café 100, and then they saw the rows of wooden houses – including Kats's family home – swept clean off their stilts by the surge. Suddenly it seemed as if the whole of Hilo was under violent attack from the sea (picture 26).

In contrast to the two schoolboys, who had started to run as soon as they saw the giant wave approach, the Miyashiros were transfixed by fear as the wave came powering towards the bridge, but they both managed to cling to one of the concrete pillars as the water surged all around them. Some of the people at the front of the bridge were swept into the maelstrom below, disappearing into the blackened water, though Richard and Evelyn, holding on tight, were able to withstand the wave.

The inundation of the Wailoa Bridge was witnessed by a small crowd of people who had climbed onto the roof of the Coca-Cola bottling plant, among whom was Masao Uchima, a seventeen-year-old senior at Hilo High School, who was still in bed when the first wave came, but whose father had been quick to recognize the pattern of events unfolding in Hilo Bay. 'He's from Okinawa, Japan', as Masao later recalled; 'they experience a lot of tidal waves, and he knew that that's the only type of building can sustain the force of that kind of tidal wave; so he went on top of the Coca-Cola building, on the roof, and started to yell at all the people around the neighbourhood, you know, to come up to the building, because that was the only safest building.' Dozens of people joined him there, including his son Masao, and together they witnessed the widespread destruction as the second and then the third waves hammered into the town below:

And another wave came, the second wave. And we saw people was in the river going up and down . . . and you trying to help them, go for rescue, but you can't because the river itself – the current – was strong. And there was no way you actually can help them. And a lot of families, like I said, were in the river being swept away and all that. You hear people screaming for help, and it was really an eerie feeling. You know, more like – really hard to explain. You hear people, adults, yelling for help, and some people just screaming, and you can hear screams and cries. And I mean, really, you want to help them, but there's no way that you can help them because you weren't prepared. There were no ropes, no boat, you know, things like that . . . in the meantime the third wave was coming. That's the hugest wave so far – it was coming again, and we're on the roof, and we saw this. So huge the wave that we were afraid that the wave was gonna come onto the roof.

The third wave did reach as high as the roof, although the fact that the plant was built of solid concrete saved it from structural damage; but the water carried on round it, 'rumbling in like a bull-dozer', as Masao described it, crashing into the surrounding houses – 'the cottages just deteriorated like a matchbox, you know' – scattering their contents across the drowning landscape as the black waters raced inland for a kilometre or more, with the entire weight of the Pacific Ocean behind them. Masao remembers seeing one of his neighbours, who had been trapped in her house by the waters of the second wave, 'and when the third wave came, that house just started to float away, and from the window, she was like saying goodbye, waving. And that's the last we seen or we heard.'

When the wave finally started to retreat, many of the surviving Shinmachi residents were left struggling in the water. Among them was twenty-three-year-old Fusae Takaki, who had been just about to leave for work in the nearby soy-sauce factory when her mother hurried home from a neighbour's house, saying: 'Tsunami ga kiyoru!' ('A tsunami is coming!'); a few seconds later the third wave struck, smashing the family house into pieces and flinging Fusae and her mother into the sudden raging surf:

Mama and I, we were in the water already. Then we were covered up with houses, all pieces of houses right above my head. I was buried. I saw Mom swimming, I looked in the back and

Mama was swimming. She told me when she was in Fukuoka Prefecture [in Japan] she used to go out swimming, so she knew how to swim. So when I look at her I say, "Oh Mom, you all right. Keep on swimming and we'll be okay." But as soon as I thought of that we both were buried under the wreckage of the buildings all in pieces. And I thought, I hope Mom didn't get hurt. Because you die if you hit your head and you unconscious, there's no way you can get up.

But the current was so strong that Fusae soon lost sight of her mother, and now she was alone, struggling to keep afloat amid the swirling wreckage as the incoming surge dragged her further inland. She kept choking on the water – 'stinking kerosene dirty water' – and more than once her head was held under by the weight of the moving debris. She was certain she was going to drown:

And I thought to myself, this is what you call death. I'm not afraid to die when the time comes. Well, if I'm going to die I'm going to say my last prayer. And I thought Christian was the easiest way to die, say "Amen" and that's all. But I said "*Namu amida butsu, namu amida butsu*" [a Buddhist mantra] three times. Not one time, you know, I said it three times. When I said the third one my body went up and I looked around, "Ah, I can see by myself now, I'm up now." So I swam.

Eventually Fusae made it back onto dry land, more than a kilometre away from where her house had once stood, but her mother was nowhere to be seen. She looked all around for her, with no success, before staggering to a nearby doctor's surgery, where, a few years before, she had worked as an administrator. After receiving treatment herself, she spent the rest of the morning helping at the surgery, tending to the stream of casualties that kept arriving, asking each of them in turn if they had heard any news of her mother. It wasn't until later in the afternoon that she learned that her mother's body had been found floating near the Coca-Cola bottling plant – the only structure still standing amid the waterlogged ruins of Shinmachi.

Meanwhile, just off Laupahoehoe Point, some fifty kilometres (thirty miles) up the coast, the young schoolteacher Marsue Mc-Ginnis was slowly drifting further out to sea. Two hours earlier she had been clinging to the roof of the oceanside cottage she had shared with her three colleagues, but now she was alone in the fast-moving sea, in pain from the injuries she had received when the outgoing wave dragged her over a reef of pahoehoe lava.* The impact had driven the roof-timbers apart, pitching Marsue into the water, but the sea beyond the reef was full of smaller pieces of debris – 'trees and boards and everything' – and she had been able to grab hold of a floating plank and pull herself half out of the water: 'I thought, every bone in my body must be broken. But I could tread water and my arms moved. And I said, "Well, nothing's broken; I'm bruised but not broken." And I kind of clung on to this.' Her next priority had been to move away from the rocks in case another big wave came and dragged her towards them, so she paddled further out with the wreckage-strewn current until she was too exhausted to go on.

By now it had started to rain, and the ocean was growing colder and rougher the further out Marsue drifted. Worse, she had bitten through her lower lip earlier in the day, and it had swollen so badly she could no longer close her mouth. Every few minutes a swell would duck her under the water, and she'd swallow a mouthful, before retching it up at the surface.

It must have been some time in the early afternoon that she caught sight of other survivors stranded in the water, a hundred

---

* There are two kinds of lava produced by Big Island volcanoes, the local terms for which, *a'a* and *pahoehoe* (pronounced 'ah-ah' and 'pa-*hoy*-hoy'), are now used worldwide in lava classification. A'a is the rough, sharp, clinker-like variety, while pahoehoe (from which the settlement of Laupahoehoe took its name) resembles coils of silvery-grey rope.

or so metres away. 'I counted seven of them', she recalled: 'Some were clinging to remains of broken buildings; two were holding on to an uprooted *lauhala* tree. "Hey!" I yelled. But they didn't shout back – they just stared as if in a coma.' All seven were children from Laupahoehoe School.

Marsue was now completely certain that she was going to die out there in the darkening water, and as evening descended she found herself increasingly preoccupied by her strong conviction – now renewed beyond all doubt – that there truly is no God. 'This is something that was very important to me at the time', as she later explained in her interview with Warren Nishimoto (of the University of Hawaii's Center for Oral History), 'and it was very important to me when I had boyfriends or dates and everything, that they felt the same way':

> But there were a lot of military men, men we met on the boat, in the navy and the marines who were up there and we had a lot of contact with them. And they'd say, "Oh, you say that now but just wait till you're faced with death and then you'll pray, you'll go back to God, you know there is . . ." But I said "No." So here I was, faced with death, I knew I was going to die. And I still knew there was no God. And I couldn't tell anybody. That was really one of my main thoughts: I couldn't tell anybody.

Just as Fusae Takaki's repetition of the Buddhist mantra '*Namu amida butsu*' seemed to give her the strength to overcome the wave, so Marsue's vigorous atheism seemed to help her maintain her spirits as darkness fell across the sea. She was shaking with cold, and growing weaker by the minute, when suddenly she became aware of a navy seaplane, flying low, 'and he was going around like this, and going around, and I kept going like this (waving), but he didn't buzz his motor, he didn't dip down, he didn't do anything for about – it seemed to me like forever.' Finally the seaplane dropped a bundle into the water, and Marsue struggled painfully towards it: 'Stencilled on it in large black letters were the simple instructions:

"To inflate, unsnap and pull handle." That's all there was to it. Swish! Like magic the raft inflated and I climbed aboard.'[5]

The last survivors to make it back to shore were three boys from Laupahoehoe School – Asao Kuniyuki, Herbert Nishimoto and Takashi Takemoto – who had spent the whole day clinging to wreckage as they drifted slowly northwards towards Upolu Point. Late in the afternoon, one of the US Navy seaplanes had spotted the boys, and dropped a rubber life raft into the sea, but by then they were too exhausted to paddle it to shore, so they kept drifting as night began to fall – a strangely peaceful experience, as Herbert

SEISMIC WAVE HAVOC

MANY DEATHS IN HAWAII

FROM OUR OWN CORRESPONDENT

NEW YORK, APRIL 2

First fears that thousands of lives had been lost yesterday when huge waves created by an earthquake in the ocean bed off Alaska swept a great part of the eastern Pacific have happily not been borne out, and it seems likely now that the number

of dead will not much exceed 200, if it rises that high. The total of known dead as late as mid-afternoon to-day was still under 100, but scores of persons are still missing.

Most of the known dead—60 out of the 93 reported—are at Hilo, in the Hawaiian Islands, where the waves struck hardest and where property damage ran into millions of dollars.

Figure v. Newspapers around the world reported the event within twenty-four hours. As is clear from this article, from the London *Times* for 3 April 1946, there was no mystery over the cause of the tsunami, a powerful undersea earthquake in the Aleutian Trench.

Nishimoto later recalled – and by the following dawn they were in sight of the north Kohala coast, sixty or seventy kilometres (forty miles) north-west of Laupahoehoe Point. The seaplane was circling again, some distance away (in fact it was picking up Daniel Akiona's mother, who had floated all night on a cottage door); a few hours later, the boys in the dinghy finally made landfall, having been in the water for twenty-eight hours, refugees from a disaster that had claimed the lives of sixteen of their classmates and four of their teachers, as well as another hundred and thirty-nine people along the devastated coastline of Hawaii.

III

Once the waters around Hawaii had finally calmed down, the people of Hilo ventured into town to find a scene of total devastation (see picture 27). The waves, powering inland at more than a hundred kilometres per hour, had swept eight-tonne blocks from the stone breakwater and hurled them into the bay-front area, smashing through the wood-framed buildings like a naval cannonade. Almost all the buildings along the seaward side of Kamehameha Avenue had been pushed twenty metres (sixty-five feet) across the road and crushed against the buildings on the opposite side. Nearly five hundred shops and houses had been completely destroyed, with a further thousand sustaining serious damage; many of the coastal region's bridges, railway lines, roads and docks had also been put out of action; the total cost of damage was estimated to be more than $26 million.

By the following day, however, a relief operation swung into action across the whole of Hilo and the surrounding area under the stewardship of General George F. Moore, Commanding General of Army Forces in the Pacific. When the general – a survivor of the 1942 Bataan death march – arrived to take charge of the operation, he was quoted in the press as saying, 'This is incredible – I didn't

imagine it was this bad',* and he ordered tanks, bulldozers and
rubber life rafts to be brought in to help survivors cross the still-
flooded remnants of Shinmachi and Keaukaha. Meanwhile, teams
of volunteers from across Hawaii, from Boy Scouts to members of
the International Longshore and Warehouse Union, set about the
awesome task of clearing the ruined city (see picture 28).

But first there was the upsetting business of dealing with the
bodies of the victims. The town morgue soon ran out of space, so
the majority of the dead were sent to a commercial icehouse to
await identification. The policeman Robert Chow recalled being
asked to look in at the icehouse later that afternoon, where he was
shocked to find that many of the corpses had already started to
decompose. 'I couldn't identify the bodies', he remembered, 'but
it was real sickening to see small ones, several years old, among
the victims. You could smell the decomposed body – I was told
later that salt water causes it to decompose faster.' Masao Uchima
also remembered being asked to identify some of his Shinmachi
neighbours, but found it next to impossible 'because of the facial
expression or the terror in the face or whatever, and the hair is not
combed, the face is discolored, you know, bluish and white . . . so
even if you know the person it's kind of hard to identify because of
the condition they're in.'

As always seems to happen after major disasters, competing
stories of miraculous survival soon began to circulate. One particularly striking tale involved the Kuwahara Store building, the only
bay-front structure on Kamehameha Avenue to survive the inundation. A few days before the tsunami, according to the story, an
elderly Hawaiian woman had shuffled into the store and asked
the owner if he could spare her some food. The shopkeeper, Mr

---

* This was a sentiment that was later recalled by the American Foreign Secretary
Colin Powell after a helicopter flight over the tsunami-stricken province of Banda Aceh
in January 2005: 'I've been in war and I've been through a number of hurricanes, tor-
nadoes and other relief operations', said Powell, 'but I've never seen anything like this'
(*Guardian*, 6 January 2005).

the Red Cross coming to the school to see if anything could be done. 'What can they do, eh?' There were funerals for those who were found, a memorial service for those who weren't and plans were put in place for the school to be relocated higher up the hill, which happened, eventually, in 1952. 'The wheels of the legislature turn slowly', observed Masuo Kino, who had graduated from the original school building in 1947, where now only the playing field is left, along with a memorial tablet built at the edge of the abandoned site, overlooking the ocean, inscribed with the names and ages of the twenty-four children and adults who were lost at Laupahoehoe Point (picture 29).

The origin of the waves that had smashed into the Hawaiian coast lay more than 3,700 kilometres (2,300 miles) away, on the northern slope of the Aleutian Trench, a 3,200-kilometre (2,000-mile) subduction zone that curves along the Alaska Peninsula. Here, the northern edge of the Pacific plate creeps beneath a section of the North American plate at a rate of nearly four centimetres (one and a half inches) per year, causing regular earthquakes and volcanic eruptions along the length of the Aleutian Island chain. As is the case along the Java Trench, the majority of these near-continuous tremors cause little in the way of damage or disruption, but the minute-long shallow-focus earthquake that occurred at 12:29 GMT (2:29 a.m. local time) on 1 April 1946 was fated to be different. Measuring 7.8 on the recently devised Richter scale, its vibrations appear to have triggered an underwater landslide several kilometres east of the earthquake's epicentre, which in turn generated a powerful tsunami that radiated through the surrounding water. Forty minutes later, the southern shore of Unimak Island, 144 kilometres (90 miles) north of the epicentre, was hit by a thirty-metre (hundred-foot) wave of displaced water, the force of which destroyed the newly built Scotch Cap Lighthouse, killing all five members of its crew. The lighthouse, which had only been in operation since 1940, was a five-storey reinforced-concrete installation that had been specifically designed to cope with the regular storm

surges and undersea earthquakes that batter that stretch of the
Alaska Peninsula, but it proved no match for the massive tsunami,
which swept the structure clear from the rocks.

Meanwhile, the shockwaves continued south through the open
ocean, picking up speed as they headed into deeper waters. Soon
they were racing across the Pacific at nearly 800 kilometres (500
miles) per hour in the form of a wave train, a series of distinct vibrations, the shallow crests of which were now some hundred kilometres apart. The waves reduced in height as they entered deeper
waters, but even in the form of high-speed ripples they lost none of
their destructive potential. In contrast to typical wind-driven surface
waves, in which only the top layer of water is disturbed (and much
of the wave energy is thereby lost through surface friction), tsunami
waves are as deep as the ocean itself, since they are usually created
by the displacement of an entire water column, shifted from the sea
floor up. Their greater depth means that hardly any wave energy is
lost through friction – in fact far from losing their impetus at sea,
tsunami waves actually *gain* speed as the water deepens, flattening
out at mid-ocean into a series of imperceptible pulses that race at
the speed of a jet airliner until they begin to approach land, where
the shelving coastline and shallower waters give rise to increased
levels of friction that effectively slam on the brakes. As in a motor-
way pile-up, the sudden shoaling at the front slows down the leading edges of the waves, so the rear sections suddenly catch up,
shunting into the stalled water, transforming the tsunami from (in
this instance) a sequence of 800-kilometre-an-hour trans-oceanic
ripples into 200-kilometre-an-hour walls of water advancing onto
the Hawaiian shoreline, five hours on from the distant scene of the
originating submarine earthquake.*

---

* Although the Lisbon earthquake and the Krakatau eruption both caused tsunamis to
form, these would have travelled much more slowly than the Aleutian Islands tsunami,
due to the shallower waters through which they passed. Much of the Pacific Ocean is
c. 4,500 metres + (15,000–20,000 feet) deep, while the average depth of the Atlantic is
c. 3,300 metres (11,000 feet), and that of the Sunda Strait less than 110 metres (360 feet).

As is clear from the eyewitness testimonies, the Fool's Day tsunami took the majority of Hawaiians completely by surprise, even though tsunamis are a familiar feature of Pacific island life, the oral and written cultures of which are replete with the kinds of detailed observations that derive from centuries of exposure to the sea. The Hawaiian word for tsunami, for example – *kai e'e* – refers specifically to the mountainous appearance of the incoming wave, and is distinct from both *kai hohonu*, the Hawaiian term for a high tide, and *kai ea*, an unusually fast-rising sea; there is even a term for the characteristic withdrawal of the water that occurs before each wave – *kai mimiki*.[6]

Hawaiian folktales bear similar witness to a long history of tsunami observation. One such story tells of an illicit affair between the reigning chieftain, King Konikonia, and a mer-woman who lived in the sea off Waiakea. The woman was persuaded ashore by the love-struck king, who took her to live in his waterside palace, but the next day she warned him that her angry brothers were likely to come and take her home by force. These brothers, she explained, were *pao'o* (blenny fish), and in order to get across the beach to the palace, they would seek help from an incoming sea; ten days later, according to the legend, 'the ocean rose and overwhelmed the land from one end to the other', until it reached the door of King Konikonia's palace, from where the mer-woman was seized by a shoal of her brother-fish, while many of Konikonia's unfortunate subjects were swept out to sea to their deaths. Hilo Bay was quickly abandoned, but some years later survivors of the king's tsunami began to return and resettle the area, vowing never to anger the ocean or its inhabitants again.[7]

The tsunami created by the Lisbon earthquake would thus have travelled at around 300–400 kilometres per hour, while those generated by Krakatau would have travelled at about 120 kph (70 mph). But as we have seen, even these less powerful tsunamis carry enormous destructive potential, while their relatively slow transit speeds are, of course, still too fast to outrun.

In spite of their vow, coastal Hawaiians remain highly susceptible to long-range tsunamis generated along the Aleutian Trench, as well as those from the west coast of Chile – another troublesome subduction zone, created, in this case, by the eastern edge of the Nazca plate as it dives beneath the South American plate at around seven centimetres per year, causing frequent earthquakes and volcanic eruptions all along the 7,000-kilometre (4,400-mile) Andean mountain chain. Chile itself is routinely battered by powerful offshore earthquakes, which, due to the particular movements of the subduction zone, send irregular tsunamis speeding out across the Pacific Ocean. Of all the islands positioned within the Pacific tsunami flight path, the Hawaiian group, and especially the Big Island, remains the most vulnerable, being largely unprotected by intervening coral reefs and atolls – in contrast to the more fortunate Tahiti islands, some 4,000 kilometres to the south, which are virtually tsunami-proof, surrounded as they are by uninhabited atolls and reefs, that, like the mangrove swamps of the Indian Ocean, do much to absorb long-period wave energy (or do when they are left in their natural state – which is reason enough to preserve them from the ongoing destruction that continues to be their fate).

Since the early nineteenth century, when written records began, the Hawaiian islands have suffered the effects of at least a dozen trans-Pacific tsunamis, the majority of which originated from earthquakes off the coasts of Chile, Japan and the Aleutians:

Date	Source	Description
1819 (12 April)	Chile	The earliest recorded tsunami on Hawaii; extent of damage unknown.
1835 (20 February)	Chile	Moderate damage.
1837 (7 November)	Chile	A severe tsunami; fourteen people killed in Hilo, two on Maui. Wave height 6 metres (20 feet). Many houses and livestock washed away.

Date	Source	Description
1868 (2 April)	Hawaii	A tsunamigenic earthquake SE of the Big Island killed forty-seven people; thirty-one others were killed in a land slide. The wave reached heights of 18 metres (60 feet).
1868 (13–14 August)	Chile	Severe damage and flooding caused by *c.* 4-metre (12–15-foot) waves. Oscillations continued for three days.
1869 (25 July)	Prob. Chile	Tsunami came ashore in Hilo and Puna, destroying houses and two kilometres of shoreline road.
1877 (10 May)	Chile	Severe tsunami (which also struck Japan), destroyed every house near the mouth of the Wailoa River in Hilo, killing five people. Waves reached 4.2 metres (14 feet).
1883 (26–27 August)	Krakatau	Small waves reached Hawaii, but no damage caused there. Nearly forty thousand killed in Indonesia.
1896 (15 June)	Japan	Twenty-seven thousand killed by 30-metre (100-foot) waves in Sanriku, Japan; the waves reached Hawaii, but caused little in the way of damage.
1906 (16 August)	Chile	Valparaiso earthquake sent 3.6-metre (12-foot) waves which damaged the south coast of Maui.
1923 (3 February)	Kamchatka	Kuril Trench earthquake sent a powerful tsunami that killed one person in Hilo, and caused $1.5 million worth of damage. Waves reached 6 metres (20 feet) in Hilo.
1933 (2 March)	Japan	5-metre (17-foot) waves reached the Big Island from an earthquake in Sanriku, Japan.

So why, given the islanders' close familiarity with the characteristic behaviour of long-range tsunamis, was there no inkling of the
disaster to come on the morning of 1 April 1946? One factor may
have been the much-reduced status of indigenous culture, which –
as was also the case in the Dutch East Indies – made it difficult for
those who actually recognized the danger signs to make their voices
heard. The team of Hawaiian road-workers at Laupahoehoe Point,
for example, had noticed the first *kai mimiki*, and knew it portended
a dangerous sea, but had been unable to persuade the school bus
driver not to continue his journey to the shore.

But theirs was not the only kind of local knowledge to have
been disastrously overlooked, for twenty-three years earlier a
Hawaiian volcanologist named Thomas A. Jaggar had attempted to
introduce a tsunami warning system, based on the traces of distant
earthquakes that registered on his office seismograph. Had Jaggar's
insights been attended to – much of the necessary technology was
already in place – Hawaii would have had several hours to prepare
for the Fool's Day tsunami.

The inception of the warning system can be dated to the
morning of 3 February 1923, when Jaggar, Director of the Hawaiian
Volcano Observatory (founded on the slopes of Kilauea in 1912),
arrived for work at eight o'clock, and noticed a series of spikes on
the seismographic printout, which registered that a powerful earthquake, somewhere to the north, had occurred at 5:23 a.m. Given the
size and location of the tremor, Jaggar predicted that a trans-Pacific
tsunami was a likely consequence, and warned the Hilo harbour
master that a series of big waves was likely to be on its way, but – to
Jaggar's incredulity – the warning was dismissed. So when the
waves began to batter Hawaii shortly after noon, seven hours after
the earthquake itself, no precautions had been taken against the violence that ensued. The biggest wave, some six metres (twenty feet)
in height, slammed most of the Waiakea tuna fleet into the Wailoa
road bridge, killing one of the fishermen, and destroying dozens of
riverside houses. Jaggar and his colleagues were understandably
downhearted, for they had known for some time that while earth-

quakes are unpredictable, long-range tsunamis are not: given that
the time in hours taken by tsunamis to cross the Pacific is roughly
equal to the time in minutes that the faster-moving seismic shock-
waves take to cover the same distance, a sixty-fold window of warning would usually be available. By using the minutes for hours rule,
as Jaggar's colleague, R. H. Finch, pointed out in an article published in 1924, 'it should be possible to predict the arrival time of
tsunami waves from all parts of the Pacific' (though since the majority of seismographs were only inspected once a day, Finch suggested
they be fitted with some kind of alarm bell to warn of bigger
quakes).[8] The concept of tsunami warnings had thus been introduced to Hawaii by Jaggar and Finch, and the idea was actually put
into practice ten years later, on 2 March 1933, when a magnitude
8.6 earthquake off the north-east coast of Japan sent twenty-three-
metre (seventy-five-foot) waves crashing into the Sanriku coast,
killing more than three thousand people and wrecking more than
eight thousand boats. The seismographs on Kilauea had registered
the earthquake at 07:10 Hawaiian time, with analysis of the
printouts indicating an epicentre just off the north-east coast of
Japan, some 6,350 kilometres (3,950 miles) away. As was the case
ten years earlier, the observatory notified the local port authorities
that a tsunami was likely to arrive later that day, and this time the
authorities acted on the warning: the fishing fleet was moved into
Hilo Bay, while on the Kona side of the Big Island, which directly
faces distant Japan, stevedores began removing cargo from the
docks, where, at 3:20 p.m. – eight hours on from the earthquake
itself – the sea withdrew in the characteristic *kai mimiki* pattern,
before the first of the waves rushed in, causing serious flooding
along the coast. Fifteen minutes later, the waves reached Hilo,
although, since it faces away from Japan, these 'wraparound' waves
were much lower and weaker, causing little in the way of damage.

So this second tsunami warning seems to have worked well,
thanks to the seismographs at the Volcano Observatory, and no
one on the Hawaiian islands was killed or injured. The problem
with such warnings, however, is that reliance on seismographic

readouts alone can lead to a tsunami alert being given out every time a major earthquake is recorded. The years following the successful 1933 tsunami warning were punctuated by disruptive evacuations of Hilo harbour based on a series of far-off earthquakes in various locations around the Pacific, although no perceptible tsunamis actually reached Hawaii for more than a decade – not until that Monday morning in 1946. By then, however, the high incidence of 'false alarms' had seen both warnings and evacuations abandoned as an expensive waste of time, while the war years had introduced apparently greater threats to life than tsunamis from distant tremors. 'Less than one in one hundred earthquakes result in tidal waves and you don't alert every port in the Pacific each time a quake occurs', explained the director of the much-criticized US Coast and Geodetic Survey in the wake of the Fool's Day disaster; yet in spite of such calculations, it was obvious that a new system of coordinated readings was the only way to generate reliable tsunami warnings in the future.[9]

But, by one of those strange coincidences that the world throws up from time to time, in April 1946 the Hawaiian islands were home to a temporary community of American oceanographers, there to observe the imminent atomic bomb tests at Bikini Atoll, 4,000 kilometres (2,500 miles) to the west. Their presence, as Walter C. Dudley observed, made the Fool's Day disaster 'the most thoroughly studied tsunami in history'; in fact, the first wave had been detected while it was still out at sea: the radio operator on one of the test-site support ships, the USS *Thomson*, which was returning to Pearl Harbor from Bikini Atoll in the early hours of Monday morning, had picked up a message from a passing patrol plane, reporting something unusual on the surface.[10] But when the pilot was ordered to investigate, whatever it was had already disappeared, having apparently outpaced the speeding aircraft; a claim that the crew of the *Thomson* dismissed as a ham-fisted attempt at an April Fool. But, not long after, a message was received that the naval fleet at Pearl Harbor had just been knocked about by an abrupt but significant tidal surge, and the *Thomson* was ordered to stay clear of the harbour until the cause of the disturbance had been established.

It was, of course, the first of the wave train, which made landfall on Oahu – the island on which Pearl Harbor is located – at 6:30 a.m., about half an hour before it reached the Big Island, 320 kilometres (200 miles) to the south-east. One of the visiting oceanographers, Dr Francis Shepard of Scripps Institute, was staying in a cottage on Oahu's north shore, when he and his wife were woken by what he described as 'a loud hissing sound, which sounded for all the world as if dozens of locomotives were blowing off steam directly outside the house.'[11] Shepard grabbed his camera and ran from the cottage to investigate, witnessing the sharp with-drawal of the first wave, which left the reef entirely exposed to view. Although aware that a series of bigger waves was likely to follow, Shepard seriously underestimated their size and ferocity, and he stayed on the beach, calmly waiting to photograph the incoming sea; suddenly he realized that the second wave massing on the distant horizon was going to be far more powerful than the first. A couple of minutes later, it had ploughed into the cottage – 'the refrigerator passed us on the left side moving upright out into the cane field', as he recalled. By the time the third wave in the train arrived, pretty much destroying the beachside house, and claiming the lives of six people further along the shore, Shepard and his wife had already made their way to higher ground.

Having witnessed the tsunami at such close proximity, and knowing that the technology needed to create a reliable warning system was already available at little cost, Shepard, along with two of his colleagues, published what would prove to be an influential paper in the inaugural issue of the journal *Pacific Science* in January 1947. After making the observation that 'there is no Hawaiian shore which is exempt from tsunamis', and noting the impracti-cality of removing all buildings and boatyards from even the most vulnerable coastline, the paper concluded by recommending the installation of a coordinated, Pacific-wide tsunami-warning system:

A system of stations could be established around the shores of
the Pacific and on mid-Pacific islands, which would observe
either visually or instrumentally the arrival of long waves of
the periods characterising tsunamis. The arrival of these waves
should be reported immediately to a central station, whose
duty it would be to correlate the reports and issue warnings to
places in the path of the waves. It should be possible in this
way to give the people of the Hawaiian Islands enough warning of the approach of a tsunami to permit them to reach
places of safety.[12]

Such technology on its own, however, would be virtually useless
if not backed up by a consistent community-wide education
programme to reinforce the agreed evacuation procedures, while
keeping them in the forefront of people's minds. If major tsunamis
occur less than once per generation, there is plenty of time for their
dangers to be forgotten. This, certainly, was one of the clearer
lessons of the 1946 tsunami, which had taken the majority of the
island population completely by surprise, with the exception of
certain wiser heads, notably the older Japanese residents of Shinmachi and Waiakea, who had known exactly what was happening,
and took steps to alert their neighbours to the dangers. Japanese
tsunami memories, like Hawaiian folk tales, are a valuable source
of tsunami lore, as in the case of a story made famous by the
nineteenth-century ethnomythologist Lafcadio Hearn. Greek-
born Hearn – who took the Japanese name Koizumi Yakumo –
had witnessed the aftermath of the 1896 Sanriku disaster, which
he described in a work entitled *Gleanings in Buddha-Fields*, a long-
forgotten volume distinguished only by the first use in written
English of the Japanese word 'tsunami': 'From immemorial time',
wrote Hearn, 'the shores of Japan have been swept, at irregular
intervals of centuries, by enormous tidal waves,— tidal waves
caused by earthquakes or by submarine volcanic action. These
awful sudden risings of the sea are called by the Japanese *tsunami*.'[13]
He then went on to relate an apparently true account of a devas-
tating tsunami that had struck the village of Hirokawa, seventy

kilometres (forty-three miles) south of Osaka, on 23 December
1854. Some time during the afternoon, according to Hearn, the
village headman, Hamaguchi Gohei, who lived on a hill overlooking the bay, felt what he knew to be an earthquake, 'a long, slow,
spongy motion', but of a kind that he had never felt before. He
rose to his feet, and looked at the sea, which 'had darkened quite
suddenly, and it was acting strangely. It seemed to be moving against
the wind. *It was running away from the land . . .* ' Soon, the rest of the
villagers had also noticed the sea's disappearance, and many of
them made their way down to the unfamiliar terrain of 'ribbed sand
and reaches of weed-hung rock left bare'. None had ever seen such
a sight before, not even Hamaguchi Gohei himself, but something
vaguely stirred in his memory, perhaps from one of the traditional
stories he had heard as a child, and he realized what the sea was
about to do.

The headman knew it would take too long for a warning
message to be sent to the village or to arrange for the priest in
the nearest temple to toll the alarm bell, so he decided on a more
radical course of action. Gohei lit a torch, went out into the fields
and proceeded to set fire to some of the enormous rice stacks that
were there, ready to be transported to market. As soon as the
villagers on the beach saw the flames they rushed inland towards
the fields, but to their amazement Hamaguchi forbade anyone to
go near the flames until all four hundred villagers had been assembled. Many feared that their headman had gone mad overnight, but
his motives became clear when Hamaguchi suddenly pointed out
to sea, where a long, dark line could be seen approaching the shore,
towering like a cliff on the far horizon:

> ' "*Tsunami!*" shrieked the people; and then all shrieks and all
> sounds and all power to hear sounds were annihilated by a
> nameless shock heavier than any thunder, as the colossal swell
> smote the shore with a weight that sent a shudder through the
> hills, and with a foam-burst like a blaze of sheet-lightning.
> Then for an instant nothing was visible but a storm of spray
> rushing up the slope like a cloud; and the people scattered

back in panic from the mere menace of it. When they looked again, they saw a white horror of sea raving over the place of their homes. It drew back roaring, and tearing out the bowels of the land as it went. Twice, thrice, five times the sea struck and ebbed, but each time with lesser surges: then it returned to its ancient bed and stayed, – still raging, as after a typhoon.[14]

Hamaguchi's decisive actions saved all but thirty of the Hirokawa villagers, and even today, long after his death, the story of the rice-beacons continues to be taught in Japanese schools as a means of passing on tsunami lore to the younger generations. Many other tsunami-prone cultures use stories as cautionary aides-memoires. The nomadic Moken people, for example, who fish the islands of the Andaman Sea off the Thai and Burmese coasts, pass on tsunami knowledge through folktales such as 'The Legend of the Hungry Wave', which describes how a powerful incoming surf was pre-ceded by the sea's empty-bellied disappearance: the classic warning sign. Such stories are clearly effective, for the majority of the Moken survived the 2004 Indian Ocean tsunami by heading inland after noticing the retreat of the sea. Similarly, a dock worker in a remote Indian coastal area, who had recently watched a *National Geographic* documentary on tsunamis, had recognized the sea's retreat for what it was, and shouted to his co-workers to run inland; his actions apparently saved several hundred lives.[15]

While folk wisdom based on direct observation continues to be transmitted in narrative form, scientific understanding of tsunami behaviour also continues to increase, in tandem with an ever-deepening understanding of earthquakes. As was noted at the end of part one, modern seismology developed in Europe in response to the Lisbon earthquake, John Michell's insights into epicentres and seismic waves proving particularly important in establishing its credentials. Thirty years later, in the wake of the Calabrian disaster of 1783, a Neapolitan earthquake commission was founded, charged (following Pombal's earlier example) with compiling a detailed report of the distribution of damage in different parts of the kingdom. The commission's chief scientist, Dr Domenico Pignataro, concluded his report by proposing the world's first earthquake-intensity scale, based on physical damage and loss of life as recorded in the aftermath. Earthquakes were to be graded in five degrees: 'Slight'; 'Moderate'; 'Strong'; 'Very Strong'; and 'Violent', with the earthquake of 5 February 1783 being graded, understandably, as 'violent'.*

It was not until the mid-nineteenth century that the new concept of wave motion through solids was applied to the science of seismic events; and in 1855, a century after the Lisbon earthquake, the first modern seismograph was constructed by the Italian earth scientist Luigi Palmieri, who installed it in the observatory that remains concealed in the base of Mount Vesuvius. Palmieri's machine featured mercury-filled U-shaped tubes arranged around the points of the compass; when an earthquake occurred, the moving mercury made an electrical contact that stopped a clock while simultaneously starting up a revolving drum that, in turn, traced the time, duration and intensity of the movement.

———————————

* In 1828 Pignataro's five-point scale was recast and expanded by the German physicist Peter Egen, who proposed the following six-point scale, based on estimates of building damage sustained during the Netherlands earthquake of 23 February 1828:

1. Only very slight traces of the earthquake are sensible.
2. A few persons, under favourable conditions, feel the shock; glasses close together jingle, small plants in pots vibrate; hanging bells are not rung.
3. Windows rattle, house-bells are rung; most persons feel the shock.
4. Slight movement of furniture; the shock in general so strong that it is felt by everyone.
5. Furniture shaken strongly, walls are cracked, only a few chimnies thrown down, the damage caused being insignificant.
6. Furniture shaken strongly; mirrors, glass and china vessels broken; chimnies thrown down, wall cracked or overthrown.

(From Charles Davison, *The Founders of Seismology* (Cambridge: Cambridge University Press, 1927), p. 40.) Egen's user-friendly scheme of damage comparison established the template for all subsequent intensity scales, which, in the decades before recording instruments, were the only means of grading earthquakes.

By 1883, the year of the Krakatau eruption, the British geologist John Milne had improved on Palmieri's prototype, producing the horizontal pendulum seismograph that continues to be the template for most of the models in use today. A large number of observatories around the world had already installed Milne-type seismographs, and all of them registered the trans-global seismic waves that were generated by the eruption. That same year – 1883 – also saw the creation of a new earthquake-intensity scale, the ten-point Rossi–Forel scale, which was an amalgamation of two earlier scales devised independently by the geologists Michele de Rossi of the University of Rome and François Forel of the University of Lausanne. The Rossi–Forel scale updated Egen's earlier scale to include seismographic information, as well as more detailed observations of the effects of earthquakes on buildings and people.*

The Rossi–Forel scale remained in widespread international use until the early 1930s, although in Italy it was replaced by a rival intensity scale proposed by Giuseppe Mercalli of the University of

---

*   I Microseismic shock. Recorded by a single seismograph or by seismographs of the same model, but not by several seismographs of different kinds: the shock felt by an experienced observer.

  II Extremely feeble shock. Recorded by several seismographs of different kinds; felt by a small number of persons at rest.

  III Very feeble shock. Felt by several persons at rest; strong enough for the direction or duration to be appreciable.

  IV Feeble shock. Felt by persons in motion, disturbance of movable objects, doors, windows, cracking of ceilings.

  V Shock of moderate intensity. Felt generally by everyone; disturbance of furniture, beds, etc., ringing of some bells.

  VI Fairly strong shock. General awakening of those asleep; general ringing of bells; oscillation of chandeliers; stopping of clocks; visible agitation of trees and shrubs; some startled persons leaving their dwellings.

  VII Strong shock. Overthrow of movable objects, fall of plaster; ringing of church bells. General panic, without damage to buildings.

  VIII Very strong shock. Fall of chimneys; cracks in the walls of buildings.

  IX Extremely strong shock. Partial or total destruction of some buildings.

  X Shock of extreme intensity. Great disaster; ruins; disturbance of the strata, fissures in the ground, rock falls from mountains.[16]

Naples, who had designed his specifically to deal with stronger quakes. The initial (1897) Mercalli scale was later extended to a twelve-point scale by Adòlfo Cancani and August Sieberg, and published as the Mercalli–Cancani–Sieberg scale (MCS) in 1917. In 1931 an English-language translation of the MCS scale appeared in the *Bulletin of the Seismological Society of America*, and such was the international approval it attracted, it was formally adopted as the standard expression of earthquake intensity around the world. It remains in widespread use today, and is known as the Modified Mercalli Intensity Scale (MM: poor old Cancani and Sieberg seem to have fallen by the wayside):

I   Not felt, except by a very few under especially favourable circumstances.

II   Felt only by a few persons at rest, especially on upper floors of buildings. Delicately suspended objects may swing.

III Felt quite noticeably indoors, especially on upper floors of buildings, but not recognized as an earthquake by many people. Standing motorcars may rock slightly. Vibration like passing truck. Duration estimated.

IV   During the day felt indoors by many, outdoors by few. At night some awakened. Dishes, windows and doors disturbed; walls make creaking sound. Sensation like heavy truck striking building. Standing motorcars rocked noticeably.

V   Felt by nearly everyone; many awakened. Some dishes, windows, etc., broken; a few instances of cracked plaster; unstable objects overturned. Disturbances of trees, poles and other tall objects sometimes noticed. Pendulum clocks may stop.

VI   Felt by all; many frightened and run outdoors. Some heavy furniture moved; a few instances of fallen plaster or damaged chimnies. Damage slight.

VII Everybody runs outdoors. Damage negligible in buildings of good design and construction; slight to moderate in well-built ordinary structures; considerable in poorly built or badly designed structures. Some chimnies broken. Noticed by persons driving motorcars.

VIII   Damage slight in specially designed structures; considerable
        in ordinary substantial buildings, with partial collapse; great
        in poorly built structures. Panel walls thrown out of frame
        structures. Fall of chimnies, factory stacks, columns,
        monuments, walls. Heavy furniture overturned. Sand and
        mud ejected in small amounts. Changes in well water.
        Persons driving motorcars disturbed.

IX   Damage considerable in specially designed structures; well-
        designed frame structures thrown out of plumb; great in
        substantial buildings, with partial collapse. Buildings shifted
        off foundations. Ground cracked conspicuously.
        Underground pipes broken.

X   Some well-built wooden structures destroyed; most masonry
        and frame structures destroyed with foundations; ground
        badly cracked. Rails bent. Landslides considerable from river
        banks.

XI   Few, if any (masonry), structures remain standing. Bridges
        destroyed. Broad fissures in ground. Underground pipelines
        completely out of service. Earth slumps and land slips in soft
        ground. Rails bent greatly.

XII   Damage total. Practically all works of construction are
        damaged greatly or destroyed. Waves seen on ground
        surfaces. Lines of sight and level distorted. Objects thrown
        upward into the air.[17]

The Modified Mercalli Scale offers a fairly comprehensive means of grading the severity of any earthquake, but like all intensity scales, however finely nuanced they may be, it constitutes an entirely subjective, nonmathematical means of gauging seismic impact. It takes no account of factors such as the observer's distance from the earthquake's epicentre, or even the duration of the event; thus, two different seismologists in two different locations would end up assigning different intensities to the same seismic event. Intensity scales are also limited by a certain cultural specificity, in that they express the effects of earthquake damage largely in terms of Western building design, or (in the case of the MM) the modern automobile; this presents a serious limitation when assess-

ing earthquakes in uninhabited areas, as well as in the developing
world.

In 1935, however, Charles Richter, a seismologist based at the
California Institute of Technology, Pasadena, devised a means of
evaluating an earthquake's *magnitude* (as distinct from its *intensity*),
by calculating the total amount of energy it released.* Richter's
new system worked by correlating two sets of figures: 1) the ampli-
tude of the maximum earthquake motion, which was established
by reading the needle traces recorded by seismographs in a number
of different locations; and 2) the square root of the ratio of the
actual distances between those seismographs and the earthquake's
epicentre. The relationship between the two sets of figures was
then expressed logarithmically on a rising scale that soon became
known as the Richter magnitude, or, more popularly, as the Richter
scale.

The key difference between Richter's magnitude scale and all
earlier intensity scales was that its unit changes were no longer
linear, like those on a thermometer, but logarithmic, using common
base-10 logarithms. Due to the complex relationship between
energy release and magnitude, however, each unit change on the
scale represented not a ten-fold increase but a thirty-fold increase of
total earthquake energy; so an earthquake measured at magnitude
8.0 releases something like thirty times more energy than one of
magnitude 7.0, which in turn releases thirty times more energy than
one of magnitude 6.0. Thus, an earthquake measuring 8.0 on the
Richter scale is not *two times* more powerful as one measuring 6.0,
but around *nine hundred times* more powerful.[18]

Richter initially devised his scale as a means of standardizing the
measurement of earthquakes in southern California, but it was

---

* An earthquake's *intensity* is an estimate of the strength of shaking experienced at a
specific location, determined subjectively from its effects on people, structures, and the
natural environment. An earthquake's *magnitude*, by contrast, is an instrumental calcu-
lation of the energy released at the earthquake's focus, and takes no account of the
structural impact of the event.

soon in use around the world, albeit slightly modified in order to take into account differences in seismograph design. In fact there are three distinct versions of the Richter scale currently in use, developed to measure the different varieties of seismic wave: firstly, there is the original 1935 scale, which is now known as the *local magnitude scale* (M_L), and tends to be used to grade smaller events; then there is the so-called *body-wave scale* (M_B), which was devised by Richter and Beno Gutenberg to determine the magnitude of small to moderate deep-focus earthquakes; and thirdly, the *surface-wave scale* (M_S), which was developed to measure larger quakes at greater distances from their foci.

More recently still, however (in 1979), a fourth scale, known as the *moment magnitude scale* (M_W), was devised specifically to measure the so-called 'seismic moment' of longer-lasting earthquakes using the enhanced capacity of modern broadband seismographs. An earthquake's seismic moment is derived from a combination of factors such as the length and type of faulting that occurs, as well as the strength of the rocks being distorted, factors which the earlier Richter scales failed to take into account. Since the moment magnitude scale was developed by the seismologists Tom Hanks and Hiroo Kanamori, it is not really a Richter scale at all – a fact which often leads to confusion during news reports, since all four scales are usually referred to interchangeably as 'the Richter scale', even though they tend to yield different results. The December 2004 Indian Ocean earthquake, for example, was initially reported to have measured 9.0 on the moment magnitude scale (M_S), but 'only' 8.9 on the (M_S) version of the Richter scale. This discrepancy became even greater when the magnitude was revised upwards (the moment magnitude scale is often subject to later amendment since it is based on a wider array of data) to between 9.15 and 9.3 (M_W), making it the fourth most powerful earthquake ever recorded.

An earthquake's magnitude is not necessarily a reflection of its intensity, since magnitude is evaluated regardless of how deep an earthquake's focus, or how much damage it inflicts on human settlements. The earthquake of 26 December 2003 that destroyed the city of Bam, in Iran, killing more than thirty thousand people, measured 'only' 6.3 on the Richter (M_s) scale, prompting a number of newspapers to express surprise that its magnitude hadn't been greater. But its shallow focus of ten kilometres (six miles) and close proximity to a densely populated clay-built city meant that its *intensity* (as distinct from its *magnitude*) would have registered as maximum XII ('damage total') on the Modified Mercalli Scale. Since magnitude is solely a index of energy released, and not an assessment of observable impact, the magnitude of an undersea earthquake offers no clear guide as to whether or not a tsunami has been triggered, or, if it has, what its size and impact might be. That kind of information requires time and equipment, which is where the tsunami-warning system comes in.

In the wake of the Fool's Day tsunami, and the published recommendations of the oceanographers, an outline warning system began to be drawn up, with approximate wave-transit times to Hawaii from various tsunamigenic hotspots around the Pacific drawn from Jaggar and Finch's hours-to-minutes rule: five hours from the Aleutian Islands; six hours from Kamchatka; ten hours from Japan, fifteen hours from South America (fig. vi). All that was needed, according to the oceanographers' report, was for the seismographs to be regularly consulted and interpreted for likely tsunami activity, as well as a reliable public communications system to pass on warnings to the local populations. The system established in Hawaii over the course of 1947–48 was intended to answer all these requirements, despite the fact that its early funding was 'on a shoestring compared to most other government agencies.'[19] Nevertheless, by the end of 1948, the Seismic Sea Wave Warning System (it was later renamed the Pacific Tsunami Warning System) was up and running in the form of a collection of seismic and tidal information exchanges located on US-owned Pacific stations including Alaska, Hawaii and Midway Island (the scene of a pivotal battle against the Japanese fleet in June 1942). Its mechanism was fairly straightforward: any earthquake of magnitude 7.0

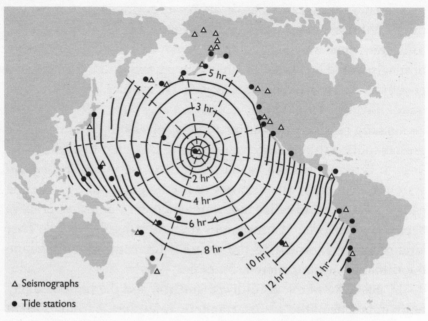

Figure vi. Map of tsunami transit times across the Pacific Ocean.

or above occurring anywhere in the Pacific (or 6.8 if the focus of the quake was located within the Hawaiian chain) would set off alarms at the monitoring stations, alerting staff to the seismic event. If the seismologists judged that a tsunami was a likely consequence – a judgement based on the quake's location as well as on its magnitude – a Tsunami Watch would be declared, and all relevant civil-defence authorities placed on high alert. This was the first, seismographic, stage of any warning cycle. The second, oceanographic, stage would depend on readings received from manned and unmanned tide gauges located throughout the Pacific, which would show whether or not the sea had been dangerously disturbed: if not, the Tsunami Watch would usually be cancelled, but if there were indications that a tsunami had been generated, then a Tsunami Warning would be issued.

The Tsunami Warning – the next level up from a Tsunami Watch – was the point at which the island population would be informed of the danger of incoming waves through the Emergency

Broadcast System, as well as through a network of outdoor sirens installed throughout the coastal towns and villages (see picture 30). This was when the evacuation of low-lying areas would begin, hospitals would be placed on emergency standby and boat-owners encouraged to move their vessels beyond the hundred-fathom line, out of the line of fire.

As long as they were facing a long-range tsunami from one of the hotspots on the Pacific rim, Hawaiians would have plenty of time to batten down the hatches. And by 1949 much of this new system was in place: the network of Pacific observatories and tide gauges had been installed, the lines of communication broadly agreed and evacuation procedures drawn up by the civil-defence authorities and printed at the front of the Hawaiian telephone book. If followed to the letter, the system would in theory save hundreds, possibly thousands of lives; but how well would it actually work in practice, the next time a powerful wave train came racing across the Pacific Ocean, bound for the vulnerable shorelines of Hawaii?

IV

The warning system received its first test in earnest on the morning of 4 November 1952, when a powerful submarine earthquake, registering 8.2 on the Richter (M_s) scale, occurred off the south-east coast of the Kamchatka Peninsula, 1,000 kilometres west of the Aleutians. The peninsula, which boasts around thirty active volcanoes, lies at the apex of the Kuril Trench, a subduction zone within the same complex fault system as the adjacent Aleutian Trench. Tsunamigenic earthquakes are a regular occurrence there, the long-range results of which have washed over the Hawaiian islands on numerous occasions in the past.

This time, however, the warning system was newly in place, and when alarms attached to Hawaiian seismographs went off just after 5:00 a.m., a tsunami watch was announced within the hour, based on the severity of the recorded magnitude. Given the

distance from the epicentre, the first waves, were any to be generated, would (it was predicted) reach the shores of Hawaii by
1:30 p.m., allowing just over six hours for any evacuation to take
place. But while the seismologists in Hawaii were still assessing
incoming data, six-metre (twenty-foot) waves had already begun
crashing into the Kamchatka coast, and tide gauges off Alaska
were registering violent movements in the water. As soon as this
secondary data was in, confirming that a tsunami had indeed been
generated, a tsunami warning was given out across Hawaii, where,
just after 1:30 p.m. – exactly as predicted – the first wave reached
Hilo Bay, surging over Coconut Island, and causing widespread
structural damage along the hastily evacuated shoreline. Several
ancillary waves came in over the course of the afternoon, and
though they were nothing like as high as they had been in 1946,
they were severe enough to cause an estimated $800,000 worth of
damage. The warning system, though, had worked like a dream,
and not a single human life had been lost, despite the fact that a
party of tourists on Waikiki Beach had apparently headed towards
the water instead of away from it – so far, so good, then (the
worrying incident on the beach notwithstanding), and the three-
year-old warning system was deemed to have passed its first
significant test. And it went on to pass its next test, too, which was
to come only five years later, on 9 March 1957, when another dawn
alarm call woke duty seismologists across the Pacific. At 4:22 a.m.,
an Aleutian Trench earthquake measuring 8.3 on the Richter (M_s)
scale sent large waves smashing into adjacent islands, at which a
general Pacific tsunami warning was issued, with the head of the
wave train expected to reach Hawaii by nine o'clock that morning.
As in 1952, all island hospitals were placed on emergency standby,
while police and the military began the work of evacuating low-
lying residential areas. And, as before, the incoming waves caused
some structural damage throughout the Hawaiian islands, but
again no lives were lost. This was due not only to the implementation of the advance-warning system, but also to the fact that neither
of the 1950s tsunamis were anything like as severe as the 1946

event; also, a sizeable area of downtown Hilo below Kamehameha Avenue had never been rebuilt, leaving a wide, grassy floodplain between the ocean and the town to serve as a buffer zone.

But there was a dangerous chink in Hawaii's surrounding armour, for while seismographic information remained easily available, alerting scientists to any earthquake, large or small, anywhere in the Pacific, the vital oceanographic information was less easy to obtain. Most of it was sourced from tide gauges situated off a few rich northern Pacific coasts – those of Russia, Japan and the USA – while Pacific coastlines to the south of Hawaii, especially those of Central and South America, remained alarmingly poorly equipped. Consequently, warnings of tsunamis generated from South American earthquakes could not be corroborated by tidal reports, a situation that resulted in scientists issuing tsunami warnings rather than watches – thus erring on the side of caution, in the absence of the kind of tide-gauge data that might otherwise have caused the warnings to be cancelled. A strong Mexican earthquake in 1958, for example, had led to a tsunami warning on Hawaii, complete with evacuations from the low-lying areas, but when no tsunami arrived, the evacuees were unimpressed by the seismologists' explanations of their technical limitations. The strange fact is that people react almost as badly to false alarms as they do to unpredicted disasters, and, as had already been discovered in the 1930s, it only takes a couple of unnecessary scares to undermine the credibility of the system. This seems to have been the case when, on the afternoon of 22 May 1960, a long and powerful earthquake off the coast of Chile was detected by seismologists on Hawaii, who set about preparing an immediate tsunami warning. When the warning went out, at 6:47 p.m., most of the population of Hawaii, remembering the recent Mexican debacle, decided that they had heard it all before. 'We were always afraid of Alaska', recalled Hayato Okino, a Japanese resident of Waiakea Town, 'the Aleutian Islands. We didn't know about South America', and though some who lived in the low-lying areas did evacuate their homes when they heard the siren, the majority thought better of it and stayed where they were.

Those who stayed put were not entirely to blame for their deci-sion. The absence of tide gauges or sea-floor sensors meant that accounts of the fast-approaching waves from Chile came from eye-witnesses on islands in the tsunami flight path rather than from instrumental data. So when the nine o'clock news on Hawaiian state radio reported that Tahiti, with its protective ring of coral reefs, had just been splashed by a knee-high wave, it seemed as if the tsunami warning was just another false alarm. To make matters worse, a confusing change to the evacuation procedure had been introduced only a few months before. Where previously the warn-ing sirens had been sounded in three distinct stages, the last of which meant 'evacuate now', the new system featured only a single siren – the signal to begin immediate evacuation. But this new procedure was widely misinterpreted, and after hearing the night's first (and only) siren sounded at 8:30 p.m., many of those who did intend to leave began to get ready, while waiting for the final signal.

But: 'There was to be no second siren that night!', as Walter Dudley put it, and just after 1 a.m. wave number three of a devas-tating tsunami rushed in to Hilo Bay, where it claimed the lives of sixty-one people, badly injured two hundred and eighty-two more, and wiped out the rebuilt streets of Waiakea and Shinmachi, caus-ing an estimated $50 million worth of damage.[20] Bunji Fujimoto, who had survived the 1946 tsunami at Laupahoehoe Point, was in Hilo during the 1960s as a member of the National Guard. He described the scene the following day as 'unbelievable. The wave picked up a whole building on the bayfront on Kamehameha Avenue and just dumped it into the river. The whole bayfront and Waiakea town was virtually destroyed. Waiakea Theater was on Kamehameha Avenue right across the bridge; the wave picked it up and deposited the theater in the middle of the street. It might be hard to believe if you haven't really seen it, but that's the tsunami' (see picture 32).[21]

Richard and Evelyn Miyashiro of Café 100 had long since rebuilt their damaged café, but a boom in business during the 1950s saw them relocate to a new and bigger restaurant a little further inland.

The couple, with their three young children, now lived in a house behind the new premises, which was lucky for them, because they were among the many who had failed to evacuate when they heard the warning siren. At 1:04 a.m., when the monster wave from Chile arrived, the newly built Café 100 shouldered the worst of the violent impact, sparing the family home from instant destruction – the timber-framed house was merely shifted a short distance on the flood-tide, away from the obliterated café. The first Café 100 had only been open for three months before it was destroyed by the Aleutian tsunami; this time, the new café, which had opened at the end of April 1960, had just three weeks before it, too, was put out of business by another vast wave.*

All in all, the impact of the tsunami on Hilo was nearly as bad as the Fool's Day disaster, but additional distress derived from the fact that the world's most competent warning system had failed – far from initiating an orderly evacuation, the sirens had actually served to *draw* curious onlookers down to the harbour wall in the hope of seeing a wave (picture 31). Many of those sightseers would have remembered 1946, but the recent spate of false alarms, coupled with misleading media reports on the size of the advancing waves, created a lethal climate of unconcern. Perhaps they might have been more alarmed had they known that the 22 May earthquake would turn out to be the most powerful ever recorded, measuring at one point in its seven-minute career an astonishing 9.5 on the moment magnitude scale (M_w), and 8.6 on the Richter (M_s) scale.[†22]

It was clear that the Pacific Tsunami Warning System needed to regain its authority; indeed it was hardly worth maintaining it if

---

* Not to be outdone by the sea, the Miyashiros opened their third and final Café 100 in 1962, though this time it was properly inland. The café is still there today, on Kilauea Avenue, where its loco mocos are warmly recommended.

† The tsunami that it generated would eventually make its way across the entire Pacific Ocean, where it would go on to kill a further hundred and forty people in Japan, more than twenty-four hours after the earthquake itself. The fact that even the Japanese Meteorological Agency (the body in charge of Japanese tsunami warnings) was caught unprepared seemed to symptomize the mismanagement of the crisis.

people either misunderstood it, or, worse, felt free to ignore it. The
first problem to be remedied was the system of siren calls; instead
of the ambiguous single alert, which had caused so much confusion
that evening, a new 'attention/alert' signal – 'A STEADY THREE
MINUTE SIREN TONE', as it is described in the Hawaiian telephone
book – would be sounded at least three hours before the estimated
wave arrival time, and repeated at regular intervals. Meanwhile,
detailed evacuation instructions would be broadcast over the radio.
It was also apparent that more tide gauges were needed near southern Pacific coasts, as a means of confirming the spread of tsunamis
from there – an outcome only achieved after 1968, when, under the
auspices of the United Nations' Intergovernmental Oceanographic
Commission (IOC), all Pacific nations joined the warning-system
family.

But the real problems on Hawaii were not technological, but
psychological: people were simply not scared enough of tsunamis,
in spite of the islands' well-documented history of regular seismic
assault. In fact, many Hawaiians seemed transfixed by tsunamis,
especially the young, who not only lacked direct experience of
their dangers, but were growing up amid a burgeoning surf culture,
with its daredevil mythologies of riding the Ultimate Wave. This
new hazard became increasingly apparent during the 1980s and 90s,
when any announcement of a tsunami watch or warning would
prompt dozens of youngsters to head to the shoreline with surf-
boards under their arms. A full-scale coastal evacuation on 7 May
1986, dubbed 'Waveless Wednesday' by a disappointed local press,
had seen a column of traffic heading *towards* Waikiki Beach for
'"tsunami party time!"', in Walter Dudley's words, while later alerts
produced a series of ever more bizarre responses, including the
group of mainland tourists who demanded to know what this
'Salami Warning' was all about, and the fisherman seen casting
his line over the Waikiki breakwater, serenely ignoring the frantic
announcements of the civil-defence helicopter hovering overhead.
And, at precisely the moment that the wave had been predicted
to make landfall at Honolulu, 'a woman with dark flowing hair,

wearing a purple muumuu, crossed the street, and calmly marched
into the waves. She gazed toward the horizon while reverently
touching the water and then motioned toward her heart.'[23] Luckily
for all these people, the tsunamis that did arrive were knee-high
or less, a fact that did little to alleviate the frustration of the
civil-defence authorities in the face of their citizens' constitutional
right to endanger themselves through their own stupidity. As
Doug Carlson, a Honolulu-based tsunami blogger, pointed out in
his post for 16 November 2006, after yet another tsunami alert
had sent surfers hurrying down to Waikiki Beach, 'the loonies who
want to "ride a tsunami" are probably beyond hope' and 'officials
may have to acknowledge that they can't change those people'.[24]
It seems it cannot be reiterated often enough – even after the
tragedy of December 2004 – that tsunami waves are lethally un-
surfable.

Because the culture of non-compliance during tsunami alerts is
bolstered every time there is a 'false alarm' – a phrase that dismays
mitigation professionals, since even a one-centimetre-high tsunami
is still a tsunami, and can easily shoal into a monster given the right
conditions – efforts to fine-tune the detection system are ongoing,
with the aim of keeping unnecessary evacuations to the minimum.
The main improvement has been to replace the first generation
of near-shore tide gauges with electronic seabed sensors – known
as bottom-pressure recorders (or BPRs) – that are able to monitor
long-period waves passing through deep water. The problem with
the old harbour-side tide gauges was that their proximity to coastlines served to contaminate the tsunami signal through patterns
of bounced and reflected waves, as well as the fact that they would
often be destroyed by the very thing they were set up to measure.
They were also fairly slow at relaying information, but the use of
satellite technology to collect data transmitted from surface buoys
located directly above the seabed sensors has reduced alert times
to a matter of minutes. The hard-working buoys, which are part of
the National Oceanic and Atmospheric Administration (NOAA)'s
Deep-ocean Assessment and Reporting of Tsunamis (DART) system,

are replaced every year, while the bottom-pressure recorders are replaced every two years, making the DART system relatively expensive to maintain, although it has done much to improve the accuracy of tsunami forecasting and warning across the entire Pacific region (see picture 33). In addition, since the 2004 Asian tsunami, the Pacific Tsunami Warning Centre has extended its remit to include the Indian Ocean, South China Sea and Caribbean Sea, all of which are in the process of installing or extending their own tsunami-warning systems under the guidance of the Inter-governmental Oceanographic Commission. The process has not always gone smoothly – in July 2006 a local tsunami off the coast of Java killed nearly seven hundred people: it later emerged that the two detection buoys installed off the Sumatran coast had been removed from the sea some months before, to await repairs in a dockside warehouse – but even so, there remain plenty of reasons to be confident that an integrated warning system will one day cover every tsunami-prone coastline on the planet.[25]

But the top priority remains the need for increased tsunami awareness, a process that best begins in the classroom. A particularly forceful illustration of this is the story of the ten-year-old British schoolgirl Tilly Smith, who was on holiday with her family at Phuket, Thailand, over Christmas 2004; as soon as she saw the withdrawal of the water on the hotel beach that Boxing Day morning she knew exactly what it meant, because two weeks earlier she had been shown a video of the Hilo tsunami during a primary-school geography lesson; 'I was having visions from the Hawaiian videos that I had seen two weeks before', she recalled, and her loud insistence that a tsunami was coming persuaded her parents to ask hotel staff to evacuate the beach – the only one on Phuket island where nobody was killed.[26] Tilly's story reinforces the fact that, in spite of the expensive equipment available, one should never under-estimate the lifesaving potential of someone running away from the shoreline shouting, 'Tsunami!', and that can only be achieved through widespread education – the first line of defence against the ever-present dangers of disaster amnesia, in which the collective suppression of painful memories leads to a lack of preparedness for future hazards.

It was this need for greater public awareness – a need high-lighted by the behaviour of surfers during the tsunami alerts of the 1980s and 90s – that led to the founding of the Pacific Tsunami Museum in Hilo in 1994, its primary mission being to provide tsunami education programmes across the Asia/Pacific region. In fact the museum's first board meeting, in October that year, was postponed due to a tsunami alert prompted by an 8.1 (M_s) earth-quake off the Kuril Islands, an apt reminder of the need for such an institution. Two years later, the unexpected outpouring of tsunami recollections that marked the fiftieth anniversary of the 1946 disas-ter made it clear that the museum had another, equally important, function, as a repository for Pacific tsunami memories, and as a place where generations of survivors could meet to 'talk tsunami'.[27]

Hazard-prone communities have often sought to repress their experiences of disaster. In Lisbon, for example, there is no official memorial to the 1755 earthquake, apart from the ruined shell of a Carmelite church on the hill above the Rossio (which was never rebuilt due to lack of funds), while the only memorial to the Krakatau dead is the mooring buoy of the *Berouw* paddle steamer, lying rusting on a plinth by the Koeripan River in Lampong Bay, Sumatra; but on Hawaii, as Mike Davis has noted, 'tsunamis have come to vie with orchids and hula' as the Big Island's principal civic symbol.[28] The first thing that strikes a visitor to Hilo today is how far from the shoreline the city has retreated. Grassy expanses line the inundation zone, and where the crowded streets of Shin-machi and Waiakea Town once stood lie state parks studded with memorials to the trans-Pacific waves that destroyed them (picture 34). The Waiakea Town clock, stopped at 1:04 a.m. by the twenty-foot monster from Chile, stands at the heart of this now-vanished neighbourhood, where it marks the beginning of the Hilo Walking Tour, a 'leisurely 90-minute walk [that] will ignite your imagina-tion, particularly on a sunny day', as the *Lonely Planet* guidebook rather bathetically puts it (picture 35).[29] The walk takes you along the deserted bay-front to the Pacific Tsunami Museum itself, a solid former bank building that survived the events of both 1946 and 1960, on the roof of which a tsunami-cam keeps perpetual watch on the horizon. Inside there is plenty for the visitor to read, along with hours of video and audio testimonials to watch and to listen to, but there is little in the way of actual objects, apart from a wave-bent parking meter and a display of detection equipment that seems far too big for the room. 'A museum is supposed to have arte-facts', as the director, Donna Saiki, told me, 'but most of ours are at the bottom of the sea.' While I was there a party of junior school children were settling down for a museum talk, which began with a slide of a tsunami siren, a familiar sight around the Hawaiian islands. 'Can anyone tell me what this is?' asked the director, at which every hand in the room shot up: 'Tsunami siren, tsunami siren.' 'And what should you do if you hear it go off?' Pause. Then: 'Run, run, run . . . !'

Hilo was preparing for the next one.

AFTERWORD

'Civilisation exists by geological consent, subject to change without notice', as the philosopher Will Durant observed in 1926, but I hope that this book has shown Durant's truism to be more complex, and more disturbing, than it might at first appear. Take our efforts to second-guess nature with costly technical appliances: as was seen over the last few pages, even the best warning systems in the world are effective only when the populations under their protection are given regular reminders of what to do when threatened by natural hazards. Installing the technology is only the beginning, as the Hawaiian experience so clearly shows: long-term education and training on the ground are just as important, but unfortunately these require consistent state-level funding to be made available at the local level – just the kind of funding that tends to evaporate as soon as the equipment is in place. Thus, initiatives such as the INGO-funded Tsunami Education Project, which ran in schools throughout coastal Sri Lanka in the wake of the Indian Ocean disaster, was only in place for a year (from March 2006 to March 2007), and there is nothing currently scheduled to replace it. While a single generation of tsunami-smart schoolchildren is a promising beginning, it is unfair to have burdened them with the sole responsibility of passing on their knowledge to the coming generations – especially if the only reason for ending the programme is a lack of long-term investment.

Similar outbreaks of fiscal shrinkage can also affect international aid and reconstruction monies, which have a habit of either not turning up, or being reallocated to the aftermaths of subsequent disasters elsewhere. Much of the international aid promised to the Iranian city of Bam, for instance – devastated by an earthquake on Boxing Day 2003 – was simply moved on the following year to the areas affected by the Indian Ocean tsunami. To this day Bam remains a city in ruins, abandoned by the world in the wake of the tsunami, and it seems unlikely that it will ever be rebuilt. The global credit crisis, meanwhile, has stalled the $108m of international aid that the UN requested be made available to the storm- and flood-battered island of Haiti in the wake of 2008's unforgiving hurricane season. So far, less than half of that sum has been delivered, and by now it is probably safe to assume that the rest will never material-ize. And as for New Orleans, left to drown in the wake of Hurricane Katrina, the fact that it was not some unreported backwater in a hard-to-reach corner of the developing world but one of America's best-loved and most-visited cities turned out to offer no guarantee of protection, either before or after the event. Having refused all international offers of aid, the US government proceeded to dither, typified by the fact that it took White House officials nearly a week to federalize the National Guard, thereby freeing them to report to the city authorities. What a contrast to the events of 1906, in the wake of the San Francisco earthquake, when the government's response was unhesitating – the National Guard was federalized at the stroke of a pen within an hour of the dawn catastrophe, and by 7 a.m. the troops had reported to the San Francisco mayor's office and were already being put to work among the city's burning ruins. Naturally, such decisiveness in 1906 had nothing to do with the kinds of technology or resources available a hundred years before Katrina, but was a consequence of the calibre of political judgement so miserably lacking in the White House of 2005.

The tragedy for Louisiana, as for so many other disaster areas, was that advance warnings had been repeatedly given by teams of scientists and engineers, which, had they been acted upon, would have averted much of the carnage that ensued. In the case of New Orleans, decades of published findings by, among others, the

US Army Corps of Engineers, had warned that the city's federally built flood defences offered no protection against the kind of storm surges associated with hurricanes above category 3 on the Saffir–Simpson Hurricane Scale (a five-point intensity scale that grades tropical cyclones according to their sustained wind-speeds). When Katrina made landfall to the east of the city on 29 August 2005, it had only just weakened to a category 3 (with sustained wind speeds of around 200 kilometres (125 miles) an hour, but it propagated a nine-metre (thirty-foot) storm surge that overwhelmed the levees in more than fifty places, flooding the city with the pent-up waters of Lake Pontchartrain and the Mississippi River, with the loss of nearly two thousand lives. As Michael Brown, the former director of the Federal Emergency Management Agency (FEMA), declared on NBC's *Nightly News* on 2 March 2006, 'I never like to say I told you so, but I told you so . . . and if we don't learn from this, then shame on us.'

As Brown implied, the lessons that the world still needs to learn are not just those of disaster preparedness, but those of disaster prevention. In fact the very term *natural disaster* is much misapplied, since nature usually plays an incidental role in creating the conditions for catastrophe. If there is one thing that the history of disaster consistently shows, it is that few of the victims have ever been the casualties of nature alone. From the Lisbon earthquake to Cyclone Nargis – which killed more than a hundred and thirty thousand people in Burma's Irrawaddy Delta in May 2008 – the real culprits have always been civic and ecological mismanagement, which have contributed far more to human vulnerability than any natural hazard. The overcrowded fire-trap that was pre-quake Lisbon was a catastrophe in waiting, built as it was above a known earthquake hotspot, while the development of the Sumatran and Javanese coasts by the Dutch colonial authorities during the nineteenth century put a collection of new towns with significant populations right on the doorstep of Krakatau, the most unstable volcanic island on the planet. Of course, eighteenth- and nineteenth-century planners and policy-makers had little or no conception of environmental

prudence, but in spite of everything that has been learned in the
centuries since, the same pattern of recklessness continues: building
regulations in earthquake hotspots around the world, from Lisbon
to Sichuan, are routinely ignored, while the agricultural clearance
of much of the Indian Ocean's fresh-water swamps and mangrove
forests has left coast and delta communities exposed and defenceless
against not only tsunamis, but the regular storm surges brought
about by cyclones such as Nargis. As recent events have shown,
where swamps and mangroves are left intact, such surges tend to
dissipate quickly, but where they have been stripped away, as is the
case throughout Burma's Irrawaddy Delta (where they have been
largely replaced with rice plantations), a catastrophic situation is set
in train, creating in effect a frictionless bowling alley for cyclones and
tsunamis, allowing waves and surges to power inland with nothing
to hinder their progress.

In neighbouring Bangladesh, by contrast, the vast Sundarbans
mangrove forests at the mouth of the Ganges – a UNESCO world
heritage site since 1997 – have been lovingly preserved for centuries;
and while their natural fisheries provide a sustainable livelihood
for tens of thousands of Sundarban families, they also act as an effective defence against high tides, storms and tsunamis. When severe
Cyclone Sidr hit Bangladesh in November 2007, it propagated a
storm surge twice the height of that of Nargis, yet the casualty rate
(less than three thousand people) was a fraction of that suffered in
coastal Burma, despite the Sundarbans being just as densely populated as the Irrawaddy Delta. This outcome, due as much to the
large-scale evacuations organized by the Bangladeshi authorities
as to the presence of the mangrove barrier, is a powerful example
of the interconnections between responsible government, environmental management and disaster prevention and preparedness –
none of which is necessarily dependent on First World levels of
resources. Bangladesh, hit by cyclones every year, many of which
(like Sidr) produce powerful storm surges, remains poor and
densely populated, yet its government has managed to invest wisely
and well in a variety of disaster-mitigation strategies, and is able

to organize mass evacuations more efficiently than the majority of first-world nations – including the United States, which in spite of its wealth and advanced technology is woefully underprepared for natural hazards, and remains decades behind developing nations such as Bangladesh when it comes to managing disaster and its aftermath.

It doesn't have to be this way. Sixty years ago, when the Pacific Tsunami Warning System was unveiled in Hawaii, public opinion remained broadly aligned with a prevailing spirit of technological optimism. Since then, however, the mood has changed, and when the same eighteenth-month time-frame for installing an interim warning system across the Indian Ocean was agreed at a United Nations conference on disaster reduction in early January 2005, the plans attracted weary scepticism from a news media habituated to reporting mission delays, critical overspends and other such instances of implementation failure. Eighteen months seemed too little time for such a complex set of arrangements to be put in place, especially as a number of Indian Ocean governments had already begun formulating their own local plans, in defiance of the recommendations of the Intergovernmental Oceanographic Commission (IOC) – 'the number of competing proposals and attempts to coordinate various efforts could scupper the project', as the *Guardian* warned on 20 January 2005; but nevertheless, in June 2006, UNESCO announced that its $30 million interim warning system was up and running as projected, with twenty-six national tsunami-information centres receiving data from twenty-five newly built seismographic stations arrayed across the Indian Ocean. A trio of deep-ocean sensors, meanwhile, had been installed in selected locations along the Java Trench, ready to detect the telltale pressure-signals of any future long-range tsunami.

As the debacle of 17 June 2006 made clear, however, installing such equipment is one thing, maintaining it is another: that was the day that a deadly tsunami evaded detection by Indonesia's pair of DART buoys, both of which had been removed from the water and were awaiting repairs onshore. Since these buoys cost around $250,000 each, and require at least $125,000 worth of annual maintenance per unit, tsunami preparedness is proving a costly undertaking for developing nations such as Indonesia, which has made painfully slow progress in its subsequent attempts to extend its coastal warning system; by November 2008 there were only twenty-two detection buoys to monitor the six thousand inhabited islands of the sprawling archipelago. And, at the time of writing (July 2009), deep-sea buoys and sensors have still not been installed off northern Sumatra – one of Indonesia's most vulnerable regions, and the scene of the highest losses of life during the 2004 disaster, where the death toll in Aceh province alone exceeded a hundred and thirty thousand. The IOC, however, is continuing to expand the UN-funded warning system, which by 2010 is set to comprise a hundred and sixty seismological stations, numerous additional DART buoys and sensors and a network of automated warning sirens ranged along the region's more populous coastlines, including those of northern Sumatra. With similar arrangements being put in place across other tsunami-prone waters, notably the Caribbean, the Mediterranean and the north-eastern Atlantic, it will soon be hypothetically impossible for another long-range tsunami to creep up on the world by surprise. Too late for those who lost their lives along the shores of the Indian Ocean, of course, but not for the millions, perhaps hundreds of millions, whose lives will benefit from enhanced disaster preparedness in the future.

There have, of course, been other disasters since the Asian tsunami – Hurricane Katrina (August 2005), the Kashmir earthquake (October 2005), Cyclone Nargis (May 2008), the Sichuan earthquake (May 2008), the Haitian floods (September 2008) – each of which shared common features with the quartet of historical disasters I had first set out to describe. Footage of the Chinese Prime Minister (and former geologist) Wen Jiabao clambering over the ruins of Beichuan in May 2008 was shown continuously on Chinese state television, which, with his uplifting motto – 'as long as there is a glimmer of hope' – echoed Pombal's earlier displays of compassionate pragmatism in the face of the destruction of Lisbon; and under 'Uncle' Wen's direction, there was much that was praiseworthy in the official Chinese response to the disaster. Less heartening was (and remains) the ongoing politicization of aid and rescue work in Burma and elsewhere, which recalls the conduct of the Dutch colonial authorities in the aftermath of the Krakatau eruption, when emergency supplies were withheld from Sumatran villages considered hostile to the colonial regime. 'First the hurricane – then the disaster', as graffiti in New Orleans succinctly put it, and the same could be said of many of the other episodes that I've mentioned, given that the 'disaster' is rarely the natural event itself, but the catastrophic decisions made before and after that conspire to make the situation worse.

And as a growing global population settles in ever more vulnerable locations, our collective exposure to natural hazards continues to increase. It goes without saying that we cannot prevent volcanoes, earthquakes and tsunamis from occurring – they are, as William Golding described them, 'terrors of nature's fact' – but we can at least undertake to act in ways that mitigate their effects and thereby hasten recovery. Perhaps it's a cliché to say that future generations are dependent on us to learn from the lessons of the past, but it is nonetheless the case that we owe them that, just as we owe an incalculable debt to those who experienced the earth in extremis, and who responded by seeking to understand its workings. For what these four true stories reveal is not only the circularity of the earth's deep connections – the earthquake precipitated a tsunami; the strange weather was caused by a volcanic eruption; the volcano was responsible for a tsunami; the tsunami was precipitated by an earthquake – but the personal and social origins of scientific thought, and the indomitable spirit of human creativity in the face of the terrors of the earth.

NOTES

Epigraph from William Golding, *The Paper Men* (London: Faber & Faber, 1984), p. 89.

PART ONE: THE LISBON EARTHQUAKE

1 The clergyman's story was told, anonymously, in *An Account of the late Dreadful Earthquake and Fire, Which destroyed the City of Lisbon, the Metropolis of Portugal, in a Letter from a Merchant Resident there, to his Friend in England* (London: J. Payne, 1755), pp. 28–32.

2 *A Genuine Letter to Mr. Joseph Fowke, From his Brother near Lisbon, Dated November 1755* (London: M. Collyer, 1755), p. 3.

3 *Gentleman's Magazine* 25 (1755), p. 561.

4 Rose Macaulay, *They Went to Portugal* (London: Cape, 1946), p. 91.

5 Cited in Martin Battestin, *Henry Fielding: A Life* (London: Routledge, 1989), p. 596.

6 George Whitefield, *A Brief Account of some Lent and other Extraordinary Processions and Ecclesiastical Entertainments Seen last Year at Lisbon* (London: W. Strahan, 1755), pp. 4; 13–14.

7 For Brazilian gold see A. J. R. Russell-Wood, 'Colonial Brazil: the gold cycle, *c.* 1690–1750', in *The Cambridge History of Latin America*, ed. Leslie Bethell, 10 vols (Cambridge: Cambridge University Press, 1984–95), II, pp. 547–600.

8 Whitefield, *A Brief Account*, p. 18.

9 José Saramago, *Journey to Portugal*, trans. Amanda Hopkinson and Nick Caistor (London: Harvill, 2000), p. 316. Saramago's great novel *Memorial do Convento* (Lisbon: Caminho, 1982), translated into English as *Baltasar & Blimunda* (London: Cape, 1988), tells the extraordinary story of the building of the Mafra monastery.

10 See C. R. Boxer, *Some Contemporary Reactions to the Lisbon Earthquake of 1755* (Lisbon: Universidade de Lisboa, 1956), p. 5.

11 Charles Davison, *Great Earthquakes* (London: Thomas Murby & Co., 1936), p. 2.

12 Aristotle, *Meteorologica*, Bk. II. 8. 366b. 20.

13 *Gentleman's Magazine* 25 (1755), p. 554.

14 This, along with the following extract, is taken from *An Account of the late Dreadful Earthquake and Fire*, pp. 11–18.

15 Collected in Rose Macaulay, *They Went to Portugal*, pp. 268–70. A copy of the original letter is now in the library of Syon Abbey, South Brent, Devon, Record: 1812, box 25: Other Houses: Letter (copy): K. Witham: Lisbon [1756].

16 The Braddock account appears in Charles Davy, *Letters, addressed chiefly to a Young Gentleman upon Subjects of Literature*, 2 vols (Bury St Edmunds: for the author, 1787), I, pp. 12–60, and was later reprinted as *An Account by an Eye-Witness of the Lisbon Earthquake of November 1, 1755* (Lisbon: British Historical Society of Portugal, 1985).

17 *Gentleman's Magazine* 25 (1755), p. 591.

18 João Duarte Fonseca, *1755: The Lisbon Earthquake* (Lisbon: Argumentum, 2005), p. 130.

19 *An Account of the Late Dreadful Earthquake and Fire*, p. 20.

20 *Gentleman's Magazine* 25 (1755), p. 560.

21 The letter was printed after Thomas Chase's death, over three consecutive issues of the *Gentleman's Magazine* 83 (1813), pp. 105–10, 201–6, and 314–17, from which the following extracts are taken.

22 *An Account of the Late Dreadful Earthquake and Fire*, pp. 30–31.

23 Thomas Prince, *An Improvement of the Doctrine of Earthquakes, Being the Works of God, and Tokens of his just Displeasure* (Boston: D. & Z. Fowle, 1755), p. 3.

24 In Macaulay, *They Went to Portugal*, p. 270.

25 John Biddulph, *A Poem on the Earthquake at Lisbon* (London: W. Owen, 1755), pp. 6–7.

26 Portuguese State Papers SP 89/50, f. 114, National Archives, Kew.

27 *Gentleman's Magazine* 25 (1755), p. 594.

28 Cited in T. D. Kendrick, *The Lisbon Earthquake* (London: Methuen, 1956), p. 41.

29 Portuguese State Papers SP 89/50, f. 114.

30 Cited in Elias Nason, *Sir Charles Henry Frankland, Baronet: or, Boston in the Colonial Times* (Albany, N.Y.: J. Munsell, 1865), p. 62. The British diplomat Sir Charles Frankland was badly injured by a collapsed building during the earthquake, but was rescued later that afternoon by his American mistress, Agnes Surriage, whom he married on board a vessel bound for England a few days later. The dramatic story went on to inspire a number of historical novels, including Edwin Bynner's *Agnes Surriage* (Boston: Ticknor & Co., 1886); Sir Arthur Quiller-Couch's *Lady Good-for-Nothing: A Man's Portrait of a Woman* (London: Nelson, 1910); and Thomas B. Smith's *Yankee Cinderella* (North Attleboro, Ma.: Covered Bridge Press, 1996).

31 Cited in Marcus Cheke, *Dictator of Portugal: A Life of the Marquis of Pombal 1699–1782* (London: Sidgwick & Jackson, 1938), p. 66. See also C. R. Boxer, 'Pombal's Dictatorship and the Great Lisbon Earthquake, 1755', *History Today 5* (1955), pp. 729–36.

32 Cited in John Smith, *Memoirs of the Marquis of Pombal*, 2 vols (London: Longman, Brown, and Green, 1843), I, pp. 92–4.

33 Cited in Kendrick, *The Lisbon Earthquake*, p. 89.

34 *Gentleman's Magazine* 25 (1755), p. 594. The British contribution is cited in Smith, *Memoirs of the Marquis of Pombal*, I, p. 104.

35 George Whitefield, *A Letter from a Clergyman at London to the Remaining Disconsolate Inhabitants of Lisbon: Occasioned by the Late Dreadful Earthquake, and Conflagration, by which that great and populous City, with many other Parts of that late flourishing Kingdom, have been laid in Ruins* (London: R. Griffiths, 1755), p. 18.

36 John Wesley, *Serious Thoughts Occasioned by the late Earthquake at Lisbon* (London and Bristol: E. Farley, 1755), pp. 5–9.

37 Peckard and Herring are cited in Kendrick, *The Lisbon Earthquake*, pp. 159–61.

38 Ibid., p. 157.

39 John Michell, *Conjectures concerning the Cause, and Observations upon the Phænomena, of Earthquakes; particularly of that great Earthquake of the first of November 1755, which proved so fatal to the City of Lisbon, and whose Effects were felt as far as Africa, and more or less throughout almost all Europe* (London, 1760), p. 6.

40 Ibid., pp. 37–8.

41 Clyde L. Hardin, 'The Scientific Work of the Reverend John Michell', *Annals of Science* 22 (1966), p. 30. See also Archibald Geikie, *Memoir of John Michell* (Cambridge: Cambridge University Press, 1918).

42 *Selected Works of Voltaire*, trans. Joseph McCabe (London: Watts & Co., 1935), p. 1.

43 *Voltaire's Correspondence*, ed. Theodore Besterman, 107 vols (Geneva: Institut et Musée Voltaire, 1953–65), XXX, p. 115.

44 *Candide* was an immediate Europe-wide success, with two rival English translations appearing within months of the original: *Candid: or, All for the Best* (London: J. Nourse, 1759), and *Candidus: or, the Optimist*, trans. W. Rider (Dublin: Hoey and Smith, 1759). This extract is from the former, pp. 17–18.

45 Cited in Nancy Mitford, *Madame de Pompadour*, 2nd edn (London: Hamish Hamilton, 1968), p. 252.

46 Walpole and Delany quoted in Kendrick, *The Lisbon Earthquake*, pp. 148; 163.

47 Thomas Hartley, *God's Controversy with the Nations. Addressed to the Rulers and People of Christendom* (London: R. Manby, 1756), p. 15.

48 For the life of William Stephens see Jenifer Roberts, *Glass: The Strange History of the Lyne Stephens Fortune* (Chippenham: Templeton, 2003). Also among the swarm of British merchants who entered the post-quake building trade was John

Parminter, a Devon-born wine exporter, who had turned to the manufacture of quick-drying cement within days of the disaster. The fortune he made would later pay for the building of an extraordinary sixteen-sided house near Exmouth – 'A La Ronde' – now in the care of the National Trust.

49 For Pombal's questionnaire in full, see Fonseca, *1755: The Lisbon Earthquake*, pp. 120–21.

50 *Gentleman's Magazine* 25 (1755), pp. 589–90.

51 See Davison, *Great Earthquakes*, pp. 15–18.

52 Joseph Baretti, *A Journey from London to Genoa, through England, Portugal, Spain, and France*, 2 vols (London: T. Davies, 1770), I, p. 101.

53 For further details of the reconstruction see Kenneth Maxwell, *Pombal: Paradox of the Enlightenment* (Cambridge: Cambridge University Press, 1995), pp. 24–35; and Fonseca, *1755: The Lisbon Earthquake*, pp. 86–93. The Pombal experiment was only the first of many; following the Iran earthquake of December 2003, in which thirty thousand people died under collapsing mud-built structures, a new lightweight foam building material was successfully tested in the USA, during a trial simulation of a magnitude 10 earthquake, 'stronger than the world has ever experienced.' See *New Scientist* 2484 (29 January 2005), p. 4.

54 Robert Southey, *Letters Written during a short Residence in Spain and Portugal*, 2 vols (Bristol: Joseph Cottle, 1797), II, pp. 260; 389.

55 Henry Matthews, *The Diary of an Invalid; being the Journal of a Tour in Pursuit of Health; in Portugal, Italy, Switzerland, and France in the years 1817, 1818, and 1819* (London: John Murray, 1820), p. 12. Matthews detested the city, claiming that 'the abominations of Lisbon are incapable of exaggeration' (p. 11), although some of his frustration seems to have stemmed from his failure to encounter any of the 'licentious feastings and debaucheries' which his reading of George Whitefield's sermons had apparently led him to expect (p. 24).

56 Saramago, *Journey to Portugal*, p. 334.

PART TWO: EUROPEAN WEATHER PANIC

1 Quoted in Claude-Anne Lopez, *Mon Cher Papa: Franklin and the Ladies of Paris*, 2nd edn (New Haven and London: Yale University Press, 1990), p. 202.

2 Cited in Esmond Wright, *Franklin of Philadelphia* (Cambridge, Mass.: Harvard University Press, 1986), p. 263.

3 Letter to Captain Nathaniel Falconer, dated 28 July 1783, in *The Writings of Benjamin Franklin*, ed. Albert H. Smyth, 10 vols (New York: Macmillan, 1905–7), IX, p. 77.

4 Benjamin Franklin, 'Meteorological Imaginations and Conjectures', *Memoirs of the Literary and Philosophical Society of Manchester* 2 (1785), pp. 357–61; also in *Writings* IX, pp. 215–18.

5 Robert Paul de Lamanon, *Journal de Physique* 24 (1784), p. 12; later translated as 'Observations on the Nature of the Fog of 1783', *Philosophical Magazine* 5 (1799), p. 83.

6 Ibid.

7 Arago cited in J. A. Kington, 'July 1783: The warmest month in the Central England temperature series', *Climate Monitor* 9:3 (1980), p. 71; Toaldo cited in *Philosophical Magazine* 4 (1799), pp. 418–19.

8 In G. R. Demarée and A. E. J. Ogilvie, '*Bons Baisers d'Islande*: Climatic, Environmental, and Human Dimensions Impacts of the *Lakagígar* Erup-tion (1783–1784) in Iceland', in *History and Climate: Memories of the Future?*, ed. Jones et al. (New York and London: Kluwer Academic, 2001), p. 234.

9 Cited in John Grattan and Mark Brayshay, 'An Amazing and Portentous Summer: Environmental and Social Responses in Britain to the 1783 Eruption of an Iceland Volcano', *The Geographical Journal* 161:2 (1995), p. 128.

10 Cited in Demarée and Ogilvie, *Bons Baisers d'Islande*, p. 231.

11 *Gentleman's Magazine* 53:2 (1783), p. 620.

12 *The Letters and Prose Writings of William Cowper*, ed. James King and Charles Ryskamp, 5 vols (Oxford: Clarendon, 1979–86), II, pp. 143–4.

13 Ibid., p. 146.

14 Ibid., pp. 148–9.

15 Ibid., p. 149.

16 *The Yale Edition of Horace Walpole's Correspondence*, ed. W. S. Lewis, 48 vols (Oxford: Oxford University Press, 1937–83), XXXIII, pp. 404–5.

17 Cited in G. R. Demarée, A. E. J. Ogilvie, and D. Zhang, 'Further Documentary Evidence of Northern Hemispheric Coverage of the Great Dry Fog of 1783', *Climatic Change* 39 (1998), p. 729.

18 Cited in Demarée and Ogilvie, *Bons Baisers d'Islande*, p. 233.

19 *Journal de Paris*, 2 July 1783.

20 'Weatherwise' saying in *Poor Richard's Almanack* (Philadelphia: B. Franklin, 1735); 'Meteorological Imaginations and Conjectures', p. 60.

21 Cited in Demarée and Ogilvie, *Bons Baisers d'Islande*, p. 225.

22 *Philosophical Transactions* 73:1 (1784), pp. 169–208. Extracts from this account were widely circulated, appearing, for example in the *General Evening Post* for 17–19 July, and in the *Gentleman's Magazine* 53:2 (1783), pp. 785–6.

23 *The Yale Edition of Horace Walpole's Correspondence*, XXXV, p. 373.

24 Cited in Demarée and Ogilvie, *Bons Baisers d'Islande*, p. 237.

25 *Gentleman's Magazine* 53:2 (1783), p. 787.

26 This translation appeared in almost every newspaper in Britain during July 1783, as well as in monthly periodicals such as the *Gentleman's Magazine* 53:2 (1783), p. 613.

27 Quoted in the *Dictionary of Scientific Biography*, ed. Charles Coulston Gillespie, 18 vols (New York: Scribners, 1970–81), VII, p. 579.

28 *The Journal of the Rev. John Wesley, A.M.*, ed. Nehemiah Curnock, 8 vols (London: Robert Culley, 1909–16), VI, p. 433.

29 *Journal de Physique* 24 (1784), p. 21; *Philosophical Magazine* 5 (1799), p. 83.

30 Burnett cited in Kington, 'July 1783: The warmest month', p. 71.

31 See Rudolf Brázdil, Hubert Valáöek, and Jarmila Macková, 'Climate in the Czech Lands during the 1780s in Light of the Daily Weather Records of Parson Karel Bernard Hein of Hodonice (Southwestern Moravia): Comparison of Documentary and Instrumental Data', *Climatic Change* 60:3 (2003), pp. 297–327.

32 All cited in Demarée and Ogilvie, *Bons Baisers d'Islande*, p. 228.

33 *Gentleman's Magazine* 53:2 (1783), p. 622.

34 Ibid., p. 714.

35 Gilbert White, *The Natural History of Selborne*, ed. Richard Mabey (Harmondsworth: Penguin, 1977), p. 264.

36 Cited in Demarée and Ogilvie, *Bons Baisers d'Islande*, p. 236.

37 Ibid.

38 Cited in Claire Witham and Clive Oppenheimer, 'Mortality in England during the 1783–4 Laki Craters eruption', *Bulletin of Volcanology* 67 (2005), p. 24.

39 *The Yale Edition of Horace Walpole's Correspondence*, XXXV, p. 373.

40 Ibid., XX, pp. 119–20.

41 Cited in Kendrick, *The Lisbon Earthquake*, p. 4.

42 Oliver Goldsmith, *The Good Natur'd Man: a Comedy. As Performed at the Theatre-Royal in Covent-Garden* (London: W. Griffin, 1768), Act 1, line 293.

43 *General Evening Post*, 17–19 July 1783.

44 *Journal de Physique* 24 (1784), p. 9; *Philosophical Magazine* 5 (1799), p. 82.

45 Ibid. (1799), pp. 82–3.

46 Ibid. (1799), pp. 86–7.

47 White, *Natural History of Selborne*, p. 261.

48 Ibid., p. 265.

49 *Philosophical Transactions* 74:1 (1784), pp. 284–5.

50 *The Journals of Gilbert White*, ed. Francesca Greenoak, 3 vols (London: Century, 1986–89) II, p. 505.

51 *Gentleman's Magazine* 53:2 (1783), p. 661.

52 Ibid., p. 712.

53 Ibid., p. 711.

54 *Philosophical Transactions* 74:1 (1784), pp. 116–17.

55 *Gentleman's Magazine* 53:2 (1783), p. 712.

56 Ibid., p. 713. The artist Paul Sandby, who had witnessed the meteor's progress from the terrace of Windsor Castle, made a watercolour drawing of the scene from memory, complete with detailed annotations describing its journey through the sky until 'it disappeared from the interposition of a Cloud'. The watercolour is reproduced in Jane Roberts, *Views of Windsor: Watercolours by*

Thomas and Paul Sandby from the Collection of Her Majesty Queen Elizabeth II (London: Merrell Holberton, 1995), pp. 68–9; for a full description of the meteor as seen from the terrace at Windsor Castle see Tiberius Cavallo's eyewitness account in *Phil. Trans.* 74:1 (1784), pp. 108–11.

57 *The Yale Edition of Horace Walpole's Correspondence*, XXV, p. 427; *General Evening Post*, 17–19 July 1783.

58 *The Poems of William Cowper*, ed. John D. Baird & Charles Ryskamp, 3 vols (Oxford: Clarendon, 1980-95), II, pp. 137–40. Was Cowper also thinking of Hotspur's words in Shakespeare's *Henry IV, Part 1*: 'Diseased nature oftentimes breaks forth / In strange eruptions: oft the teeming earth / Is with a kind of colic pinch'd and vex'd / By the imprisoning of unruly wind / Within her womb; which for enlargement striving, / Shakes the old beldame earth, and topples down / Steeples and moss-grown towers'? [Act 3, Scene 1.]

59 Quoted in Wright, *Franklin of Philadelphia*, p. 262.

60 Ibid., p. 290.

61 Ibid., p. 269.

62 *Writings*, II, p. 302. See also Patricia Fara, *An Entertainment for Angels: Electricity in the Enlightenment* (Cambridge: Icon Books, 2002), pp. 67–75.

63 *Writings*, II, p. 303, and in Benjamin Franklin, *Experiments and Observations on Electricity, Made at Philadelphia in America* (London: E. Cave, 1751–53), p. 10.

64 *Writings*, III, p. 255.

65 Franklin, *Experiments and Observations*, p. 63.

66 Ibid., pp. 62–3.

67 Cited in Wright, *Franklin of Philadelphia*, p. 67. Abbé Nollet, Franklin's most persistent opponent on the matter, declared that 'bells, by virtue of their benediction, should scatter the thunder-storms and preserve us from strokes of lightning . . . it is as impious to ward off God's lightnings as for a child to resist the chastening rod of the father.' Cited in I. Bernard Cohen, *Benjamin Franklin's Science* (Cambridge, Mass.: Harvard University Press, 1990), pp. 120; 158.

68 *Writings*, V, p. 398. See also Fara, *An Entertainment for Angels*, pp. 76–81.

69 Cited in *Writings*, I, p. 107.

70 See Franklin, *Writings*, I, p. 108; footnote from the *Guardian*, 19 May 2005, p. 30.

71 *Writings*, I, p. 105. See also Ralph Korngold, *Robespierre: First Modern Dictator* (London: Macmillan, 1937), pp. 33–5.

72 For the ballooning episode see *Writings*, IX, pp. 79–85, and Carl van Doren, *Benjamin Franklin* (New York: Viking, 1938), pp. 700–702.

73 Cited in van Doren, *Benjamin Franklin*, p. 423.

74 Franklin, 'Meteorological Imaginations and Conjectures', pp. 60–61.

75 Saemund Magnussen Holm, 'Account of a remarkable Fiery Eruption from the Earth, in Iceland, in the Year 1783', *Philosophical Magazine* 3 (1799), p. 116.

76 Cited in Richard B. Stothers, 'The Great Dry Fog of 1783', *Climate Change* 32 (1996), p. 80.

77 Svante Arrhenius, 'On the Influence of Carbonic Acid in the Air upon the Temperature of the Ground', *The London, Edinburgh and Dublin Philosophical Magazine and Journal of Science* 41 (1896), pp. 237–76; reprinted in H. Rodhe and R. Charlson (eds), *The Legacy of Svante Arrhenius: Understanding the Greenhouse Effect* (Stockholm: 1998), pp. 173–212.

78 Intergovernmental Panel on Climate Change, *Climate Change 2007: The Physical Science Basis: Summary for Policymakers* (Geneva, 2007), p. 10.

79 Ibid., pp. 4–8 (their emphasis).

80 For a thorough yet accessible overview of the science see Mark Maslin, *Global Warming: A Very Short Introduction*, 2nd edn (Oxford: Oxford University Press, 2008); and Mike Hulme, *Why We Disagree About Climate Change: Understanding Controversy, Inaction and Opportunity* (Cambridge: Cambridge University Press, 2009). In his bicentennial lecture on Franklin at the American Philosophical Society in April 1906, Cleveland Abbe read out Franklin's 1784 report in full, describing its author as 'the pioneer of the rational long-range forecasters'. See Abbe, 'Benjamin Franklin as Meteorologist', *Proceedings of the American Philosophical Society* 45 (1906), p. 128.

81 James Lovelock, *The Revenge of Gaia: Why the Earth is Fighting Back* (London: Allen Lane, 2006). Lovelock apparently believes that the point of no return has already been reached, and that governments around the world need to start preparing survival packs for the few human beings who will still be around at the end of the twenty-first century.

82 *Writings*, VIII, p. 10.

83 Writings, IX, pp. 572–3.

PART THREE: THE ERUPTION OF KRAKATAU

1 In common with several other eyewitness accounts cited in this chapter, this transcript of Baker's interview is sourced from Tom Simkin and Richard S. Fiske's definitive study, *Krakatau 1883: The Volcanic Eruption and its Effects* (Washington, D.C.: Smithsonian Institution, 1983), pp. 98–101.

2 Ibid., p. 216.

3 Seaman R. J. Dalby, of the Liverpool barque *Hope*, in a BBC radio interview given in 1937, a transcript of which was published in the *Listener* 17: 427 (17 March 1937), pp. 496–98. He was seventy-five years old at the time of the interview.

4 Simkin and Fiske, *Krakatau 1883*, p. 14.

5 Simon Winchester, *Krakatoa: The Day the World Exploded 27th August 1883* (London: Viking, 2003), pp. 374; 393.

6 See Henry and Elizabeth Stommel, *Volcano Weather: The story of 1816, the year without a summer* (Newport, R.I.: Seven Seas Press, 1983).

7   Winchester, *Krakatoa*, p. 317.
8   Cited in Simkin and Fiske, *Krakatau 1883*, p. 286.
9   Ibid., p. 308.
10 For Javanese volcano legends see Lorne Blair, *Ring of Fire: An Indonesian Odyssey* (London: Inner Traditions, 1991), pp. 46–8; and Jelle Zeilinga de Boer and Donald T. Sanders, *Volcanoes in Human History: The Far-Reaching Effects of Major Eruptions* (Princeton: Princeton University Press, 2002), pp. 184–5.
11 See Tom Simkin and Lee Siebert, *Volcanoes of the World*, 2nd edn (Tucson: Geoscience, 1994), pp. 64–79; 167–70.
12 See Rupert Furneaux, *Krakatoa* (London: Secker & Warburg, 1965), pp. 10–13.
13 Cited in Verbeek, *Krakatau*, p. 88; Simkin and Fiske, *Krakatau 1883*, p. 59.
14 Ibid.
15 Furneaux, *Krakatoa*, p. 11.
16 Winchester, *Krakatoa*, p. 168.
17 Cited in Simkin and Fiske, *Krakatau 1883*, p. 60.
18 The Schuurman account was collected by R. D. M. Verbeek in his official government report, *Krakatau* (Batavia: Landsdrukkerij, 1885), pp. 17–23; this translation is from Simkin and Fiske, *Krakatau 1883*, pp. 63–6.
19 *The Graphic* 715 (11 August 1883), p. 145. The caption reads: 'A Volcanic Eruption at the Island of Krakatau in the Straits of Sunda, Midway between Java and Sumatra'.
20 Simkin and Fiske, *Krakatau 1883*, p. 67.
21 Ferzenaar's report was first published in Verbeek, *Krakatau*, pp. 25–7; this translation is from Simkin and Fiske, *Krakatau 1883*, p. 67–8.
22 Simkin and Fiske, *Krakatau 1883*, p. 68.
23 Ibid., p. 73.
24 Captain Watson's account first appeared in the *Liverpool Daily Post* in October 1883; then in *Nature* 29 (1883), pp. 140–41, and *Atlantic Monthly* 54 (1884), pp. 387–9, before being published in Verbeek, *Krakatau* (1885), pp. 70–72, and subsequently in Simkin and Fiske, *Krakatau 1883*, pp. 102–105.
25 Simkin and Fiske, *Krakatau 1883*, p. 102.
26 Schruit's account first appeared in the Dutch-language *Bataviaasch Handelsblad* on 9 September 1883, and subsequently in this English translation in the *Ceylon Observer* for 2 October 1883. See Simkin and Fiske, *Krakatau 1883*, pp. 69–73.
27 Cited in Furneaux, *Krakatoa*, p. 78.
28 Simkin and Fiske, *Krakatau 1883*, pp. 72–3.
29 Cited in Furneaux, *Krakatoa*, p. 81.
30 Simkin and Fiske, *Krakatau 1883*, p. 79.
31 Philip Neale, 'The Krakatoa Eruption', *Leisure Hour* 34 (1885), p. 637; Simkin and Fiske, *Krakatau 1883*, p. 77.
32 Furneaux, *Krakatoa*, p. 89.

33 Extracts from Captain Lindemann's logbook (a manuscript copy of which is lodged in the National Archives at Kew, ref. MT 10/409) were published in the *Proceedings of the Royal Society of London* 36 (1884), pp. 199–203; see also Simkin and Fiske, *Krakatau 1883*, p. 91.

34 Ibid., p. 94.

35 Ibid., p. 91.

36 Ibid., p. 101.

37 Ibid., p. 103.

38 In Verbeek, *Krakatau*, pp. 480–81; and Simkin and Fiske, *Krakatau 1883*, p. 99.

39 Furneaux, *Krakatoa*, p. 105.

40 Simkin and Fiske, *Krakatau 1883*, p. 92

41 Ian Thornton, *Krakatau: The Destruction and Reassembly of an Island Ecosystem* (Cambridge, Mass.: Harvard University Press, 1996), p. 1.

42 Furneaux, *Krakatoa*, p. 138.

43 Ibid., p. 106.

44 Simkin and Fiske, *Krakatau 1883*, p. 76.

45 Furneaux, *Krakatoa*, p. 100.

46 Simkin and Fiske, *Krakatau 1883*, p. 102.

47 Cited in Winchester, *Krakatoa*, p. 276. The tsunami was referred to by Major Baird of the Royal Society as a 'supertidal' wave, while the withdrawal of the sea was referred to as a 'negative supertidal wave'; see the 'Report on the Tidal Disturbances caused by the Volcanic Eruptions at Java, August 27 and 28, 1883, and the Propagations of the "Supertidal" Waves', in *Proceedings of the Royal Society of London* 36 (1883), pp. 248–53.

48 Both cited in Simkin and Fiske, *Krakatau 1883*, pp. 95; 105.

49 Furneaux, *Krakatoa*, p. 167.

50 *The Times*, 30 August 1883, p. 3.

51 *Liverpool Daily Post*, 4 September 1883, p. 6.

52 Neale, 'The Krakatoa Eruption', p. 556.

53 Cited in Furneaux, *Krakatoa*, p. 138.

54 Neale, 'The Krakatoa Eruption', p. 556.

55 Furneaux, *Krakatoa*, p. 136.

56 Simkin and Fiske, *Krakatau 1883*, pp. 91–2; 96.

57 Ibid., p. 101.

58 Ibid., p. 271.

59 Winchester, *Krakatoa*, p. 269.

60 Robert Scott, 'Notes on a Series of Barometrical Disturbances which Passed over Europe between the 27th and 31st of August 1883', *Proceedings of the Royal Society of London* 36 (1884), p. 139. Scott's article was followed by a 'Note on the foregoing Paper' by Richard Strachey, FRS, in which the global nature of the phenomenon ('it had travelled before its extinction more than 82,200 miles, and had passed 3¼ times round the entire circuit of the earth') was reiterated.

Idem., p 149. See also E. R. Weston, 'Atmospheric waves from Krakatoa', *Science 3* (1884), p. 531.

61 E. L. Layard, in *Nature* 29 (1884), p. 461, cited in Simkin and Fiske, *Krakatau 1883*, p. 154.

62 G. M. Hopkins, 'The Remarkable Sunsets', *Nature* 29 (1884), pp. 222–3. It has also been surmised that Tennyson's poem *St. Telemachus* (1892) makes reference to the Krakatau sunsets: 'Had the fierce ashes of some fiery peak / Been hurled so high they ranged about the globe? / For day by day, thro' many a blood-red eve'. See Simkin and Fiske, p. 395.

63 Joseph Wharton, 'Dust from the Krakatoa Eruption of 1883', *Proceedings of the American Philosophical Society* 32 (1894), pp. 343–5.

64 G. J. Symons, et al, *The Eruption of Krakatoa, and Subsequent Phenomena: Report of the Krakatoa Committee of the Royal Society* (London: Trübner & Co., 1888). This volume was the product of an unprecedented worldwide interdisciplinary endeavour, described by Symons as 'altogether very heavy, for it has not only extended back to the year 1500, but it has ramified through many branches of physics, and has involved extensive correspondence with all parts of the globe' (p. vi).

65 Cited in Simkin and Fiske, *Krakatau 1883*, p. 18.

66 Verbeek, *Krakatau*, p. v. A summary of Verbeek's initial findings was published (in English) in *Nature* 30 (1884), pp. 10–15; a translation of the foreword to the final report appeared in *Nature* 33 (1886), pp. 560–61. See Simkin and Fiske, p. 455.

67 Translation from Thornton, *Krakatau*, p. 132.

68 Winchester, *Krakatoa*, p. 351.

69 Ian Thornton, *Krakatau: The Destruction and Reassembly of an Island Ecosystem* (Cambridge, Mass.: Harvard University Press, 1996), p. 5.

70 Ibid., p. 175.

71 Ibid., p. 282.

72 Mike Rampino, speaking in the Channel 4 film *Krakatoa* (120 mins, 2005), broadcast on 22 January 2005.

73 See Matthias Dörries, 'Global science: the eruption of Krakatoa', *Endeavour* 27:3 (2003), p. 115.

PART FOUR: THE HILO TSUNAMI

1 Most of the eyewitness accounts in this chapter are sourced from the two-volume collection of interview transcripts produced by the Center for Oral History at the University of Hawaii at Manoa: *Tsunamis Remembered: Oral Histories of Survivors and Observers in Hawai'i*, 2 vols (Honolulu: Social Science Research Institute, 2000). The interviews were conducted by Warren Nishimoto and Nancy Pi'ianaia, to whom I am extremely grateful for permission to

quote from their transcripts, as well as to the individual interviewees themselves, whose voices give life to this chapter: the late Bunji Fujimoto; Masuo
Kino; Marsue McGinnis McShane; Kapua Heuer; Alexander Riviera; Robert
"Steamy" Chow; Jimmy Low; Masao Uchima; June Odachi; Fusae Takaki;
Hayato Okino; Herbert Nishimoto; and Jeanne Branch Johnson. Unless noted
otherwise, the eyewitness accounts quoted throughout this chapter are derived
from this University of Hawaii collection. Many other details, particularly when
it comes to the Pacific Tsunami Warning System, are sourced from Walter C.
Dudley and Min Lee's exhaustive study, *Tsunami!*, 2nd edn (Honolulu: University of Hawaii Press, 1998).

2 Cited in *April Fool's . . . The Laupahoehoe Tragedy of 1946: An Oral History* (Hawaii:
   Laupahoehoe School, 1997), p. 12.

3 See the entry on 'rain' in Mary Kawena Pukui and Samuel H. Elbert, *Hawaiian
   Dictionary* (Honolulu: University of Hawaii Press, 1973), at the end of which the
   reader is directed to the entry on Hilo ('*See* downpour, Hilo'), which describes
   the city as 'famous in song as the home of Chief Hanakahi, and for rain.' *HD*,
   II, p. 73; p. 124.

4 From an information panel in the Pacific Tsunami Museum, 130 Kamehameha
   Ave., Hilo, Hawaii.

5 Marsue McGinnis Fernandez, 'Swept to Sea by a Tidal Wave', *Reader's Digest*
   (April 1959), pp. 27-32.

6 See *Hawaiian Dictionary*, I, p. 109. According to Walter Dudley and Scott C.
   Stone, the phenomenon of the seismic seiche (the sequence of resonant oscilla-
   tions in enclosed or semi-enclosed bodies of water, which occurred throughout
   Europe on the morning of the Lisbon earthquake) has also been observed in
   Hilo Bay, where it is referred to by the locals as *kai ku piki'o*. See Walter Dudley
   and Scott C. S. Stone, *The Tsunami of 1946 and 1960 and the Devastation of Hilo
   Town* (Virginia Beach: The Donning Company, 2000), p. 28.

7 From another information panel in the Pacific Tsunami Museum.

8 R. H. Finch, 'On the prediction of tidal waves', *Monthly Weather Review* 52:3
   (1924), cited in Dudley and Lee, *Tsunami!*, p. 102.

9 Ibid., p. 104.

10 Ibid., p. 105.

11 Cited in ibid., p. 5.

12 G. A. Macdonald, F. P. Shepard, and D. C. Cox, 'The Tsunami of April 1, 1946,
    in the Hawaiian Islands', *Pacific Science* 1 (1947), p. 36.

13 Lafcadio Hearn, *Gleanings in Buddha-Fields: Studies of Hand and Soul in the Far
    East* (London and New York: Harper Brothers, 1897), p. 16. The word *tsunami*
    translates literally as 'harbour wave'.

14 Ibid., pp. 20–25.

15 See Donald and David Hyndman, *Natural Hazards and Disasters* (New York:
    Thomson, 2006), p. 101.

16 From Charles Davison, *The Founders of Seismology* (Cambridge: Cambridge University Press, 1927), p. 103.

17 H. O. Wood and F. Neumann, 'Modified Mercalli Intensity Scale of 1931', *Bulletin of the Seismological Society of America* 21:4 (1931), pp. 277–83.

18 See Matthys Levy and Mario Salvadori, *Why the Earth Quakes: the Story of Earthquakes and Volcanoes* (New York: Norton, 1995), pp. 77–8.

19 Dudley and Lee, *Tsunami!*, p. 107.

20 Ibid., p. 145.

21 Cited in *April Fool's. . .* , p. 15.

22 Edward Bryant, *Tsunami: The Underrated Hazard* (Cambridge: Cambridge University Press, 2001), pp. 152–6.

23 Dudley and Lee, *Tsunami!*, pp. 253; 272.

24 http://tsunamilessons.blogspot.com/2006/11/hawaii-tsunami-was-real-but-some.html; accessed 27 March 2008.

25 See Eli Kintisch, 'Global Tsunami Warning System Takes Shape', *Science* 307 (21 January 2005), p. 331.

26 BBC News 24, 9 September 2005, 15:17 GMT.

27 See Mike Davis, 'Tsunami Memories: Disaster-Tourism on the Big Island', *Landfall* 201 (2001), p. 54.

28 Ibid., p. 53.

29 Conner Gorry and Julie Jares, *Hawaii: The Big Island* (Melbourne: Lonely Planet Publications, 2002), p. 177.

ACKNOWLEDGEMENTS

I have incurred many debts during the research and writing of this book, not least to the libraries, archives and museum collections which generously supplied its raw materials; so it's a pleasure to thank the staff of the British Library; the Newspaper Library, Colindale; the University of London Library; the National Archives, Kew; the Department of Manuscripts and Special Collections, University of Nottingham; the Royal Geographical Society; the Royal Institution; the Science Museum, London; and York City Archives. In Lisbon, the staff of the Biblioteca Nacional and the Museu da Cicade were helpful beyond the call of duty, as was Dr João Duarte Fonseca of the Lisbon Technical University, who kindly presented me with a copy of his superbly illustrated dual-language study *1755: The Lisbon Earthquake* (Lisbon: Argumentum, 2005). In Hawaii, Genevieve Cain and the rest of the staff and volunteers at the Pacific Tsunami Museum, Hilo, were exceptionally generous in sharing their knowledge and expertise, as was Dennis Dungochi at the Lyman Museum and Mission House, Hilo, and Doug Connors at the Laupahoehoe Train Museum. While staying in Hilo, I was lucky enough to meet and 'talk story' with Robert 'Steamy' Chow, a key eyewitness of the 1946 tsunami, and, since 1999, an officially recognized Living Legend of Hilo. His eyewitness testimony of the Fool's Day tsunami, as were most of the others cited in part four, were recorded by Warren Nishimoto and Nancy Pi'ianaia of the Center for Oral History at the University of Hawaii at Manoa, and I am extremely grateful to Dr Nishimoto for granting me permission to quote from the Center's unparalleled collection of tran-

Acknowledgements

261

scripts. I would also like to thank Dr Richard S. Fiske of the Smithsonian Institution's National Museum of Natural History, who kindly retrieved the 130-year-old photograph of Sidney Tucker Baker (see picture 14) from a long-buried box file in the Museum's archives and passed it on to me.

Some of the material in part one was published in different form as 'Notes from Underground: Lisbon after the Earthquake', in a special issue of the journal *Romanticism* (vol. 14.2, 2008) that was devoted to the theme of 're-imagining the city'; I am grateful to the journal's guest editor, Gregory Dart, for the opportunity to preview some of the Lisbon material, as well as to the other contributors for their insightful comments and advice.

Family, friends and colleagues have also been a constant source of encouragement and good sense, especially Jo, Ben and Jessica Hamblyn, Markman Ellis, Gavin Jones, Piers Russell-Cobb and Peter Straus, as well as Jon Adams, Giles Bergel, Stephen Daniels, William Fiennes, Angie Foster, Michael Griffiths, David Hamblyn, Judith Hawley, Noah Heringman, Megan Hiatt, Robert J. *'Haole'* Howell, Betsy Hurley, Anthony & Paula Lynch, Mark Maslin, Robert McSweeney, Beth Moore, Michael Newton, Marian Peglar, Lynda Pratt, Julie Sanders, and Adrian & Emma Simpson. A thousand thanks are also due to everyone at Picador, especially my wondrous editors, Andrew Kidd and Sam Humphreys, whose patience and forbearance have been much appreciated throughout the time that it has taken me to work out how to finish this book.

INDEX

Note: References in *italics* refer to Picture Sections.

Account of the late Dreadful Earthquake and Fire . . .,
    An 19–22
Aceh province 244
Aden 163
aid, international 43, 165–6, 239–41
Akiona, Daniel 186, 205
Aleutian Islands 209–10, 212
Aleutian Trench 204, 209, 212, 229, 230
Alps 92
Alvares da Silva, José 48–9
American Civil War 191
American War of Independence 65, 66, 102, 103,
    108
Anak Krakatau 176–80; *21*
animals 90
Anjer, Java 127, 129–30, 138, 139, 146, 149–50,
    152–4, 157, 162, 165, 168–9
aphids 85–6
Arago, Dominique François 68
Archimedes 103
Aristotle 16
Arrhenius, Svante 117–18
Atlantic Ocean 17, 25, 51, 56
    Mid-Atlantic Ridge 13, 114
atmosphere 173–4
    (1783) *see* fog (haze) over Europe
    after Krakatau eruption 126, 135, 171–4;
      19
    pollution 87, 91–3, 114, 116–19

Baker, Captain Benjamin C. 125, 126, 159, 169
Baker, Sidney Tucker 125, 126, 127, 128, 131,
    144–5, 158, 169; *14*
balloons 109–10, 121, *12*
Bam, Iran 227, 240

Bangladesh 242–3
Banten 165
Barcelona 86
Barker, Thomas 95, 96
barographs 170
Baschi, Comte de 53
Batavia (Jakarta; Java) 126, 129–30, 139–40, 142,
    144, 146, 149, 153, 165, 166, 168
Bataviaasch Handelsblad 149, 152
Bath Chronicle 83, 86
Bazingham, Abbot of 86
Beichuan, China 244
Belém, Portugal 36, 40
bells, church 81–2, 107
Beneawany village 164
Berbice (paraffin-ship) 145, 148–9, 158, 162, 169
Berouw (paddle-steamer) 151, 155–6, 157, 161,
    237; *17*
Beyerinck, Anna 139, 144, 161–2, 167–8
Beyerinck, William 140, 144, 150, 155, 167–8
Bible: disaster prophecies 76–7
Biddulph, John 35–6
Bikini Atoll: observation team xix, 216
Blanchard, Jean-Pierre 111
Book of Kings, Javanese 134–5
Boston 125, 128
Braddock, Daniel 23–4, 26–7, 28–9
Brazil: gold 8–9, 54–5
Bridgettine nuns 22–3, 38
Bristowe, William 178
Britain
    and American War of Independence 65, 66,
      102–3, 108
    and Lisbon earthquake 43, 54
Brown, Michael 241
Buijs, Thomas 153
Buitenzorg (Bogor) 126, 146

Burma 220, 241, 242, 245
Burnett, Janet 81

Calabria, Italy 73, 75, 220
calderas 175–6
Cambridge 49, 51, 86–7
Cancani, Adòlfo 223
Caribbean 56
Carlson, Doug 235
Castres, Abraham 37–8
Catherine of Braganza, Princess 6, 11
Cavendish, Henry 111
Ceylon Observer 163
Charles, Jacques-Alexandre-César 110–11
Charles Bal (British cargo barque) 145–8, 157–9, 163
Chase, Thomas 30–2
Chile 212, 213, 231–2
China 72, 244–5
Chow, Robert 'Steamy' 196–7, 206, 207, 260
climate change xviii, 73, 112, 117–19
Coimbra, Portugal 37
Collinson, Peter 106
Conrad (Dutch mail steamer) 140
Cooper, Revd William 99–100
Cotteau, Edmond 177
Cowper, William 69–71, 101–2, 172
The Task 101–2
Cremnitz, Hungary 82
Cyclone Nargis 241, 242, 244
Cyclone Sidr 242
Czechoslovakia 81–2

Danan crater 176
Davis, Mike 237
de Rossi, Michele 222
de Vries (Straits pilot) 153
de Zipj (Dutch yacht) 134
Deep-ocean Assessment and Reporting of
Tsunamis system (DART) 235–6, 243–4;
33
Delany, Mary 54
disease 86–7
Douglas, Lord Charles 38
Drake, Dorothy 186, 187, 189, 208
Dudley, Walter C. 216, 232, 234
Durant, Will 239
Dutch East India Company 8, 137
Dutch East Indies, government 137–8, 166, 214, 241, 245

earth 245
crust 12, 131–2, 133

formation 12
Gaia hypothesis 119, 174
global warming 116–19
hotspots 114
see also tectonic plates
earthquakes
(1783) 88, 90, 96–7
causes, supposed 75–6, 89–90
formation 12–18
grading 221–6
Indian Ocean 226
Indonesia 135–6
Iran 227, 240
Italy 73–6, 79, 88, 92, 220–1
Japan 213, 215, 219
Kuril Trench 213
London 88–9
Mexico 231
Portugal 12
San Francisco 240
study 49–51
tsunamigenic xvi, 212–13, 229
Chile 212, 213, 231–2
Indian Ocean xvi, 132–3, 226
Indonesia 134–6
Lisbon (1755) 25–7
Pacific 209–10, 227, 229
see also Lisbon earthquake (1755)
Edinburgh Advertiser 76
Egen, Peter 221
electrical storms 80–5
electricity: experiments 103–6
see also lightning
Elisabeth (German warship) 138–9, 140
Enlightenment 42, 45
Evening News 69

Ferzenaar, H. J. G. 143
Fielding, Henry 7
Finch, R. H. 215
fire
Cremnitz 82
Lisbon (1755) 30, 31–3, 35–6, 58
and refracting mirrors 103
see also volcanoes
floods 241, 244
see also tsunamis
fog (haze) over Europe (1783) 66–73, 76–81, 116
Fonseca, João Duarte 25, 260
Fool's Day tsunami (1946) *see under* Hilo Bay,
Hawaii
Forel, François 222

France
   and American War of Independence 65, 102,
      103
   earthquakes 88, 96–7
   and Lisbon earthquake 43, 53–4
   weather (1783) 66–9, 76–9, 81, 86, 96–7
      investigations 91
   see also Paris
Franklin, Benjamin 65–7, 72–3, 102–9, 110–13,
      116, 118, 119–21, 174; 9
French Academy of Sciences 77, 91, 109
Fujimoto, Bunji 183, 184, 186, 188, 208–9, 232

Gaia hypothesis 119, 174
Gazeta Warszawska 82
Gazette van Antwerpen 84
Gazette van Gent 73–4, 82
General Evening Post 81, 87, 88, 90, 101
Gentleman's Magazine 93
   (1755) 5, 19, 24, 27–8, 37, 56
   (1783) 69, 76, 84, 98, 99, 100
George III, King 108
Germany
   and Lisbon earthquake 43
   weather (1783) 76
Geuns, Mathias van 86
Glatz 82
global warming 116–19
Gloucester Journal 79–80
Gohei, Hamaguchi 219–20
Golding, William vii, 245
Goldsmith, Oliver 89
Gouverneur-Generaal Loudon (mail steamer) 140–2,
      144–6, 150, 151, 155, 156–7, 159–61, 163, 168
Graphic 142
Grenoble, France 91
Gulf Stream 119, 120
Gunung Bromo 136, 140
Gunung Kaba 139
Gunung Kelut 137
Gunung Merapi 135–6, 139, 140
Gunung Ringgit 137
Gutenberg, Beno 226

Haiti 240, 244
Hamilton, Sir William 74–5
Hanks, Tom (seismologist) 226
Hawaii 186, 190, 227
   history 190–2
   surf culture 234–5
   tsunamis 211–12, 213, 216–18, 229, 234–5,
      237–8

   (1868) 213
   (1923) 214–15
   (1933) 215
   (1952) 229
   (1957) 230
   (1960) 231–3 .
   in World War II 192, 193–4
   map 185
   see also Hilo Bay, Hawaii; Pacific Tsunami
      Warning System
Hawaiian Volcano Observatory 214–15
Hayashida, Katsuyoshi 195, 198–9
haze *see* fog
Hearn, Lafcadio 218–19
Hecla, Iceland 98, 113
Hein, Karel 81
Herring, Revd Thomas 47
Heuer, Kapua 189, 207–8
Hilo Bay, Hawaii 190, 192, 216, 260
   Kamehameha Avenue 194–7, 205, 208, 232;
      23
   Kuwahara Store 206–7
   Laupahoehoe Point 183–9, 202, 208, 214; 22,
      30
      memorial tablet 209; 29
   Laupahoehoe School 183–4, 185–9, 192, 203
   Pacific Tsunami Museum 208, 237, 238, 260
   tsunamis 212, 213, 214
      (1923) 214–15
      (1933) 215
      (1946) xviii–xix, 183–9, 194–205, 214,
         216–17; 24, 25, 26, 27
         aftermath 205–9; 28
         origin 209–10
      (1952) 229–30
      (1960) 231–3; 31, 32
   in World War II 192, 193–4
   map 185
Hirokawa village, Japan 218–20
Hirshorn, Barry xvi
Holm, Saemund Magnussen 115
honeydew 85
Hopkins, Gerard Manley 172, 179
hot-air balloons 109–10, 121, 12
Hurd, Richard 47
Hurricane Katrina 207, 240–1, 244, 245
hurricanes 240, 241

Iceland 114
   volcanoes 112, 113–14
      Laki Fissures 113–16, 171; 13
      new island 97–8

India 162
Indian Ocean xvi, xvii, 130, 212, 242
   (1883) 126, 162–3, 168, 169–70
   (2004)
      tsunami xv–xvii, 45, 132–3, 136, 166, 220,
        236
      earthquake xvi, 132–3, 226
   Tidal Survey of India 162
Indonesia 130–1, 135–7, 243–4
   see also Java; Sumatra; Sunda Strait
Intergovernmental Oceanographic Commission
   (IOC) 234, 243, 244
Intergovernmental Panel on Climate Change
   (IPCC) 118, 119
international aid 43, 165–6, 239–41
Ipswich Journal 80–1, 84, 85
Italy: earthquakes 73–6, 79, 88, 92, 220–1

J. E. *Ridgeway* (cargo steamer) 173
Jaggar, Thomas A. 214–15
Jakarta *see* Batavia
Japan 212, 213, 215, 218–20, 233
Java 132, 134–7
   (1883) tsunami 125–8, 129–30, 138, 139–40,
      142, 144, 149–50, 152–5, 157
     aftermath 163–9
   (2006) 236
Java Sea 137, 145
Java Trench xvii, 132, 136, 209, 243
Jeffries, John 111
Jesuits 41, 87
João V, King of Portugal 9–10, 11, 36–7, 39–40
Johnson, Fay 186, 187, 189, 208
Johnson, Jeanne Branch 208
Journal de Paris 72, 77–8
Journal de Physique 68, 80, 91

Kali Antoe village 167
Kamchatka 213, 229
Kanamori, Hiroo 226
Karang Antoe 164
Kashmir 244
Kedirie (barge) 168, 175
Ketimbang, Sumatra 139, 144, 150–1, 155, 161
Kiessling, Johann 174
Kingseed, Helen 186, 187, 188, 208
Kino, Masuo 183–4, 187, 188–9, 209
Kirkjubæjarklaustur, Iceland 115
Klatovy, Bohemia 82
Kłodzko 82
Krakatau 129, 130–1, 132, 138, 140–2, 143; *15*
   early eruptions 134–5

(1883)
   eruptions xviii, 125–30, 133–4, 138–43,
      146–52, 157–62, 169–70; *16, 20*
   tsunamis following 152–7, 161–3, 169,
      210, 211, 213
   aftermath 163–71
   aid following 165–6, 245
   effect on atmosphere 171–4; *19*
   subsequent study 174–6; *20*
   Anak Krakatau 176–80; *21*
Krakatau (report) 175; *20*
Kruse, Fred 186, 408
Kuniyuko, Asao 204
Kuril Islands 237
Kuril Trench 213, 229

La Pérouse expedition 93
Laki Fissures, Iceland 113–16, 171; *13*
Lalande, Joseph-Jérôme Lefrançais de 77–80, 90,
   96–7, 111
Lamanon, Robert Paul de 68, 80, 91–3
Lang island 130, 135, 175, 176
Lausanne, France 81
Leicester 83
Leyden jar 103–4, 106
Liège, Belgium: bell foundry 11
lightning 80–5, 97, 105
lightning rods 65, 105, 106–10
Lima, Peru 49
Lincoln 84
Lindemann, Captain 141, 150, 151, 156, 157, 158,
   160, 168
Lisbon, Portugal 241, 260, 261; *1, 4, 5, 6, 7, 8*
   before (1755) 3–12
   auto da fé 33; *4*
   earthquakes 12
   geographical position 13
   Royal Opera House 54; *7*
   see also Lisbon earthquake (1755)
Lisbon earthquake (1755) xvii, xviii, 4, 12, 17–36;
   5, 6, 7, 8
   tsunami following 25–7, 35, 56, 210, 211
   fire 30, 31–3, 35–6, 58
   after-shocks 36–8, 43–4, 55, 60
   death toll 38–9
   international aid and reaction 43, 53–4, 58–61
   accounting for 43–55
      questionnaire 55–6, 57–8, 59
   and literature 51–3
   global effects 56–7
   reconstruction 39–43, 58–9
   subsequently 49–51, 237
Liverpool Daily Post 166

Logan, Captain William 145–6, 148–9, 162, 169
London
    (1783) weather 71, 84–5; *19*
    earthquakes 88–9
    lightning rods 108
London Recorder 71, 90
looting 41, 207; *6*
Lovelock, James 119, 174
Low, Jimmy 197–8

Macaulay, Rose 6, 8
McGinnis, Marsue 186–8, 189, 192, 202–4, 208
Mafra, Portugal 10–11, 54; *2*
Malagrida, Gabriel 41–2, 47
Maldá, Barón de 86
Manchester Literary and Philosophical Society
    112
Marie (salt barque) 155–6
Matthews, Henry 61
Mauna Loa, Hawaii 193–4
Merak village, Java 154–5, 163
Mercalli, Giuseppe 222–3
Messina, Sicily: earthquake 73–6, 79
meteor 98–101; *11*
Mexico 231
Michell, John 49–50, 220
Mid-Atlantic Ridge 13, 114
Milne, John 222
Miyashiro, Evelyn 193–4, 199, 232
Miyashiro, Richard 194–5, 199, 232
Montgolfier, Joseph-Michel and Jacques-Etienne
    110; *12*
Moore, George F. 205–6
Morning Herald 69, 96, 97, 98
Mount Laki, Iceland 113–16, 171; *13*
Mount Pinatubo 116
Mount Tambora 132
Mount Toba 132
Mount Vesuvius 74, 221

National Oceanic and Atmospheric
    Administration
    Deep-ocean Assessment and Reporting of
        Tsunamis system (DART) 235–6, 243–4;
        33
Nature (journal) 172
Nazca plate 212
Neale, Revd Philip 154–5, 166, 167
New Orleans 240–1, 244, 245
Newton, Revd John 69, 70
Nishimoto, Herbert 204–5
Nishimoto, Warren 203, 260

Nollet, Jean-Antoine 103–4
Norham Castle (British mail ship) 145, 146, 158,
    159

Oahu xvi, 217
    see also Pearl Harbor
Okino, Hayato 231

Pacific Ocean xvi, 200, 204, 210, 211, 212, 215,
    227
    La Pérouse expedition 93
    tsunamis 209–11, 212–13, 216, 229–33
        transit times 215, 227–8
        warning system *see* Pacific Tsunami
            Warning System
    US forces in 193–4, 205, 227
    map 204
Pacific Science (journal) 217
Pacific Tsunami Museum 208, 237, 238, 260
Pacific Tsunami Warning Center xvi, 236
Pacific Tsunami Warning System xv, xvii, xix,
    227–8, 229–30, 233–4, 235–6, 243; *30*
Palmieri, Luigi 221–2
Paris, France 65–6, 78–9, 111
    weather (1783) 67–8, 96
Passy, France 65–6, 103, 111
Pearl Harbor 193, 194, 216–17
Peckard, Peter 47
Perboewatan crater 176
Percival, Thomas 112
Philadelphia 104, 106, 120–1, 173
Philippines 116, 125, 169
Phuket Island, Thailand 236
Pignataro, Domenico 221
Pigott, Edward: notebook *10*
Poederlé, Baron de 72
Pombal, Marquis of 39–44, 48, 55, 58, 60, 245
Pompeii 131
Portugal 6–11
    and Brazil 8–9, 54–5
    Seven Years War 53
    tsunamis 25, 56
    see also Lisbon; Mafra
Portuguese traders 137
Powell, Colin 206
Prince, Revd Thomas 34–5
Princess Wilhelmina (mail steamer) 144
Pringle, Sir John 108
Pulo Soengan 130
Purfleet naval depot 108

Quetta (British mail steamer) 143
quinine 87

Rabelais, François 120
Rajah Bassa, Sumatra 134, 139, 151, 155, 161, 167
Rakata 131, 133, 175, 176, 177, 178, 179
Rampino, Prof. Mike 179
Ranggawarsita 134–5
Read's Weekly Journal 36
Richter, Charles 225
Riviera, Alexander 195, 198–9
Robespierre, Maximilien 109–10
Robinson, Thomas 38
Rodriguez island 170
Romanticism (journal) 261
Rousseau, Jean-Jacques 52
Royal Society of London 93, 95
    and Krakatau 170, 175
        Krakatoa Committee 171, 173
    and Lisbon earthquake 49, 74
    and lightning rods 108

Saiki, Donna 238
Samoa (ship) 164; *18*
Sampson, Captain 159
San Francisco 240
Sanriku, Japan 213, 215, 218
Saramago, José 10, 61
Schruit (telegraph master at Anjer) 149, 152–3,
    162
Schuurman, A. 140–2
Schwarz, Gottlob 76
Scotland
    (1755) 56–7
    (1783) 116
Scott, Robert H. 170
Sebesi 130, 138, 140
Sebuku 130
Seismic Sea Wave Warning System 227
    see also Pacific Tsunami Warning System
seismology 220–6, 231
    in Hawaii 227–31
    after Lisbon earthquake xviii, 48–51, 55–8,
        220
    seiches 56–7
    seismographs 214–16, 221–5, 227
    waves 13, 16–18, 25, 50, 57–8, 204, 221
        measuring 226
        diagram 16
Selborne, Hampshire 85, 94, 96
Serang 129, 164, 165
Seven Years War 53
Seymour Conway, Henry 54
Sheffield 99
Shepard, Dr Francis 217–18

Sherlock, Revd Thomas 89
Shinmachi, Hilo Bay 192–3, 202, 206, 232; *34*
Sichuan, China 244
Sieberg, August 223
Simeon, Charles 87
Sir Robert Sale (British merchant ship) 145, 158
Smith, Tilly 236
South Africa 163
South America 231
Southey, Robert 60–1
Sri Lanka xvi, 6, 162–3, 169, 239
Steingrímsson, Jón 115
Stephens, William 55
Stormont, Viscount 102
Suez Canal 131
Sumatra 130, 132–3, 137–8, 237
    (1883) 128, 138–40, 144, 150–1, 155–6, 161–2,
        163–4, 166–8, 245
    (2004) xvi, 133, 136
    (2006–9) 236, 244
Sunda Arc 132–4, 137
Sunda Strait 130–5, 137
    (1883) 126–9, 138–41, 143–51, 155–60, 162–4,
        166, 168–9; *18*
    (1928–31) 176, 178–9
    map 145
surf culture 234–5

Tahiti 212, 232
Takaki, Fusae 200–1, 203
Takemoto, Takashi 204
Tambora 172
Tanara village 164
tectonic plates 12–16, 114, 132–3, 209, 212
    sea-floor spreading 114
    subduction 13; *3*
    map 14–15
Telok Betong 130, 144, 151, 155, 156, 157, 161
Thailand xvi, 169, 220, 236
Thomson (US support ship) 216
Thornton, Ian 177–8, 179
Tidal Survey of India 162
Times, The
    (1883) 164–5
    (1946) 204
Toaldo, Giuseppe 68
Tsunami Education Project 239
Tsunami Watch 228
tsunamis 25, 245
    awareness and education 236–7, 239
    Indian Ocean (2004) xv–xvii, 45, 132–3, 136,
        166, 220, 236, 239, 243, 244

tsunamis (*cont.*)
  Japan 215, 219–20, 233
  following Krakatau eruption 152–7, 161–3,
    169, 210, 211, 213
  following Lisbon earthquake 25–7, 35, 56,
    210, 211
  transit times 25, 215, 227–8
    map 228
  trans-Pacific 209–13, 216
  tsunamigenic earthquakes xvi, 212–13, 229
    Chile 212, 213, 231–2
    Indian Ocean xvi, 132–3, 226
    Indonesia 134–6
    Lisbon (1755) 25–7
    Pacific 209–10, 227, 229
    Sumatra (2004) 136
  warning systems 214–16, 217–20, 227
    DART system 236, 243–4; *33*
    see also Pacific Tsunami Warning System
  waves 210, 211
  see also Hawaii; Hilo Bay
Turku, Finland 69
Turner, J. M. W. 171–2
Tutuila, Samoa 93

Uchima, Masao 199–200, 206, 207
Unimak Island 209–10
United Nations 240, 243, 244
  Intergovernmental Oceanographic
    Commission 234, 236
  UNESCO 242
United States forces 194–5, 205, 227

Valparaiso earthquake 213
van der Stok, Dr 139
van Sandick, R. A. 156, 163, 168
Verbeek, Rogier 174–6; *20*
  Krakatau (report) 175; *20*
Verlaten island 130, 135, 175, 176
Versailles 104
Vissery, M. de 109

volcanoes 245
  alert grades 176–7
  and atmosphere 116–18
  causation 133
  Iceland 97–8, 112, 113–17
  Java Trench xvii, 132–3, 136, 209, 243
  Mid-Atlantic Ridge 13, 114
  Pompeii 131
  Vesuvius 74, 221
  see also Krakatau
Volcanological Survey of Indonesia 176
Voltaire 51–3, 55
  Candide 52–3

W. H. Besse (American barque) 125–8, 144, 157–8,
  159, 168–9
Waiakea Town, Hilo Bay 192, 193, 214, 218, 231,
  232–3; *35*
Waikiki Beach, Oahu 230, 234
Wales 86
Walpole, Horace 54, 71–2, 75–6, 88, 89, 101
Waluran village 162
War of the Spanish Succession 11
Warburton, Revd William 47–8
Watson, Captain W. J. 146–7, 158–9, 163
weather in Europe (1783) xviii, 66–88, 90–7, 99,
  101–2, 112–13, 116
Wesley, Revd John 46, 47, 48, 80, 87
Wharton, Joseph 173, 179
White, Gilbert 85–6, 94–5, 96, 116
Whitefield, Revd George 8, 10, 44, 47, 48
Whitehall Evening Post 39, 90
Wilson, Benjamin 108
Winchester, Simon 131, 133, 170, 176
Witham, Catherine 22–3, 35, 38
Witney, Oxfordshire 80
World War II 192, 193–4, 227

Yogjakarta, Java 135
York Courant 81, 82, 83

Zaclar, Bohemia 82